Look,

This living hand, now warm and capable
Of earnest grasping, would, if it were cold
And in the icy silence of the tomb,
So haunt thy days and chill thy dreaming nights
That thou wouldst wish thine own heart dry of blood
So in my veins red life might stream again,
And thou be conscience-calmed—see here it is—
I hold it towards you.

John Keats

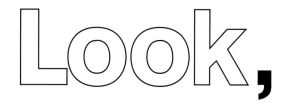

Look,

100 Years of Contemporary Art

Thierry de Duve

translation: Simon Pleasance & Fronza Woods

LUDION

VOICI

PALAIS DES BEAUX-ARTS, BRUSSELS

23 NOVEMBER 2000 – 28 JANUARY 2001

And what about the ribbon?

> Hamm—You've forgotten the sex.
> Clov (*vexed*)—But he isn't finished. The sex goes on at the end.
> Hamm—You haven't put on his ribbon.
> Clov (*angrily*)—But he isn't finished, I tell you! First you finish your dog and then you put on his ribbon!
> Hamm—Can he stand?
> Clov—I don't know.
> Hamm—Try.
>
> Samuel Beckett, *Endgame*

Now that six months have passed since the exhibition closed, the rather silly idea has occurred to me that an endeavor like *Voici** had something to do with the little stuffed dog's story in *Endgame*. I didn't put on the show's ribbon, but its sex— I mean, Eros, I mean the art of loving—I don't think I put it at the end, as did Clov. Beckett's little dog is what the psychoanalyst D. W. Winnicott would have called a transitional object. It is with the help of such objects that infants learn how to negotiate with absence. When they grow up, some inconsolable children become art lovers, and, if they are wealthy, art collectors. The curator of an art exhibition is someone fortunate enough to be able to gather together, for a limited time span, a more-or-less ideal collection of his transitional objects, and who wagers that others, too, will find something there to negotiate absence with. This might not be the most scientific definition of a curator's job, but it is the one I applied to myself, without much ado, when curating *Voici*.

Naturally, Beckett does his best to make sure that his little dog fails in his role as a transitional object. He only has three legs, he's missing his sex and his ribbon, he's black although blind Hamm thinks he's white, and the third time that Clov, on Hamm's orders, goes off to fetch him, he uses him to smash Hamm right on the head. For sure, Beckett speaks for the entire century. *Endgame* is not the only screeching comedy about a world in which mediation with absence is denied or which refuses it. Twentieth-century art as a whole was striving to make things that, to varying degrees, managed not to be transitional objects. So we might describe the challenge, with respect to the public, of an exhibition sub-titled *100 Years of Contemporary Art* thusly: in each viewer, search out the inconsolable child who then

---

* *Voici* is the original title of the exhibition. Etymologically, the word "*voici*" derives from "*vois ci*," or "*vois ce, ici*," which literally means: "see this, here." While the most satisfactory English translation of *Voici* might have been: *Here it is*, we nevertheless settled for *Look*, concise and elegant, reserving the "Here I am—Here you are—Here we are" construction for the show's three parts, *Me voici*, *Vous voici*, and *Nous voici*.

is given objects that offer no solace. It would hardly have been surprising had no one come to see the show. The public did come. 82,000 people saw *Voici* in a little under ten weeks, and most of them went home happy. The outside world did not for one single second cease to be as black as in the last century, and artists to be as abrasive as Beckett. Such a success, therefore, must be based on a misunderstanding.

Could it have been otherwise? When a success is said to be based on a misunderstanding, it means that it is founded on a biased social pact that suits both parties. This is stated a bit bluntly, but so be it. Given that unbiased social pacts are exceptional, a misunderstanding is at least an honest one. The pact that gives art its place in the community has been biased since the dawn of time: no society whatever tolerates works of art being transitional objects designed to fail without wrapping them in misunderstanding. You must be talking about avant-garde art?—there is indeed an abyss between a little stuffed dog and a marble Venus. No, I am speaking of works of art of all times. Artists have been driven to madness paying court to beauty because they're no less human than any other mortal, and mortals cannot relinquish the desire to negotiate with Absence and cannot refrain from providing themselves with transitional objects to do the mediation. But artists have always known—and when they haven't, their work has—that beauty is the veil for non-mediation, and that one can't cut a deal with Absence. This truth is intolerable without a biased social pact. In their mad utopianism, the avant-gardes dreamt they might do without such a pact—no more misunderstanding! down with nostalgia! let's be inconsolable, but with ferocious joy!—and failed. *Endgame* does not end ending. With the same works, *Voici* might have been an exhibition faithful to the avant-gardes in their utopianism. Its staging would have been intransigent, purist, without pedagogic concessions, and more concerned with historical precision than aesthetic pleasure. But *Voici* rests on a different conception of faithfulness to the avant-gardes and on an analysis that puts their refusal of misunderstanding in perspective. The avant-gardes mistook the misunderstanding they rejected for misunderstanding as such—so long had it been the rule—whereas it was only one particular biased social pact they sought to do without: the one that made the artist the partner of the priest—and which presently threatens to return in the guise of the society of the spectacle.

Misunderstandings that oil the gears of society go unnoticed as long as society lives according to common beliefs. And as long as these common beliefs are a shared faith, art has its natural place within a religious relationship to the world no one would even think of doubting. Wherever we go on this planet, and from time immemorial, art has been an integral part of the rituals and myths by which humans have tried to communicate with the invisible and the great beyond. Everywhere, priests have enlisted artists to provide the community with fetishes, idols, icons, cult objects, holy images—all transitional objects intended to mediate the Absence. And everywhere the artists—the great ones, at least—responded a little to the side of the demand, in delivering things that give us a glimpse of the terrifying beauty of non-mediation. I suspect that the artist and the priest always knew that the pact uniting them was biased. Perhaps this explains why it was maintained for so long. But it doesn't work any more, since when, and why, everyone knows. We even take for granted that it doesn't work anymore, whereas it is its extraordinary longevity that gives the harsh novelty of the avant-gardes' advent in history its true salience. While the priests were waiting for Godot, the artists have been playing *Endgame* since the word go. Maybe the avant-gardes arrived to tell us the time has come to switch misunderstandings.

The public came to see *Voici* because they sensed that it was a child of love. Oh we aren't any more innocent than Beckett. Love is a misunderstanding too. It speaks to our need to truck with absence, even if it doesn't mediate Absence. But it is not a biased social pact because it is not a social pact at all. The love relation is one-to-one. And when you live by the rules of love, sex never comes last. For the lovers of art, Beckett's little dog and those of his avant-garde colleagues—things wobbling on three feet, lacking their ribbon, black when thought to be white, even things used to give great bangs on heads—are transitional objects. To acknowledge this required an avowal of weakness which, I now realize, formed the basis for what I would call, for want of a better term, my humanism: the love of art, in my personal experience, makes me a little more human than I would be without it, perhaps. In trying to share this, my only naïveté has been in thinking that art makes humans human, collectively, and that it has always been so, without interruption. The whole "strategy" of the exhibition, starting from this premise, was to pretend the question was reversed: what is it, to begin with, that humanizes these transitional objects, which the twentieth-century avant-gardes went out of their way to make as little human as possible? Then to activate the seesaw that reverses the answer with regard to the question: to present the works in such a way that they present themselves, that they address themselves to us, their viewers, and that they speak about us, all of us. Hence the three-part division of the show: *Me voici*, where the work speaks and presents itself; *Vous voici*, where the work addresses itself to the men and women facing it; and *Nous voici*, where the works testify to what we, human beings, have in common.

The essay in the book follows the same three-part division, and addresses the same issues. But it does so at a remote, resting mostly on works that were not in the exhibition. The short texts accompanying the images cater to the broadest possible audience and are close to the audioguide. The catalog is interspersed with installation shots, acting as the show's memory.

Brussels, August 2001

Here I am

Here you are

Here we are

Here I am

Édouard Manet

Le Christ aux anges
(Le Christ mort et les anges), 1864

There are two voices, as in a fugue. One says: "This isn't art," while the other says at the same time: "I am Art."

Roland Barthes

Presentations

What if we were to go straight to Manet, where the adventure of modern art takes off? And what if we decided to embark on our adventure not with *Olympia* or *Le Déjeuner sur l'herbe*, but rather with a less well-known yet altogether extraordinary painting, *Le Christ aux anges (Christ among the Angels)* painted in 1864? An unexpected choice, and all the stranger, actually, because, together with *Christ Mocked* and the Zurburán-inspired *Monk at Prayer*, both from 1865, this painting is one of just three religious works dating from Manet's mature years. There are no others. So why on earth go looking for the beginning of modern painting in a religious canvas, and one not even typical of its painter? For all we know, the 136 years that have elapsed between that moment and now have hardly been the historical period most favorable to religious sentiment. Faith, for us, has become a private matter to be settled according to individual conscience. And religious practice is no longer the social mortar it once was. Aren't we needlessly complicating our efforts to understand modernism in painting by starting with a religious picture, when modernity is so typified by a waning of religion in every field, and art itself has not escaped the overall secularization of human relationships? No one has ever been seen kneeling in front of *Christ among the Angels* in New York's Metropolitan Museum, where the painting hangs. Nor for that matter in front of a Van Eyck *Madonna* in Bruges' Groeninge Museum. People possibly commune and contemplate quietly in museums, but they don't pray in them.

One thing is certain, though: the religious fervour of the painter bears enormously on the aesthetic quality of a Van Eyck *Madonna*. It is visible, and even, as it were, palpable. It emanates from the painting. And the fact that the *Madonna* participated in the rituals of the church where it hung, before being moved to the Groeninge Museum in Bruges, has a bearing on its aura as well. The same cannot be said of Manet's *Christ*. First and foremost, because it was never intended for church use, and secondly, because it is both visible and palpable that what emanates from it is not religious fervor, but rather human compassion. Manet painted his *Christ* for the 1864 Salon. Unlike *Le Déjeuner sur l'herbe*, submitted the year before, it was not rejected. The Salon's audience was even more heterogeneous than any church congregation, despite the Christian credo that everyone, regardless of class or education, is admitted to the house of God, where the common man's faith deserves no less a place than that of the theologian. From here, it's a very short leap of faith indeed to say that the Salon was a modern church … Why not?—insofar as we can think of a football stadium as a church, and liken a World Cup match to the celebration of a mass broadcast by television to the "cathodic" Church in its entirety. The doors of those 19th-century painting Salons were open to the masses, who flocked to them in droves. Perhaps the Salons foreshadowed the great confusion marking the end of the 20th century, with its leisure-oriented society, its thirst for things spiritual, and its lavish consumption of art all thrown together to form a massive cocktail substitute for the religion which we are lacking.

Le Christ aux anges is still called *Le Christ mort et les anges (Dead Christ and the Angels)*. Unnecessary to be a practising Christian to appreciate the painting, but you do need a modicum of Christian culture to grasp its meaning. At the very least, you should know that Christ is the Son of God incarnate among men, that he died on the Cross to atone for humanity's sins, and that he rose from the dead three days later. You need also a basic acquaintance with iconography, and know that although angels are invisible, they are traditionally depicted as young, winged, androgynous beings. Visitors to the 1864 Salon—even those who believed in the God of Abraham or in no God at all—possessed this rudimentary Christian culture. Manet must not have been too sure whether they had much more of it, for, on a stone in the foreground of the painting, he engraved the reference to the Gospel according to St. John, xx, xii, which refers to the episode when Mary Magdalene stood in tears beside Christ's open tomb, then peered inside and saw two white-clad angels, "sitting there where Jesus had lain, one at the head, the other at the feet." Unless, of course, by including this reference, Manet simply wished to underline that he had veered off from the text. The angels in St. John's Gospel watched over an empty tomb, after the resurrection; the dead Christ, for his part, was alone in his grave. Manet conflates the two moments. Art history has produced quite a few dead Christs, most of them prone and in profile (think of those by Grünewald, Holbein, and Philippe de Champaigne, and even, to stay closer to Manet, by his contemporary Jean-Jacques Henner). The famous exception to the profile would be Mantegna's rendering, where the painter shows Christ with his feet foremost, strikingly foreshortened. Dead Christs seated are rare, but they do exist, and two, at least, are supported by a pair of angels, one painted by Veronese, the other by Ribalta. It has been shown that Manet could well have known about them through engravings published in Charles Blanc's *Histoire des peintres*, and once we are familiar with Manet's propensity for quoting painters he admired without imitating them in any way, we may rest assured that his *Christ* alludes to a marginal pictorial tradition breaking with the text. What does Manet make it say that is new?

Let's compare *Dead Christ and the Angels* with Ribalta's *Dead Christ held by two Angels*. What is straightaway striking about Manet's painting is the head-on depiction of Christ. He is looking at us, whereas Ribalta's Christ has a writhing mannerist pose lending him elegance yet not quite touching. It is the angel to the left who, in Ribalta's work, makes eye contact with the viewer, whereas, in Manet's painting, he is engrossed in sadness and pays us no attention. The angel to the right is turned away from Christ in the Spanish painting, while, in the Manet, his gaze is lost in the space between the painting and us. And with Manet it is Christ who makes eye contact with the viewer! His eyes are open, whereas in the Ribalta the eyelids are lowered. On closer inspection, his right eye is open and his left one half-shut, like a dazed person waking from a nasty dream. Manet's Christ looks at us, but doesn't see us. And for a very good reason, too: he's dead. We don't know if Manet had read Ernest Renan's *The Life of Jesus*, published scarcely a year before he painted *Le Christ mort*, but there is no denying the fact that, with this picture, the painter offers us a Christ complying with the "critical and rational Christianity" that Renan had been fostering, a human more than a divine Christ, a Christ in whose twofold nature it would no longer be necessary to believe for a religion of love to spread, nonetheless, in this world. Everything happens as if, in order to appreciate this painting for its true worth and get right inside its meaning, belief in Christianity had become superfluous, even if knowledge of the Christian narrative was still called for. God is dead, Manet seems to be saying, thus beating Nietzsche to it, and his painting is an *Ecce homo*, but *post mortem*.

It cannot be said that Manet had anticipated, with the same lucidity as Nietzsche, that the "death of God" would inevitably be followed by the "death of man." Nor that the dreadful 20th century would drag human affairs through the minefield that humanism has become when men have lost their Father and tear each other apart. Two World Wars and an endless litany of local and regional conflicts, the Shoah and Hiroshima, and genocide perpetrated everywhere, all have left the figure of man more than riven—and none of this is Manet's legacy. But the modern painting he so forcefully helped to create—once, thanks to him, it had been set on the track of non-figuration—was hard pressed, indeed, to defend itself against the charge of anti-humanism that was levelled at it time and again. Cézanne painted his wife's face as if

Engraving after Ribalta
Le Christ mort soutenu par deux anges,
in Charles Blanc,
Histoire des peintres

it were an apple or a mere thing, and it was not just the critics who made this accusation, he himself also claimed responsibility for it. We reckon nowadays that, far from reducing a face to a thing, he lent the thing the dignity of a face, but this would have been less obvious to him than to us. Great artists have their own ways of plunging headlong into their doubts, the better to overcome them. Like Plato's pharmakon, their work is both the poison and the antidote. We might call this the vaccine strategy: being inoculated with an infective agent in order to develop the relevant anti-bodies and strengthen the immune system. Artists felt this need before medicine understood its mechanism. It is this selfsame vaccine strategy which prompted the Expressionists to distort the human figure beyond all recognition, the Cubists to smash to smithereens the Euclidean space wherein the figure stands and moves, and non-figurative painters to do away with the figure altogether. With them, anti-humanism appeared to win the day. Abstract art has bumped off man. The truth is quite different, however. The best modern art has endeavored to redefine the essentially *religious* terms of humanism on *belief-less* bases. In 1913, when Malevich painted his *Black Square on a White Ground*, which was exactly that, a black square on a white ground, who could then have understood that he was inoculating the tradition of the Russian icon with a vaccine capable of preserving its human meaning, for a period which faith in God could no longer keep alive? Well, as Marie-José Mondzain, a great expert in orthodox iconophilia, said: "Those who refuse the icon refuse to rise from the dead." We've reached this point.

A letter from Baudelaire to the Marquis de Chennevières, curator at the Louvre and in charge of the Salon, vouches for the title which, it would seem, Manet himself gave to this painting, today titled *Le Christ mort et les anges* or *Le Christ aux anges*, and given to the 1864 Salon as *Les anges au tombeau du Christ*. It used to be: *Le Christ ressuscitant, assisté par les anges (Christ Rising from the Dead, Helped by Angels)*. Which radically alters our interpretation of it. Christ's dead yet awakening gaze is not pulling him out of a bad dream, but showing him coming back from the hereafter, with, in his vacant pupil, the knowledge of the unknowable, and disbelief before the spectacle of the world in which he is being reborn. This particular Christ is a Christ proceeding without transition from the *Eli eli lema sabachtani* which he cried to his Father on finding that he was mortal and abandoned, to the status of that human, all too human (as Nietzsche would have said) man, upon whom his task weighs immensely. This is a Christ touched by loss of faith and by despair, whom only the beholder's gaze can bring back to life. Even though Manet died a good Christian having received the holy sacraments, it is not easy to turn him into a mystic or a priest. Manet was a painter, period. His *Christ Rising from the Dead* is not a pious image, it's a *morceau de peinture* offered to the hordes jockeying their way into the Salon to see some art, pass the time, be seen and flaunt their attire, and, in the best possible scenario, brush up on culture a little, maybe even seek out the soul which the materialism of modern life has deprived them of—but definitely not to perform their devotions. Everything hung on the public's reaction. Either the bedazzled crowd would see just an altarpiece totally inappropriate to this free-for-all called the Salon, an out-of-place treatment of the subject, painted with an irreverent brush and making no sense whatsoever. And exclaim, like that "very distinguished lady" whose comments were recorded by Thoré-Bürger: "Who would have thought of such a thing! It's an aberration!" Or, alternatively, the crowd would manage to really look—like Thoré himself, who had a discerning eye—and accordingly find "the whites of the shroud and the flesh tones to be extremely true" and, in their enthusiasm, think of Titian, Rubens, El Greco, and Velázquez. And wonder about the Christ in this astounding painting: "Perhaps he's in the throes of rising from the dead under the wings of two attendant angels." As if the mere willingness to let oneself be visually touched by the picture were tantamount to an act of faith.

Thoré was the exception. As was their wont, the critics were for the most part incredulous. To them, Manet's dead Christ seemed more than dead, he seemed inert, dirty, and flat, like a *thing* that had never lived and never should have lived, for that matter. "The livid aspect of death is mixed with grimy half-tones, with dirty, black shadows which the Resurrection will never wash clean, if a cadaver so far gone can ever be resurrected, anyway," said Théophile Gautier. Not only is this Christ no longer a God, he isn't even a man. His flesh has never been alive: it's as similar to the surface of an inert thing as you can imagine, above all when you compare it to Titian's exquisite renderings of flesh or, to compare comparable things, the vile and festering flesh of Grünewald's *Dead Christ* or the dark and gloomy flesh, albeit imbued with a velvety mystique, of Jean-Jacques Henner's. It's common knowledge that Manet was invariably accused, Salon after Salon, of painting rubber instead of flesh. Olympias as whores instead of lively and alluring odalisques. Playing-cards instead of people. The same has been said of Cézanne—and similar things have been said of a whole host of artists whose work, with time, we have learnt how to look at—and still is being said about some of our contemporaries for whom time has not yet had the chance to do its thing. What are we to do with such verdicts, these days? It's too easy to rely on time, as if historical distance trained the eye all by itself. A little effort is called for, especially if we don't want our contemporary artists to have to wait as long as Manet did to be appreciated—and understood, which could take more time still. From this viewpoint, *Le Christ ressuscitant* hasn't had the last word, yet.

Belief or non-belief in the Gospel doesn't play much of a role in the judgment of the critics of the day. Cultural habit and mental sloth, on the contrary, do play quite a considerable part. We think we're seeing a church painting because that's just what it looks like, and that's enough to stop us from asking what meaning a church paint-ing, *painted for the Salon*, might have. Or else, we find plenty of fault with it, in which case it no longer looks like a church painting at all. We think we're seeing *The Angels at Christ's Tomb* because we read the title in the booklet, and we forget to check out St. John's chapter xx verse xii, which tells us that Christ shouldn't have been in his tomb at the same time as the angels. Or else, having checked things out, we accuse the artist of incoherence, unless we prefer to grant artists and poets the license to fantasize, so as not to have to ask ourselves questions. Critics have excuses. With two thousand paintings per Salon to write up, they're a bit over-extended. But historians? They are in a league of their own when it comes to picking images to bits and going through writings with a fine-tooth comb. It's thanks to historians, for example, that we know Baudelaire warned Manet against liberties taken with the Scriptures, not in the matter of the passage in St. John, but over the wound on the right side, which Manet painted on the left: "By the way, it would seem that the spear blow was inflicted on the right. So you will have to change the position of the wound before the opening. Confirm the matter in the four evangelists. And be mindful of giving malicious people cause to mock!" Manet didn't change the place of the spear blow, either before the Salon opened or after, and he protracted his mistake in the etching and the (mirror-reversed) watercolour he made a few years later, based on the painting. Historians have been at great pains to take due note of all of the above. Some have emphasized the degree to which Manet is a painter of deliberate anomalies. Most of them take refuge behind the texts to avoid interpreting the images in ways misconstruing their meaning for the day and age to which they belonged. Few and far between were those who ventured to offer explanations. Virtually not a single one, pounced upon Baudelaire's above-mentioned letter to Manet, proof enough that the poet was definitely well-informed about the painter's intentions, even before the Salon opened, to conclude that if he talked in his letter to Chennevières about a painting titled *Le Christ ressuscitant, assisté par les anges*—whereas the critics would refer to a painting titled *Les anges au tombeau du Christ*—this was because Manet had decided, in the meantime, not to provide his audience with the clue which would have enabled them to know that, in this painting, Christ is as if snapped at the precise moment when he is travelling back along the road leading from life to death.

Manet probably learned from Courbet how to refrain from giving his audience the clues to his work. For many an artist coming after Manet—the champion among them being Duchamp—this became second nature. We may well grumble, because this exclusionary tactic justifies the hermetic reputation that has clung to the coat-tails of modern—or avant-garde—art among the general public. But there is cause to wonder about the strategies that have been abetted by such avant-garde tactics. Are we not, as ever, talking about the vaccine strategy? We all know the witticism: "God is dead, man is sick, and as for me, I'm not feeling any too good, either." To get better, avant-garde artists had to infect themselves with the disease in small doses. Inevitably, the public has had to be inoculated, too. This disease is called doubt—the opposite of faith. The avant-garde wants the public not to *believe* in appearances. Thus far things are pretty clear, and help explain why the hermeticism of the avant-garde is often perceived as a form of intellectualism. But they are distinctly less clear when it comes to grappling with the paradox of the vaccine strategy, wondering how doubt might vaccinate someone against a loss of faith. Yet it is here, in this very issue, that the true hermeticism, and the real difficulty, of avant-garde art lie. Painters are manufacturers of appearances, and appearances are all they have available to invite the public to go a step further. So, paradoxically, no longer believing in appearances is to give in to them. This calls for something other than intellectual endeavor, questioning, and skepticism; much more to the point, it requires an openmindedness that has as much to do with an openness of the body and the heart: letting oneself be *touched* emotionally and aesthetically by the painting, and by what it shows. That most distinguished lady, who cried aberration before what she naïvely took to be a

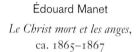

Édouard Manet
Le Christ mort et les anges,
ca. 1865–1867

church painting, feels excluded, for sure, but not solely because she didn't make the effort to think beyond appearances. What she knew or thought she knew about appearances prevented her from yielding, without putting up any resistance, to what so evidently appears in the painting. Had she done so, what might she have seen?

The spear blow, placed on the left despite Baudelaire's admonition, went straight to the heart of that man whose stigmata prove that he has to be recognized as Christ after the Passion, the Crucifixion and the Deposition—the dead Christ. To be that much surer, Manet sketched in a halo for him, as if to reassure himself that our doubts don't stray where they shouldn't. This Christ most probably died with his eyes open, and without any illusions. But no distortion of the holy scripture can get us to accept that no one closed his eyes after death. We must not muddle the vaccine of doubt and the improbability of the image. For today's beholder as well as for those Salon visitors, eye contact with Christ's lifeless pupils cannot make us forget the fact that at the moment of picking up his body at the foot of the Cross, either the Virgin, or St. John, or Joseph of Arimathea must have closed his eyelids. Once we have seen and understood as much, we may well wonder how it is possible to see this Christ other than rising from the dead, and there is no other explanation for the blindness of critics and the caution of historians than their dread before that still dead gaze which stares deep into our eyes, after having looked death in the face. Not to see it is to repress the terror it stirs within us. Seeing it is to let the terror touch us. So the willingness to let ourselves be aesthetically touched can have wide ramifications. Doubt, pulled from the depths of dread in the face of death, becomes the vaccine against the loss of faith. Needless to say, one is reluctant to talk of religious faith, which is still a private matter settled according to individual conscience, but there is no hesitating if it's faith in Manet and faith in his paintings one is talking about. The painting, after all, revealed the clues to its interpretation—all it required was a close look. Christ's hands are moving; they open one after the other, like the eyelids, and in the same order, the stigmata duplicating the half-shut, half-open drawing of the eyes. You just have to compare them with the dangling hands of Ribalta's *Dead Christ* to be left in no doubt. The split-second that Manet "snaps" is suspended between the already-dead and the not-yet-risen-again. The angel on the left is still engrossed in lamentation, while the one on the right is responding to life being reborn. It feels the flesh quiver beneath its hand laid on the nape of Christ's neck and in the muscles of its left arm hidden by the shroud. There is no effort required. In a flash, Christ will get to his feet unaided; his left foot is already braced, while his right foot shifts forward. What an amazing painting! In a flash, this Christ, who is no longer a God but just a man, will rise again from the dead.

Thoré didn't have the clue that Baudelaire had, but he rated the painting as persuasive. More or less out on a limb among the various critics, by letting himself be moved by "the extremely true flesh tones," he stood, poised and hesitant, on the threshold of the act of faith that had him saying of the Christ figure in this painting: "Perhaps he's in the throes of rising from the dead." Perhaps … Gautier, whom Baudelaire had apparently let into the secret, had the clue, though this didn't stop him wondering, skeptically, whether "a cadaver so far gone can ever be resurrected, anyway." Anyway … Manet put himself into the hands of his critics, and it is *his* act of faith that is gauged by the yardstick of *their* doubts. Faith in the faith that his critics may or may not invest in his painting, trust in his public's verdict, which went against him, and in the verdict of posterity, which found in his favor. Herein, it goes without saying, lies his living modernity. But doubt is a fearsome bug which doesn't inoculate against loss of faith once and for all. With hindsight, we may say that Manet must have had an untarnishable faith in himself to keep going the way he did in the face of the repeated gibes of the critics, and that he must have had unshakeable confidence in his public not to offer it the facile insights into the work which it expected. Yet nothing could be less certain. He actually had the wonderful naïvety of great artists who cannot even imagine that the public might expect less of art than they, and who, for this very reason, make no compromises. And he very likely thought, in all good faith, that he had put into the painting all the necessary visual clues—eyes stirring to life, hands opening, feet moving, calf muscles flexing—so that entitling his painting *Christ Rising from the Dead* would have seemed to him to be an insult to the public's sensibility and intelligence. But what about his own doubts? Was he that sure that his Christ would rise again from the dead? Or that Christ had actually risen? Not for nothing did he give us a Christ dead to his divine nature, then born again, as the man Jesus, to his human, too human, nature. We cannot separate faith in God from faith in painting, nor faith in man from faith in God, as easily for the 19th century as we think we can do nowadays. It's not because Manet unwittingly nudged Renan in the direction of Nietzsche that he wasn't troubled by the idea of making a religious painting whose aesthetic quality owed nothing to religious fervor. And he was aware how risky it was to call upon human compassion while throwing his painting to the inattentive and mocking Salon public. Is his Christ really about to get to his feet? He is, after all, locked in the moment before—and painting doesn't have the possibilities of film. Is the tremor of life really coursing already through his flesh? It's only made of oil on canvas, after all. Is the picture really spirited enough so that the Christ it *represents* introduces himself—*presents* himself—to us all on his own?

Presentational devices

To present or introduce oneself is to say: "Here I am." To say: "Here I am" is to introduce oneself. Only a living being endowed with language can do this; inanimate things can't. Works of art, however, are things. We lend them human properties; we deem them to be alive and we call them eloquent when they're successful; we treat them with the respect due human beings; and we reckon it's barbaric to destroy them. But none of all this is self-evident. For a long time, in the fact that works of art resemble us, people have seen proof that they talk to us. Anthropomorphism in the visual arts tallied with humanism in the culture, and vice versa. In this sense, humanism is much, much older than the Renaissance humanism of Erasmus and Giordano Bruno, Copernicus and Galileo, Tasso and Thomas More, and all those people who ferried the West along the path that would prompt human beings to do without God. The humanism we are talking about is as old as hominization. And the same goes for anthropomorphism. The very first hand-print on the wall of a prehistoric cave testifies to the inaugural apparition of the human form, just as the red ocher found in palaeolithic tombs is evidence of the fact that art came into being at the same time as the cult of the dead—the earliest sign of the irrepressible need in human beings to fabricate gods in order to palliate their dread before their own mortality. There is no good reason why that fundamental humanism should not survive the cultural wear and tear of Renaissance humanism, provided one weighs up the novelty of this latter and the intensity of the crisis inflicted upon it by the 19th century—the century of Manet and Nietzsche—and then the fearsome 20th century—the century of the Shoah and Hiroshima. How short is our experience of life without God, when measured against the history of humankind! A couple of hundred years if we date it back to the French Revolution? Five hundred if we go back to the Renaissance? Ridiculous. Well, it's this ridiculousness that modern art has come up against, and that the best contemporary art is still up against—in the mourning for God for many artists, and in the resurrection of God-less man for the more radical among them. This is not to be sniffed at. The scope of the task is such that there is some doubt about whether it can be achieved in painting, which brings us back to Manet. Does his Christ really rise from the dead? Does he really come forward on his own, unaided? Though Manet has given us the aesthetic clues to his act of faith, he has given us the clues to his doubt just as much. It could well be that his Christ isn't strong enough to present himself without the help of some presentational device.

Let's note the extreme ingeniousness and artifice of the device. The large white shroud, against which Christ's body stands out with a frontality never before seen in the treatment of this subject, seats him as if on some monumental throne, but with not a trace of realism. Who has so elegantly arranged beneath his posterior the shroud which he's not even supposed to have extricated himself from yet, if not a theater director who doesn't give a damn about verisimilitude? The lighting, which can easily be linked with the tradition of Caravaggio, and which also pulls off the paradox of leaving Christ's face in dark shadow while his chest and the face of the angel on the right are fiercely lit, would seem to be the work of a stage electrician, painstakingly angling halogen spots, when electric light had not even been invented. The encompassing gesture of the same angel, who appears to be lifting Christ up as if to introduce him to us, but apparently without suffering in the slightest from the muscular effort implied in hoisting this dead weight, vanishes into the folds of the shroud. So where does its forearm end up—a forearm which anatomical verisimilitude ought to show us emerging beneath Christ's left elbow? Manet doesn't really care. He doesn't want to interfere with the exemplary symmetry of Christ's arms, parted like the ones of those Sulpician Sacred Hearts who absolutely have to show you the stigmata, and resting lifelessly on the armrests that the painter—stopping at nothing when it comes to ploys—has provided for them. The arms and the hands are the presentational device for the stigmata; the throne-like shroud that of the arms; and the angel, that of Christ. We should almost skip from Manet straight to Brancusi, with whom we never know where the sculpture starts and the pedestal stops, in order to gauge the pleasure going hand-in-hand with doubt. Obviously, Manet can't help taking back with one hand what he gives us with the other. He shouldn't have grumbled if his audience didn't get it. No sooner are we of a mood to believe that his Christ is coming forward all on his own and addressing us with his "here I am," than Manet pulls the rug from under our feet by showing us a Christ pathetically supported by a "this is my dead—or rising-from-the-dead—Christ; up to you to decide," which is his presentational device.

We might say that the presentational device is what lives on of God the Father when God is dead—fascination with Power in its almightiness. We might say that it's Art with a capital A, the authority of the Museum, the room in the Met where the *Dead Christ* is coming back to life. We might also say that Manet had his heart set on his bit of Power, and that he painted for the Museum, while pretending to paint for the Salon. Were this so, Manet would have remained on this side of Renan who, for his part, had the cheek to make the resurrection dependent on the "Divine power of love! Sacred moments when the passion of a hallucinated woman gave the world a resurrected God," and the nerve to claim that it's not God the Father who brought Christ back to life, but the love of a woman. The hallucinated woman is Mary Magdalene, the sinner, the woman in love, who—let's recall St. John, xx, xii—discovers the empty tomb and doesn't believe her eyes when, two verses later, Christ appears before her, alive. Like St. Thomas she wants to touch him. "*Noli me tangere*," Christ says, "don't touch me." Showing surprising and problematic modernity, Renan doesn't realize that he is harbingering Freud and Lacan when he makes the power of the Father reliant on the desire (Renan says "imagination") of the hysteric upholding the Father's very own desire. For the time being, let's note that the presentational device is not God, but rather love. Love of art, as it so happens. And that if it is true that Manet painted the *Dead Christ* under Renan's influence—or, alternatively, that his sensibility to his time unwittingly drew him to Renan—then it makes no difference whether he painted it for the Museum or the Salon. He had already realized that museums would one day become what the Salon already was—a free-for-all absorbed by the leisure industry, an entertainment specializing in "spirituality," a secular mass just like a World Cup match broadcast on TV. And that, in this context, the works must fiendishly appeal to the love of art if they are to come back to life. The Museum, the 19th-century Salons and the Palais des Beaux-Arts in Brussels are only temples of artistic power for those who submit to it as they enter. For art-lovers, they are erotic cabinets where you go to indulge your passion. Those who have railed against the museum are legion. They accuse museums of being cemeteries, filled with works whose life has been drained from them, and arrayed as in a morgue in the drawers of styles and periods. They claim, further, that we must be pretty sick and spineless to visit them so religiously and pay our two cents to the death-dealing cult of art. And they're quite right, if God is dead. Van Eyck's *Madonna* in the Groeninge Museum in Bruges no longer radiates the faith of the assembled faithful. We're left with the painter's faith. Yet we don't commune in it, but rather, in the sheer aesthetic pleasure into which it has changed. We are taking part in a dead religion whose relics we venerate. How hard modernity has striven to snatch our relationship to art from the fate of this religion which no longer can—and no longer wants to—be coped with as such, but to which the museum returns all the more perversely because it is the place of worship of a cult that is no more. The earliest such efforts at secularization date back to the very birth of museums, in the 18th century, finding a foothold in the invention of aesthetics, which started out by theorizing over our love affairs with beauty-*qua*-beauty. In the 19th century it was art rather than beauty which became the object of aesthetics. There then emerged the art-for-art's-sake theory, which failed to avoid deteriorating into a religion of art. What's the point of having made art autonomous, if it's still not independent of religiosity! What's the point if, meanwhile, Van Eyck's *Madonnas* have left their churches one by one and ended up in museums—unless we're talking about Ghent's cathedral drawing more tourists who have come to gaze at the *Mystic Lamb* than people attending Sunday mass! Museums have become churches while churches have become museums, as if religiosity, determined not to die, obeyed a strange law of communicating vessels. The 20th century heroically took up the slack, and it was formalism, from Roger Fry to Clement Greenberg, which expected to complete the secularization of aesthetics. Wasted effort. These days, most art theoreticians see formalism as just one more chapel in the history of art doctrines, and not the least dogmatic, either. "Chapel," "doctrine," "dogma," the vocabulary is eloquent. The more formalism singles out so-called autonomous and "pure" aesthetic quality, free of the dross of the religious being-in-the-world, the more its detractors accuse formalism of fetishizing it. But if aesthetic quality is a fetish, then love of art is altogether akin to both sexual perversion and mystic superstition. We might as well prefer art which—and we're back with the vaccine strategy again—exposes the fetish for what it is.

Presenters

And what if we now went to the fetish-work of all fetish-works and the man through whom scandal was ushered in? In 1917, a French artist who'd been living in New York for two years—and was more famous there than in his own country for having shown at the 1913 Armory Show (the biggest art bazaar of all time) a painting in the Cubist vein decked out with a title which his Cubist friends deemed heretical, *Nude Descending a Staircase*—discreetly submitted, under the pseudonym Richard Mutt, a lowly men's urinal to the hanging committee (chaired by none other than himself, what's more) for the first show to be put on by the Society of Independent Artists. It should be said that the Society of Independent Artists, which had been created six months earlier, had, at the prompting of the same French artist—Marcel Duchamp, not to mention names—modeled its statutes on those of the French *Société des artistes indépendants*, created in 1884 (a year after Manet died) by a group of French painters united around Seurat and infuriated by the discretionary powers of the Salon jury. The same Parisian motto was adopted in New York as in Paris: "No jury, no prizes," "*Ni récompense ni jury*." So the hanging committee had no power of censorship, and it was not asked to exercise its aesthetic judgment. Anyone who had taken out his or her Society membership card (for the modest sum of six dollars) was entitled to show two works in its show, a right which the mysterious Richard Mutt used—or misused—to submit for the approval of the New York public a thing which no one or nothing had ever been prepared to grant the dignified status of a work of art: a urinal! A vulgar urinal which, though spanking new and unused, smelt symbolically of piss and sexuality and, although titled *Fountain*, and duly signed and dated as artworks are, shamelessly sported its *thing*-like character. The *thing* was spirited away before the show and the New York public was not called upon to pass judgment, which hasn't stopped it from acquiring in art history books the status of an avant-garde icon, comparable, prestige-wise, solely with Malevich's *Black Square*. It was a photo, signed "Alfred Stieglitz" and published, once the exhibition was over, in a small magazine called *The Blind Man*, which was responsible for handing the work on to posterity. The photo leaves us in no doubt as to the nature of the *thing*. It was neither a painting nor a sculpture *representing* a urinal, no. Had it been a representation, the hanging committee, trained at the Ash Can School (the name of the first avant-garde movement in the United States), would probably have gone along with it. But no, it was a urinal, period. The *thing* was clearly not made by the hand of this Mr. Mutt, who dared to claim it as his own work. It was ready-made. A genuine urinal which the artist—if artist there indeed was—had contented himself with *presenting* for all to see on a stand, in a position which excluded any use of it and appeared to invite only its contemplation.

It is, of course, pure coincidence that the shape of Duchamp's urinal in Stieglitz's photo roughly matches that of Christ on his funereal throne in the Manet painting.

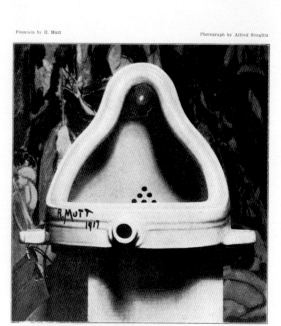

Fountain by R. Mutt

Photograph by Alfred Stieglitz

THE EXHIBIT REFUSED BY THE INDEPENDENTS

Marcel Duchamp
Fountain, 1917
Page from *The Blind Man*, 1917
photo Alfred Stieglitz

But it is most probably not a coincidence when the article accompanying the photo in *The Blind Man* calls the urinal by the name of a god in the title (*Buddha of the Bathroom*) and the mother of God in the text (which refers to *Madonna of the Bathroom*). There is every reason to suspect that the article was penned by an accomplice, and that the religious allusions smack deliberately of heresy. The *thing* doesn't appear designed to resurrect, either as a God or a man. For all this, we don't get away from the alternative imposed to aesthetics—either superstition or fetishism—once belief in God-man incarnate is lost. The *thing* swings either in the direction of the dead Father haunting the museum-temple, or towards "specialty" collectors come to the museum to enjoy their little perversions. Boy, how we've turned Duchamp into the parodying officiating priest of a cult which focuses, like the Christian mass, on the consecration! "*Hoc est corpus meum*, this is art," and that's done the trick. All the public has to do is to share, rapturously, in the belief in the Duchampian transsubstantiation, at the risk of seeing the museum-temple occupied by that nihilist god, the power of the art institution. When art for art's sake has become power for power's sake, we've reached that stage. It is easier, today, to *deify* Duchamp's urinal—especially if it's out of derision or desecration—than to find within it *human* qualities justifying our treating it with the respect due to works of art. Its avant-garde icon status, on an equal footing with Malevich's *Black Square*, is a misinterpretation—icons,

Marcel Duchamp's studio
33, West 67th Street, New York,
1917–1918
(photographer unknown)

not to put too fine a point on it, were never consecrated. Let's rather use the term "idol" to avoid wavering between sexual fetish and profane Host, which moves us both further away from and closer to the matter of the urinal's humanness—a harder one to deal with. It is hard to decide, for example, that the urinal sufficiently resembles us for us to reckon that it incarnates us. This was the issue in the period of Cubism and budding abstraction, when Duchamp was, officially, a Cubist painter and, secretly, Richard Mutt, but not yet the high priest of the cult that today's art-world celebrates in his name. Does the urinal resemble us enough for us to lend it a life of its own and the faculty of speech? In other words, can it present itself unaided, and say: "Here I am"?

Quite obviously not. It needs a display shelf, a monstrance or some other presentational device—namely, the pedestal it rests on in the Stieglitz photo. There's something suspicious about this photo, though. The only other two photos we have of the 1917 urinal, taken in Duchamp's studio, don't show it on any kind of pedestal at all, but hanging in a doorway in the company of a snow shovel and a hat-stand, also hung up, which would go down in history together with the urinal in the new art category of readymades. Wasn't Stieglitz tampering with Duchamp's intent just a tad? Stieglitz wasn't just any old Tom, Dick, or Harry. He was a very well-known artist-photographer, a gallery director, and a great campaigner for the cause of modern art in the United States. He had also introduced the New York public to Cézanne,

Matisse, and Rodin, and in his gallery he championed a handful of some of the most promising American painters, for whom he was God the Father. In those days he considered Duchamp to be a con artist, but he wasn't aware that the con artist in question was lurking behind Richard Mutt. He agreed to take the photo as a protest against the censorship of the hanging committee, but he was as taken aback, not to say shocked, as the committee itself at the idea that anyone might want to pass off a urinal as art. So he prettied up the presentation of the *thing*, cleverly lighting it, placing it delicately on its pedestal, and using a Marsden Hartley picture as a backdrop. If the pedestal was, indeed, the thing's presentational device, then Stieglitz was the presenter of the thing *with* its pedestal. In a nutshell, he played, out of loyalty, the part of ringmaster—*Monsieur Loyal*. The only thing motivating him was actually to make the brand new art institution, the Society of Independent Artists, comply with its statutes, which it had been in such a hurry to betray. Stieglitz was an élitist where art was concerned, but a democrat where politics were concerned, and he sincerely believed that the Society's radical egalitarianism, whereby anyone and everyone could be an artist, would, in the long run, serve the cause of the avant-garde in the United States, even if he had to give an eccentric agitator a bit of a boost to achieve as much. He was trying to find a compromise between his aesthetic standards and his democratic principles, by beautifying the *thing's* photographic presentation as much as it permitted. Poor Stieglitz. In this endeavor, he was the manipulated manipulator, for the boost in question exceeded anyone's wildest dreams. And Duchamp reaped the benefits, biding his time, slipping a readymade here and there into a Surrealist exhibition, and only owning up to Richard Mutt's true identity as the Second World War loomed, when he published the *Box in a Valise*, his portable museum. Nobody has ever since managed to remove from his famous urinal the invisible label which reads: "This is a work of art."

When we recall *how* Duchamp's urinal became art, we pay less attention to the fetishist mystique of its consecration than to the politics behind the whole affair. For it has its history, and it goes back a long way. Like its French namesake, the Society of Independent Artists came into being because artists were more than fed up with the arbitrariness of the only institution authorized to hand out legitimacy patents to anyone aspiring to the rank of professional artist. In the United States, it was the National Academy of Design, in France the *Société des artistes français*, itself a rickety offshoot of the countless crises of legitimacy afflicting the *Académie des Beaux-Arts* in the 19th century. The *Académie's* last official Salon, held in 1880, had been a complete fiasco, with a jury challenged by most of the artists involved and which, faced with the hue and cry, absolved itself of its responsibilities by accepting almost all the works submitted (7,289 in all!). Add to this a director who hung the worst artists in the best spots in order to poke fun at the jury, an unbridled criticism, a disgruntled public, and a deficit of about $120,000 in today's currency, and you will understand why, in 1881, Jules Ferry (who was not only Minister of Education but also Minister of Fine Arts) decided that the Government would no longer be involved with the Salons. And so it was that the *Société des artistes français* was founded. It took a mere three years for this body to see its jury challenged in turn by artists rallying around the "anarchists," Seurat, Signac, and Pissarro, who turned their backs on juries once and for all by founding the *Indépendants*. It's not easy for us to imagine, in our day and age, the sense of liberation that this independence represented for French artists of the day, and it's harder still for us to gauge its effects, which they themselves only half-understood. The mechanics of it all were twofold. Firstly, people realized that for virtually the first time since 1648, when the *Académie* was created, artists would be able to exhibit in public without having to be filtered by a directly or indirectly State-appointed jury, and they were delighted by this new-found freedom. Secondly, people realized that, under these conditions, anyone could be an artist, and there was alarm over the levelling down and loss of legitimacy that this might entail for serious artists. As is often the case in the history of avant-gardes, irony decreed that backward-looking art conservatives were quicker on the uptake than modernity's enthusiasts when it came to picking up on the dangers of the latter realization implicit in the liberation promised by the former. It is at such moments that the vaccine strategy becomes a matter of urgency for genuine artists, for they wish neither to take a step backwards nor to lower the standards of their art. From his own experience, Duchamp was equipped to grasp this necessity. Before his *Nude Descending a Staircase* brought him fame in New York, hadn't it been turned down by the hanging committee for the Cubist room at the 1912 *Salon des Indépendants* in Paris? (The *Indépendants* had no jury, but they had one or more hanging committees whose role was confined in principle to allocating places; here, it clearly exceeded its brief.) He developed a mood of rancor, a desire to get his own back, and a keen perception of what was at stake. The *Indépendants* had already betrayed their principles; it now remained to be seen just what purpose those principles served. So he made up his mind to toughen the test by upping the ante. Because the Americans, in 1916, were grappling with the same institutional censorship as the French in 1884, let's apply the same cure, or the same bug—they, too, must establish their own Society of Independent Artists. And because they will sooner or later be grappling with the same contradictions, let's give them the vaccine, in nothing less than small doses, and too bad if the vaccine kills the patient. This was Duchamp's strategy with his urinal. He was well-placed to sense how the New York Independents would develop—having himself been at the forefront in viewing the academization of the Parisian *Indépendants* and having borne the brunt of it. He drew up his plan well in advance, fixed things so that he was nominated chairman of the hanging committee, surreptitiously slipped a banana peel called *Fountain* under their feet, refrained from attending the stormy meeting of the said committee during which (nobody knows quite how) *Fountain* was spirited out of sight, solemnly handed in his resignation, worked it so that the *thing* reappeared as if by magic (here again, nobody knows quite how) in front of Stieglitz's lens without Stieglitz suspecting who sent it to him, published the photo in *The Blind Man*, let the storm blow over, and bided his time. The Society never got over it, and Duchamp clinched a place for himself in the 20th century which only Picasso could rival. Did you say strategy?

Yes, and vaccine strategy, too. Let commodity fetishism (as Marx would put it) vaccinate against the idolatry of Art with a capital A, and let the "anything whatever" vaccinate against the "anyone an artist." We mustn't be so naïve as to take Duchamp for a democrat when he inoculates America with the virus of artistic egalitarianism. It's when he injects the vaccine that he is one. In other words, Duchamp is an aristocrat, but an aristocrat who has understood that true nobility only makes sense in a radically egalitarian world, just as the real act of faith only makes sense in a radically belief-free world. In the same way as his *Dead Christ* was, for Manet, the vaccine for loss of faith in art, so, for Duchamp, *Fountain*, a ready-made object that anybody could have "made," was the vaccine against the levelling of aesthetic hierarchies. Likewise, though, just as Manet can only be understood in the context of the world of non-belief that his century drafted around him (with or without Renan), so we understand nothing about Duchamp if we separate the "Richard Mutt case" from the history of the *Indépendants*, in the wake of which it has become a *fait accompli* that anybody can be an artist. Needless to say, Duchamp is not just "anybody," nor just any old artist. He is the man through whom scandal was ushered in, and he deserves his place as artist of the century on a par with Picasso. For the latter half of the century—when his influence really started to make itself felt—this place has been interpreted as that of the demiurge, the great appropriator, King Midas turning everything he touches into art. People began talking of a Duchampian or a post-Duchampian artworld, a world where, indeed, anybody could be an artist, provided his strategy makes him master of the world in question. What a misreading! When at last shall we realize that the only strategic purport of the readymade is that it gave art back to anyone and everyone? Not for utopian reasons—that would be another misreading (from Novalis to Beuys, a whole Romantic tradition has dreamt that everybody would be an artist)—but quite simply because it's a *fait accompli* that art belongs to anyone and everyone the minute Salons are open to the masses as much as churches. In these conditions, what's the point of juries and their petty monopolies? The onus is upon the man-on-the-street to say who deserves to be an artist and who doesn't. Added to this is the fact that when artists are independent, in other words, liberated from the supervision of juries, the profession of artist is no longer protected and even the man-on-the-street can be an artist. The world no longer splits into the art-loving public, on the one side, and the artists' guild, on the other, and all a priori division of labour between judging art and making art has vanished. Whence the readymade—an object in front of which both the artist and the public are on equal footing, for neither has made it with their own hands. Both have just one thing to say about it: "This is art," or: "This is not art."

The readymade strategy sheds light not on the post-Duchampian but on the pre-Duchampian artworld. What Duchamp, as an artist, realized in 1917 had already been understood by Mallarmé, as a critic, in 1874. In that year, Manet (him again) submitted four canvases to the Salon. Two of them, *Masquerade at the Opera* and *Swallows*, were turned down. Mallarmé rallied to Manet's defence in an article where he wrote: "Entrusted by the nebulous vote of the painters with the responsibility of choosing, from among the pictures presented in a frame, those that truly exist as paintings, in order to put them before our eyes, the jury has nothing else to say but: this is a painting, or that is not a painting." It's worth noting the emphasis laid on the presentational device and on the presenter. Both are crucial. Mallarmé was well aware that the worst daubs can aspire to the title of painting if they are "presented in a frame," and only recognized the jury's one right, that of separating them from "those that truly exist as paintings, in order to put them before our eyes." In other words, to present them to us. Let the jury withdraw once the separation has been made; let it refrain from any judgment of taste. It is now up to us, Salon visitors, to decide which, among those pictures that *truly* exist as paintings, are *good* ones. Mallarmé required the jury to have a presenter's ethics, and was particularly keen that it didn't use its power to decide about aesthetic quality. The jury is responsible for drawing the boundary between those paintings which wouldn't even exist in its eyes without the authority of the presentational device, and those it reckons capable of presenting themselves on their own. Such is the nominal boundary between "that is not a painting" and "this is a painting." Mallarmé made these observations eleven years after the *Déjeuner sur l'herbe* (but not only the *Déjeuner*—many very mediocre paintings, too) had been labeled "that is not a painting" by the jury and "this is a painting" by … none other than Napoleon III, who may well have been no authority when it came to art, but was the emperor all the same. It was in fact under his patronage that the 1863 *Salon des refusés* was opened. The protests of the ousted artists had reached even his ears. With other fish to fry than playing arbiter of taste (but never passing up an opportunity for a little demagogy), he washed his hands of the *Académie* tiffs and opened, right opposite the official Salon, a pavilion where the masses would have to make do with the rejects. What happened next is history. No one remembers the 1863 Salon, but the *Salon des refusés* still basks in Manet's glory, Napoleon III's authority notwithstanding. Mallarmé's protest over the half-refusal of Manet at the 1874 Salon, the Impressionist exhibition at Nadar's that same year, and other "alternative" events were among the things that prompted the artists who had been barred from the 1884 Salon to join forces against the *Société des artistes français*, hold their own *Salon des Indépendants* in April, and eventually found the *Société des artistes indépendants* in June. Duchamp was mindful of all this in 1916 when, buoyed up by his prestige as both a Cubist painter and avant-garde troublemaker, he proposed setting up an American Society of Independent Artists, with its statutes modeled on those of its French namesake. He had understood all this when, six months later, he submitted to the Society's hanging committee a *thing* that it could neither include in its Salon without running the risk of discrediting all the Independents in one fell swoop, nor turn down without running the risk of creating a Salon *du* refusé for a single "work". And he had digested all that when he chose the thing in question in such a way that it banned any judgment of taste being applied to it, yet forced the hanging committee to decide whether or not it deserved to be offered to the public's judgment of taste. The Society's poor hanging committee was transformed by its chairman into a jury, but a very peculiar jury—a jury the likes of which history had not known, but the sort Mallarmé had wished for it to be. It shilly-shallied, dodged responsibility, and finally succeeded in whisking the thing away, all the while deciding nothing.

Without Stieglitz, it's not certain that Duchamp's urinal would have lived on. Hasn't the photographer, who despised Duchamp but was God the Father to his protégés, unwittingly played the part of the Mallarmean jury that the hanging committee failed to play? Or that of Napoleon III, perhaps? Out of loyalty to the Independents' maxim and counter to his own taste, he decided that the thing which landed before his lens had to be presented to the public. Not that it deserved to be. Because it couldn't be compared with anything artistic, it couldn't even be put among those "pictures presented in a frame" or sculptures presented on pedestals, from which, according to Mallarmé, the jury should select the "true" paintings and statues. This is indeed why he put the urinal on a stand before photographing it. It cried out for the presentational device in order to be a plausible candidate for the judgment of taste. And so loud that, not content with giving it just a stand, Stieglitz embellished its presentation as much as he could by using flattering lighting and the Marsden Hartley backdrop. The presenter's ethic didn't work for him unless he confused it with aesthetics. He completely failed to see that Duchamp's strategy actually relied on a presentational device other than the pedestal if *Fountain* were to go down in history—on a photo signed Alfred Stieglitz! When it was published in *The Blind Man*, it was with three captions: *Fountain by R. Mutt*, THE EXHIBIT REFUSED BY THE INDEPENDENTS, and *Photograph by Alfred Stieglitz*. We read the word "by" thrice: three authorial references, that is, references to authorities that it might be instructive to compare. Mr. Mutt may well be the "author" of *Fountain*, but he's strictly an unknown quantity; he hasn't done anything with his own hands; so he has no authority. Because of the Independents' refusal of the piece, they also lose theirs, inasmuch as the only legitimacy they ever had is bound up with the collective authority of their self-proclaimed artist members. They are left with the naked power of censorship. The only person with a real authorial ranking is Stieglitz. Of course, he isn't the author of *Fountain*, just of its presentational device—the photo which *represents* the thing and by the same token *presents* it to the posterity of its future beholders. Always one step ahead of his partners, Duchamp knew that not only are paintings and sculptures—even "true" paintings and sculptures—*things*, and things do not present themselves all on their own, but also that the frames around pictures and the stands beneath sculptures are things, too. In other words, he knew that presentational devices need a presenter; their authority is not *sui generis*. He got Stieglitz involved, and Stieglitz did have authority—the authority of God the Father within the little inner circle of artists he championed, the authority of an uncompromising gallery director in the world of art lovers, and the authority of a great photographer in the rest of the world. Stieglitz refused to exercise the first two variants, and if he did exercise the third, it was without suspecting that the unknown by the name of Richard Mutt would appropriate it. Perhaps he embodied the Mallarmé jury after all, or played the part of Napoleon III, but then against his will. He was so unconvinced that the thing was capable of presenting itself all on its own that he preferred to summon the traditional authority of the pedestal to give it a fair chance. The presenter took cover behind the convention of the presentational device. The fact remains that it's Stieglitz who must be credited, despite himself, with having propelled the thing into the museum, from which nobody, to date, has managed to flush it out.

Presentifications

Nobody, that is, except perhaps Marcel Broodthaers, Duchamp's most clear-sighted heir, in his own allegorical way. So what if we skipped to him, now? We're in 1964, exactly one century after Manet's *Dead Christ* and the selfsame year when Arturo Schwarz, a Milanese gallery owner with a passion for Duchamp, issued, with the latter's agreement, a series of a dozen readymades, with eight copies of each, plus two artist's editions. These figures tally with the number of editions of a bronze that can legitimately be considered originals. Officially rescued from the limbo accorded them, the readymades reconstructed by Schwarz (whose real "originals" had mostly vanished) thus acquired, in that very year, the same artistic dignity as a Rodin bronze, even though no one would dream of calling them sculptures. In the early 1960s we were in the thick of Pop Art and everyone, even a sculptor like Donald Judd, was happier talking about objects rather than sculptures. Duchamp's rating had never been higher. For more than ten years, his influence had been blazing an underground trail in the work of Johns and Rauschenberg in the United States, and in that of the British Pop artists, the *Décollagistes*, the *Nouveaux Réalistes*, and the *Zero* group in Europe. He had just had his first major retrospective at the Pasadena Museum in California, and it is no exaggeration to say that a whole generation of artists was feeling the need to take up a stance in relation to his. People weren't talking about Conceptual Art just yet, but the idea was gaining ground that since the readymade's invention, the concept of art had shifted. So that year, the poet Marcel Broodthaers, little read and penniless, as is the lot of poets, decided to try his luck as a visual artist, and wangled an exhibition at the Saint Laurent Gallery in Brussels. The invitation, printed on a printer's slip sheets, read as follows:

> I, too, have been wondering whether I couldn't sell something and succeed in life. It's been a while now that I've been good for nothing. I'm forty years old ... Finally the idea of inventing something insincere crossed my mind and I set to work forthwith. After three months, I showed what I'd done to Ph. Edouard Toussaint, owner of the Saint Laurent Gallery. But this is art, he said, and I'll gladly show it all. Okay, I replied. If I sell something, he'll take 30%. These are apparently normal conditions, though some galleries take 75%. What are we talking about? Objects, actually.
> Marcel Broodthaers.

Let's relish the cool wit of these few lines. It's a syringeful of vaccine that Broodthaers inoculates his potential audience with at the very start of his career. Playing ingénue, he declares deadpan that his succeeding in life depends on his commercial success, and he gives honest notice that he is driven by insincerity. When one thinks that sincerity is basically nothing other than the feeling of being honest, the turnaround has a certain piquancy. Having realized, better than anybody else, that the new disease which the vaccine strategy must vaccinate against is precisely art as strategy, he starts by flaunting his own. Since Duchamp's success has shown that anything and everything could be art, provided that it be recognized as such by the art institution, let it be proclaimed for all to hear that artists coming after Duchamp must now master no

Marcel Broodthaers

Section des figures
(Der Adler vom Oligozän bis heute),
Städtliche Kunsthalle Düsseldorf,
1972 (detail)

art other than the art of strategy, enabling them to penetrate the said institution. Thus did Broodthaers claim that he had been coopted by the artworld—he, the 40-year-old good-for-nothing who still hadn't sold a thing. It wasn't the artist, but the gallery owner who said: "But this is art, and I'll gladly show it all." Thus bolstered, Broodthaers embarked upon the production of objects, to which he affixed the ironic label "Belgian Pop Art," which were actually subtle allegorical comments on the situation of the artist who had "sold out before he'd been bought." Four years later, Broodthaers wound up his "Belgian Pop Art" phase and ushered in his "Musée d'art moderne" phase, which opened on 30 May 1968 with the occupation of the Palais des Beaux-Arts in Brussels by a group of anti-establishment artists.

In the thick of May '68, when everyone was giving in to a purely imaginary desire to break up institutions, Broodthaers realized that the artist was irrevocably compromised, and all the more so because the artworld in which he was moving was the post-Duchampian world, a world institutionalized through and through and which, with more or less cynicism and more or less thoughtlessness, had fallen in line with this one, circular, rule: a museum is a museum of art if it contains art; everything a museum of art contains is automatically art. To break the vicious circle of this tautology, Broodthaers then gave himself the status of museum director—a real director of a fictitious museum. The *Musée d'Art Moderne, Départment des Aigles* was created on 27 September 1968 at his Brussels home and inaugurated by Johannes Cladders, an authentic official of the post-Duchampian artworld. It went through several versions, one of the last being the *Section des Figures* in Düsseldorf, in 1972. In his self-styled role of museum director, Broodthaers brought together in the city's *Kunsthalle* some three hundred objects in an exhibition called *The Eagle from the Oligocene to the present*. Some of these objects were acknowledged works of art, others mere *things* taken from the vernacular culture and natural history museums. Master paintings and beer bottles, ornamented jewels and cigar bands, illuminations and advertisements, pre-Colombian sculptures and military emblems, all these objects bore the effigy of an eagle, and all had been borrowed from public and private collections. Each one of them was accompanied by a small black plastic sign stating, in three alternating languages: "This is not a work of art." In the catalog, Broodthaers pointed out that these signs "illustrate an idea of Marcel Duchamp and René Magritte," and juxtaposed on two facing pages the photo of the Schwarz version of Duchamp's urinal and the reproduction of Magritte's *La trahison des images*, the famous painting where Magritte captions the picture of a pipe with the sentence: "*Ceci n'est pas une pipe.*" Two years later, Broodthaers confirmed to Irmeline Lebeer: "'*Ceci n'est pas un objet d'art*' is a formula obtained by conflating a Duchamp concept and an antithetical Magritte concept."

Such a conflation has the kind of luminous simplicity that can, for a long time, veil the complexity of the underlying thinking: "*Ceci est un objet d'art*" + "*Ceci n'est pas une pipe*" = "*Ceci n'est pas un objet d'art.*" Broodthaers borrows from Magritte what it takes to deny Duchamp. The surprising thing is this borrowing. Had Broodthaers wanted to reverse the operation sanctioning a readymade, he didn't need to go through Magritte. Duchamp had already put forward the paradoxical idea of a *reciprocal readymade: using a Rembrandt as an ironing-board,* and had put it into practice more than once on his own work—for example, in 1950, when he exhibited in Sidney Janis' gallery a urinal similar to the one Stieglitz had photographed in 1917 in its tipped over position, but affixed to the wall in its "normal" position, and quite low down, "so that even little boys could use it." For lack of a Rembrandt to be used as an ironing-board, Duchamp used a Duchamp as a urinal instead. Broodthaers, it goes without saying, didn't use a Magritte as a pipe. Nor did he "really" want to chuck the urinal out of the museum. The exercise was of another kind, and brought into play the function of presentational devices and presenters in the post-Duchamp artworld. Any object whatsoever, provided it is presented in and by this tautology-ruled world, is automatically accompanied by an invisible label that reads: "This is art." Just as automatically, in fact, as a painting of a pipe is accompanied by an invisible label that says: "This is a pipe." An equation is thus established between the power of the institution and the power of pictures. Broodthaers has not only grasped that Duchamp's gesture with the readymade had been to reduce the work of art to the sentence sanctioning it, and that it is not the artist who has the authority to utter this sentence, but rather the institutional presenter, but he has also understood that Magritte's gesture with *La trahison des images* was to have *representation* reduced to *presentation*. Even in writing out in full: "*Ceci n'est pas une pipe*" under the depiction of a pipe, it is quite simply not possible to prevent the image from being the pipe's *presentational device*. The two gestures, Duchamp's and Magritte's, are linked together by an equation whose middle term is the notion of power, where "power" means, on the one hand, "institutional authority" and, on the other, "persuasive force of figurative images." The perception of this equation is Broodthaers' stroke of genius. It is also what makes the qualitative leap between his "Belgian Pop Art" phase and his "Musée d'art moderne" phase. Nothing records this better than the excerpt from his interview with Irmeline Lebeer, where the conversation shifts from committed art to *indifferent* art. Indifferent art is made, Broodthaers suggests, "from the moment when you're less of an artist, when the need to make thrusts its roots into memory alone. I believe

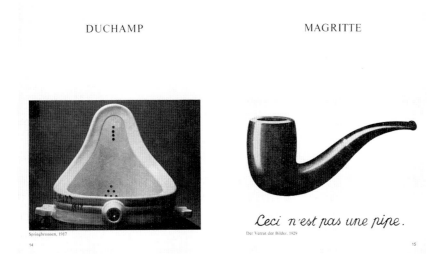

Marcel Broodthaers
Section des figures (Der Adler vom Oligozän bis heute),
Städtliche Kunsthalle Düsseldorf, 1972 : double page from the catalog

my shows depended, and still depend, on memories of the time when I used to embrace the creative situation in a heroic and solitary form. In other words—Back then: Read, look. Today: Allow me to present you …"

It would be falling for a red herring to see in Broodthaers' *indifferent* art a refusal of political commitment. There's a certain type of political commitment—the "May '68" type, or the "occupation of the Palais des Beaux-Arts" type—whose inefficiency Broodthaers had understood in the interval between 30 May and 27 September 1968. The occupation of the Palais des Beaux-Arts couldn't go on forever. The institution would always get the upper hand. None of the 1960s' utopias—street art, happenings, multiples, audience participation as advocated by Kinetic Art, Situationism, the so-called de-materialization of the art object by Conceptual Art, Land Art's flight into the desert—offered a viable alternative to art for museums. So this is what needed rethinking. Just as it made no difference whether Manet had painted for the Salon or the Museum, so it would in the end prove *indifferent* whether Broodthaers "succeeded in life" because he's had the right strategy for penetrating the art institution, or because he was a good artist. Needless to say, this particular indifference—vaccine strategy *oblige*—ought to make the difference. Its task is to neutralize the institution's power and render unto Caesar that which is Caesar's. In other words, render to the institution the ethic of the presenter that it should never have betrayed, and to the public the right to love or hate with no holds barred. Nothing truly fundamental has changed between the Salon in the days of Manet and the contemporary salons which emerged in the postwar years, the Documentas, the Venice and other Biennales, and the art fairs here, there, and everywhere—this whole spectacular absorption of art into the leisure industry and the marketing of "spirituality." Nothing's changed except that along came Duchamp, and that after Duchamp, the sentence "this is art" took on such intimidating force that it's become virtually indelible. Appealing to the love of art among a public, about which, *a priori*, we don't really know any more today than in Manet's day whether it might have a sufficiently trained mind, a sufficiently keen eye, and a heart sufficiently open to allow itself to be touched, is infinitely harder after Duchamp than before him, because the best informed chunk of this public knows, or thinks it knows, that the die is cast—if it's in the museum, it's art. The rest of the public just has the option either to give in to intimidation, or feel like philistines. Here, we're getting close to the limit where the vaccine has been injected in such doses that we can no longer tell it apart from the disease. Broodthaers is virtually the only one of his generation of artists to have understood this. He has grasped the far-reaching, altogether institutional, tautological and, for the true artist, tragic meaning of art as strategy. Making art has turned into a kind of war game played exclusively among artists, gallery owners and curators of contemporary art, with the public on the sidelines. Either the artist and the curator play the game of escalation, and the challenge is invariably knowing who has the edge over whom (Daniel Buren is a master at this war game). Or, frankly displaying his bad faith, the artist usurps the curator's role and plays the part of the man in power, the better to disempower him. Innocence comes at the price of a devious perversity. The

Marcel Broodthaers
Untitled
(commonly called
Le Général au cigare),
1970

artist as museum director? Yes, in other words, the artist as *insincere* ringmaster: "Allow me to present you ..."

Stieglitz had played the ringmaster out of loyalty to the Independents' maxim: "No jury, no prizes," and, despite himself, invested his authority as a great photographer in an unknown entity called Richard Mutt. This Mutt turned out, in retrospect, to be the artist-chairman of the Independents' hanging committee—the charismatic head presenter. Fifty years later, the entire artworld is beholden to his authority. In the late 1960s, a new figure appeared in the artworld, half-exhibition organizer, half-artist, sometimes a gallery owner and dealer, always a promoter of new trends. Seth Siegelaub in the United States, Michel Claura in France, Harald Szeemann in Switzerland, Fernand Spillemaeckers and Marc Poirier dit Caulier in Belgium, among others, have all seen their role as being that of art presenter, authorized, usually unbeknownst to them, by Duchamp. When Broodthaers created his *Musée d'Art Moderne, Département des Aigles* just a few days before Duchamp died, he responded to them by putting the post-Duchamp artworld under the anti-authority of Magritte. The "formula obtained by conflating a Duchamp concept and an antithetical Magritte concept" is the poetic and political equation which, as he said to Irmeline Lebeer, helped him "to decorate Duchamp's urinal with the insignia of the Eagle smoking a pipe." In the same interview, Broodthaers added: "I think I've emphasized the principle of authority that makes the symbol of the Eagle the colonel of art." The catalog where the interview was published contains, twice over, the image of a "dead general smoking an unlit cigar." The parallel with a "colonel of art" smoking a pipe sticks out by a mile. Under Broodthaers' eye, Magritte's pipe takes on a political significance: the colonel of art is dead and the pipe is out. In other words, the Eagle is deposed.

Of course, the same applies to Art with a capital A as it does to Eagle with a capital E. "The exhibition concept is based on the identity of the Eagle as an idea and Art as an idea." This is the identity—or, better still, the equation—that Broodthaers proceeded to present under the title *The Eagle from the Oligocene to the present*. Equations between ideas, and ideas themselves, are not presentable, though. It isn't possible to show ideas or put them on a stand, because they are mental and thus invisible (*conceptual*, as the jargon in force in the eponymous art form has it). And yet, there is a well-known technique of classical rhetoric—a *figure* of speech—which, for want of making ideas presentable, makes them representable. We're talking about allegory. Just as a blindfolded woman holding a scales represents the idea of justice, so an eagle represents the idea of power. More than one empire has availed itself of the image—whether one- or two-headed, the eagle is imperial—and to such an extent that the allegory has frozen into a symbol. Using the fact that allegory, symbol, and emblem are representations and that these can be presented as objects, Broodthaers managed to visualize the invisible, show the exhibition concept, and *presentify* what is not presentable as such. How did he manage this? The subtitle of the Düsseldorf exhibition says it all: *Marcel Broodthaers Shows an Experimental Exhibition of His Musée d'Art Moderne, Département des Aigles, Section des Figures*. Every word counts, starting with *Marcel Broodthaers Shows*. What did he choose to show? *An*

Experimental Exhibition, a test. What's the test about? Monstrance itself, presentation. What's being presented? The *Section des Figures* of the *Département des Aigles* in his own *Musée d'Art Moderne*, as if he were striving to have us believe that art responds to a taxonomy carefully hierarchized into Museum, Department, and Section. Last of all, what does the *Section des Figures* contain? Some three hundred objects systematically denied their status as art objects and for the most part decorated with the image of an eagle that *already* has the status of a figure of speech— whether allegory, emblem, or symbol of power. The emphasis is laid not so much on the objects as on the presentational devices. The exhibition walls, littered with pictures and images, the slide projectors, the stands, and, above all, the vitrines with their old-fashioned charm and their "Natural History Museum" look, are too exotic in this setting to go unnoticed. All these presentational devices *present* objects that *present* an image that *represents* an eagle. "*Publikum, wie bist Du blind!*," rails Broodthaers at the blind who forget that, meantime, Magritte had reduced representation to presentation, and who think that they're dealing with the eagle theme in all its variations: "the eagle in art, in history, in ethnology, in folklore …" Blind to ideas—and for a good reason: they aren't visible—this public cannot conceive that we are neither in the Natural History Museum, nor in the Empire Museum, nor in a "real" art museum, but in the company of an artist who takes hold of the Museum idea in general and turns it into an allegory of an allegory, presentifying his own conception of art. Even those visitors bred on the latest conceptual trends should no longer imagine that it is possible to subsume eagle *figures* under the concept of art, the way it is possible to subsume those majestic birds of prey under the concept of eagle. "The Eagle as idea" is to "Art as idea" what museum director Broodthaers is to artist Broodthaers. What both Broodthaers seem to share is a power, which means "institutional authority" for the museum director and "persuasive force of figurative images" for the artist. What they actually share is a presenter's ethic. When Broodthaers presents some three hundred objects representing an eagle, accompanying them with a sign which also presents them, but robbed of their artistic authority, he is in fact *presentifying* the equation: "Art = Eagle = Power," by emphasizing three hundred times the fact that what's involved here is an idea, and it isn't his.

Even if we climbed up the trail back to Napoleon III, the president-prince who became the first emperor of the bourgeois era, under whose supreme authority the *Salon des refusés* was opened, we would still understand only the caricature of the allegory of the Eagle that Broodthaers deposes. We should both stop much closer to us and go much further back in history to understand why Broodthaers, an unrepentant aesthete seemingly wrapped in the melancholy of bygone styles, chose to inhabit the Second Empire with such ease that he bumps into Baudelaire and Mallarmé in almost every one of his works. Closer to our time, that is, in the Third Reich: the Nazi Eagle (conspicuously absent from the Düsseldorf catalog, and we might well wonder why) tears a hole in the history of humankind in no way commensurate with the break made by Duchamp's urinal in the history of art, even if decorating this latter with the insignia of the former might have opened up a chasm of reflection about the responsibility and irresponsibility of artists in the fearsome 20th century. And further back: to the First Empire (which Broodthaers also visited, with *The Battle of Waterloo*); to the sack of Europe by Napoleon's armies and the *petit caporal*'s confiscation of the republican ideal; to the two-headed eagle of the Habsburgs; to the imperial eagles of Rome. And further away, too: to Greece, and the two eagles guarding the *omphalos* at Delphi; to Persia, to the mythical eagle of the Achaemenids; to the Americas, to the solitary eagle of the Aztecs and the Amerindian peoples. And deeper: to the myths, the myth of Ganymede, carried off by Zeus disguised as an eagle, and the myth of Prometheus, condemned by the same Zeus to watch his liver being devoured by an eagle day after day. And to religions, which have all kept a symbolic place for the eagle—not forgetting, for Christendom, the eagle that is the symbol of St. John, the fourth evangelist and author of the Apocalypse. And much more troubling: to those obscure regions of the human soul where the symbol of the eagle intermingles sexuality, submission to Power, and the need for God, inescapably justifying some holy war or other. The majesty of the soaring bird has everywhere been likened to that of a war lord, and vice versa. Even more than power, it is war—the art of war, i.e. strategy—which is the common denominator that links Art and Eagle, with a capital A and E.

It is this Art with a capital A that Broodthaers' art with a small a deposes. Admittedly, it doesn't readily yield up the clues to its understanding: an art that espouses the vaccine strategy so as to vaccinate against art as strategy is bound to be somewhat obscure. It's no longer enough to summon aesthetic emotion to touch the audience and invite it to yield before the work's appearance. This might just about suffice to see Manet's *Dead Christ* rise from the dead, but it's not enough to read the revival of "this is art" out of an exhibition that makes it a point of honor to deny it three hundred times. We may complain about this, as ever. It's not surprising that the hermeticism of the avant-garde should be at its peak when it is precisely the bellicose connotations of the word "avant-garde" from which the love of art has to rescue the works. Duchamp had been there. For the most avant-gardistic factions of the art scene in the 1970s, this meant that the work's art status no longer had a great deal to do with aesthetic emotion or quality. Hadn't the readymade shown that all that matters in a successful work is the questioning it sparks off about the concept of art? Broodthaers feigned to agree with them, and then proved them wrong, when his own questioning about the concept of art had freed up another interpretation of the readymade. The Düsseldorf exhibition was an *installation* exploiting the mania for classification that goes on in those provincial museums to which the quirks of history have entrusted collections made up of motley bits and pieces with a vague status, somewhere between art objects, ethnological artefacts, and relics of the past. The objects in the show were grouped together according to such categories and nevertheless had their differences smoothed out by the unity stemming, Eagle-wise, from the iconography, and by the very marked *indifference* permeating the arrangement, and which emanated, Art-wise, from the obsessive repetition of the signs warning that one should not always trust the conventions of classification. Rubbed up the wrong way by "This is not a work of art" when the sentence labels an eagle's head from Ingres' pencil, viewers must have wondered at the warning when it accompanies a typewriter brandnamed Adler. All this is a source of confusion. A source of reflection, too, for anyone who can be bothered. But not a source of immediate aesthetic emotion. The aesthetic—in other words, loving—relationship to art is, to all appearances, discredited in favor of the intellectual relationship to art, and it'll be hard, this time around, to turn appearances against appearances, in order to rediscover, *in fine*, the willingness to let oneself be touched. Let's say it again: Duchamp had been there. Now everything depends on the interpretation we give to his gesture.

Halfway between Manet's *Dead Christ* and Broodthaers' eagle *figures*, Duchamp's urinal is a milestone beyond which aesthetics is no longer quite what it used to be. Yet, believing that a work no longer needs to touch us to be a work of art comes from the same misapprehension as the one that sees Duchamp as the great appropriator in whose wake artists no longer have any other talent to possess and technique to master than the art of strategy opening the doors of the institution to them. To applaud them for criticizing the system from within doesn't make the misapprehension any the less tragic for art, for the public that doesn't necessarily derive its pleasure from the fact of seeing itself as part and parcel of the institution, and for those artists for whom the hope of touching the public is more rewarding than the intention of playing some coded war game with the artworld. Broodthaers indicates that there are other possible interpretations of *Fountain* and the readymade in general: aesthetic judgment invariably calls for a readiness to be touched, but it can henceforth be expressed by "this thing is art" just as much, say, as by "this picture is good". The sentence "this is art," as it can be applied *a priori* to anything and everything, redefines the loving relationship to art as a readiness to be touched aesthetically by *something*—any thing whatever—so as to judge whether or not it deserves to be called art. What Duchamp changed in the loving relationship to art wasn't much, in theory, but it was huge, socially speaking. The novelty is that *Fountain*'s status of a mere thing stemming from no artistic craft whatsoever requires on the part of the viewers a generalization process that invites them to take this particular specimen of a urinal—the one before their very eyes—for an *example* of any object whatever, within or outside established artistic categories, but a candidate for art all the same. Less clued-in viewers carry out this operation spontaneaously, helped in this by the object's industrial nature. We can even say that the less clued-in the viewers, the more spontaneously they will generalize. The layman exclaiming: "If that is art, then anything and everything can be art!" implies: "If the guy who did that is an artist, then so am I."

Mindful, like Broodthaers, of the consequences of Duchamp's gesture and eager, like him, to free contemporary art from its confinement within art as institution, certain well-intentioned critics, albeit timorous in their tastes and their "politics" alike, have acknowledged the wonderful popular wisdom of the layman, but instead of this being a cause for rejoicing, it became a cause for alarm. Needlessly. There is absolutely zero risk of anyone and everyone becoming an artist, and of art succumbing to the "anything whatever," provided we let aesthetic judgment do the sorting—given that aesthetics is no longer quite the same after Duchamp as it was before. Other critics lament the utopia which, from Novalis to Beuys, dreamt of everyone becoming an artist some day. It may be distressing to kiss it goodbye; in any event, it wasn't realistic, and no genuine art lover has ever subscribed to it other than through ideology. The only utopia worth defending is the one that starts out from what Duchamp had already realized: when artists' works are exhibited in places open to the crowd (as only churches used to be under the *ancien régime*), and when the profession of artist is no longer protected (unlike the way things were under the *ancien régime*), it is then a *fait accompli* that art belongs to anyone and everyone. In order for the layman to draw the logical conclusion that art has been rendered unto him, all that he's possibly missing is an awareness of the fact that it's up to him to deem "whether the guy who did that is an artist." Fearsome freedom this, whose correlate is the responsibility shared on an equal footing by exhibition curators, museum directors, and artists. Broodthaers was all three rolled into one, and assumed this responsibility, having grasped that all three are presenters—exhibition curators in the manner of 19th-century Salon juries, post-Duchamp museum directors in the manner of Duchamp himself, and artists in the manner of the layman whom Duchamp put in the place of the Salon jury. And the logic has come full circle, which reminds us of the ethic that Mallarmé demanded of the jury when he asked it to sort the works it would submit or refuse to submit to the public eye by "this is a painting," or "that is not a painting." Indeed this is the ethic of a presenter, who doesn't exercise his authority to make pronouncements about the quality and beauty of things "presented in a frame," but merely to draw the nominal boundary between things which, in his eyes, wouldn't exist without calling upon the authority of the presentational device, and those which he reckons capable of presenting themselves all on their own. Because no *thing* is capable of presenting itself all on its own, reckoning something to be capable thereof is to give it the same *esteem* as a talking, living being. Mallarmé wanted this *estimation* to carry the decision to present it for the public to appraise. It's been done, now that the readymade has gone down in history. In the aftermath, whoever reckons that a urinal—or any other thing, like an installation consisting of three hundred images of eagles—is art, finds himself in the position of telling the public after him: "Here it is. Your turn."

Presents

"*Voici*" (literally, "see this") is a verbal presentational device. There are others in its group. Pronouns, demonstratives, and adverbs of time and place are presentational devices, too. "I," "you," "he" and "she" are respectively presentational devices of the person speaking, being spoken to, and being spoken about. And when what you're talking about is a thing, its presentational device is "this" or "that." The words "here" and "now" present those circumstances of speech that we happen to call the present. And so on and so forth. Words such as these, which linguists call deictics, point toward the world beyond language but are nevertheless confined within language, like all words. They depend on the real, on the locutor, and on each other for us to know what they are designating. The word "I" shifts with the person talking, the word "tomorrow" with today's date, and the word "today" with time passing. The word "this" is like a forefinger pointing at something; but without a thing at the forefinger's tip, without another flesh and blood finger to show the thing, without someone to utter the word and someone else to hear it, what exactly is *this*? Deictics are presentational words under guardianship; behind them hides the authority of the presenter who appropriates them. They should be imagined left to their own devices, freed from the mouths uttering them, and as if etched by an anonymous hand on loose sheets of paper. We would then see them wandering about in the prison of language, available to one and all, and behaving like nomadic proper nouns, both detachable and detached—in a word, free. Free to select their referents. Like all words, they are also at liberty—a particularly mischievous variety in their case—to designate themselves, to be self-referential. "Nebuchadnezzar, king of Babylon, write that for me in four letters." Magritte was no stranger to such mischief. What does "this" designate in his famous "This is not a pipe"? The pipe? Its drawing? The word "this" itself? And what does it designate in the "This is not a work of art" engraved three hundred times by Broodthaers on his little black plastic signs? Itself? The sign? The object associated with the sign? The image displayed by the object? The eagle inhabiting the image? Or, alternatively, the equation "Art = Eagle = Power = Strategy"? The denial of Duchamp via Magritte? The exhibition concept? Concepts are not objects. Because they are invisible, they cannot be presented, only presentified. Yet the word "*voici*" definitely does present. It is the supreme presentational word, for it means "see this; look; everything to be understood has first of all to be seen." "*Voici*" is a word for visual artists.

In the late 1960s, when Broodthaers started to "succeed in life," Conceptual Art was the thing. A word-based art convinced that words are presentational devices for ideas, whereas words are scarcely more capable of presenting ideas than a pedestal—they can only presentify them. Visual art gets lousy press, as if its offering something to see hampered it from offering something to think about. Painters in particular suffer from this bad reputation. They are reproached for being formalists, which means stupid in the jargon of the day—they produce decoration and illustrate Greenberg's theories about "modernist painting." Poor Greenberg. For a lot of American artists, he was *the* reference at the beginning of the decade, and anybody who was anybody in the New York art scene swore by him. Ten years later, he had been deposed by Duchamp and only wielded his influence over a handful of small circles of provincial painters, like the group that regularly invited him to Emma Lake, in Canada—where we are going now. Not to rejoin Greenberg and his circle, but to catch up with a great artist, though not well-known outside his own country—the last artist in the dazzling summary that has allowed us to extract, from the history of modern art, the issue of "*Me voici*—Here I am." This artist is Michael Snow, and he is the most protean artist there is. A painter by day, by night he was a jazz pianist in a Toronto nightclub when the most perceptive critics started to take an interest in him, in the late 1950s. One of his last "Greenbergian" paintings, *Lac clair* (1960), was, even then, a parody of Greenberg's theories. A little later, he would go and live in New York, and for six years paint, sculpt, photograph, and film countless variations of his *Walking Woman* before producing, in 1967, his masterpiece of experimental film called *Wavelength*, which won an award that same year at the Knokke-le-Zoute festival. He returned to Toronto in 1974, and since then he has been involved in painting, sculpture, photography, film, installations, writing, and music, with sorties into holography and the new technologies. Being a true child of Duchamp, Snow realized that you could make art with any medium whatsoever, and that what it was henceforth important to explore was the interplay between media. His impressive film career was interrupted in 1974, after he'd made *Rameau's Nephew by Diderot (Thanx to Dennis Young) by Wilma Schoen*, the longest and most complex of all his films (four hours), and then resumed in 1980–82 with two films made in quick succession, *Presents* and *So Is This*.

The issue of presentation and all its corollaries—presentational device, presenter, and presentification—lies at the nub of *Presents* (which Snow wants us to read with the stress on either syllable). The film (16 mm color, 90 minutes) starts like a Barnett Newman-style "zip," accompanied by an electronic soundtrack. A thin vertical slit gradually opens onto a scene shot in video. The whole image is actually squeezed into the crease of light. The anamorphosis is gradually rectified as the image broadens out, and when it is as wide as the screen, we recognize a composition typically borrowed from the history of painting—a female nude lying on a bed, described by one critic as a remake of Manet's *Olympia*, but which is more reminiscent of Ingres'

Michael Snow

Presents, 1980, film 16 mm, color, sound, 90 minutes

Michael Snow
Presents, 1980
Production shots

Grande Odalisque. The image is then squeezed again, but vertically this time around, until the whole scene is compressed into a horizontal crack, and then the cycle starts all over again. At a given moment, the grain of the image changes and we realize that we've moved from a video image to a cinematographic image, whose finer resolution emphasizes the garish, artificial hues of the set. We are in a bedroom parody. The sound is now synchronized. We hear knocking at the door. The woman gets up, slips on a dressing-gown and walks to the right of the screen, her gait oddly hesistant. When she opens the door and walks into the adjoining room, it becomes obvious that the filmmaker is showing us a set with the fourth wall missing. This time we're in a combination living-room-dining-room-study—its design ludicrously amateur-ish. The furniture looks as if it's made of cardboard, and in fact most of it is. A man clutching a bunch of flowers ushers the woman in, and hands her the bouquet. She goes back to the bedroom to put the flowers in a vase, then returns, her gait still just as unsteady. All this (and what follows) is shot in a single sequence which follows the woman as she moves to and fro. The pan continues to the right while the couple seems to be having trouble staying upright, their stumbling coinciding with the jerkiness of the tracking shot, which comes across as being very badly executed. On the soundtrack, barked commands ("Forward!," "Back!") and the seemingly responding sounds of a truck's engine are overdubbed on a Bach solo cello suite interrupted by dreadful scratching sounds, as if a record-player needle had slipped, bumped by uncontrollable jolts. And this is actually what's happening. It wasn't the movement of the camera making the pan, but the movement of the set itself, heaved by two fork-lifts. It would take too long to describe the remainder of the scene, which is irre-sistibly funny and thoroughly enigmatic until we've understood that Michael Snow has presentified for us, with the first two sequences of *Presents*, the most critical reflection imaginable about our blindness in front of the conventions of presentation governing the art of cinema. No presentational device has any credibility left—nei-ther the frame of the image, elastic in the video sequence, nor the resolution of the TV image, whose coding the shift to film which starts the second sequence under-scores, nor the relative movements of camera and set, nor even the benevolent voyeurism of the camera. Indeed, at the end of the scene, the camera climbs onto the stage, elbows the characters, proceeds into the set, and violently destroys it. (A pane of glass was set up in front of the camera, itself mounted on a dolly cobbled togeth-er out of a wheelchair; it shoves and squashes the cardboard scenery as it moves for-ward.) In traditional filmmaking, the camera isn't meant to leave any signs of its pres-ence in the reality it's shooting. Yet it is Number One in the hierarchy of presenta-tional devices used by the art of cinema to depict the visible. It's the camera, more than either the script or the editing, to which all directors give the responsibility of addressing the audience with: "*Voici*. Look here." Without the camera there wouldn't be anything on movie house screens. But it is supposed to remain humble and discreet, at the beck and call of both the director's intentions and the conven-tions of representation. Some experimental filmmakers have been eager to pull it up out of its servile status and let it have the leading role, but in order the better still to subjugate it—to their *ego*. For Stan Brakhage, the camera was not just the presenta-tional device, but the organ through which the artist viewed the world—"my eye," he would say. In *Presents* it is so far from being Snow's eye that it refuses to budge, unruffled while he flaps about and uses great expenditure to make sure that it's the whole thing—stage, scenery, actors—moving about in front of it. It is said that, at the cinema, the audience is in the camera's seat. This is true with respect to the *repre-sented* scene, not so with respect to the *presented* scene—the scene that presents itself to the camera during the shooting, and for which the camera is the presentational device. The camera wears itself out while the audience sits. The director and the viewer have reached an understanding at the camera's expense to see that it will bring back images from the other side of the earth, if need be, to present them to Master viewer without his having to move. This pact is the basic convention of film repre-sentation, and everything that has to do with presentation is subordinate to it. In *Presents*, the presentational device gets its own back. It's a simple matter of fairness: since the viewer takes the place of the camera during the screening, let the camera take the place of the viewer during the shooting! It is in on the show, sovereign, even if it so upsets it that the viewer forgets the simple story being told him or her (a man offers flowers to the woman he loves …) and starts to suspect the script of actually dealing with something quite different—self-referential stories where the film talks of film conventions, period. But the camera's revenge doesn't stop here. It is even right here, in the wised-up viewer's suspicion, that it really starts, and that the enraged camera gets carried away. As if it were furious at being reduced to commenting on film conventions, it abandons its sovereign perch, invades the stage and destroys everything that gets in its way. Why on earth does it lose its cool? The camera has a lousy and cumbersome reputation. It is said to be a great image hunter—a thief and a killer, that is—whereas it feels it has a quite different calling: it is made for giving. Offering something to see, presenting. Nobody wants its generosity. So, having had enough, it counter-attacks. Experimental film is called avant-garde? Fine. *En avant*, full steam ahead. The poor thing blows its top, and its reaction is a sheer *acting out*. It doesn't have any strategy, turns into a terrorist, undiscriminatingly wrecks everything that comes before it, and ends up leaving the scene of its crime in a panic, vanishing into a hole in the set which it has made itself.

We figure that, from this point on, the artist intends to address a viewer who's not only wised-up, but stupefied by all this violence. The last part of the film (and the longest, lasting an hour) reinstates the viewer's innocence, and restores to the camera its pleasure in giving. It consists of almost two thousand shots edited together end-to-end and punctuated by a drum beat with each cut. Sequences, for the most part very short, are filmed at arm's length by an ever-moving camera "aiming" at likewise ever-moving objects and beings: a passing car, an aircraft landing, a man or a woman moving through a crowd, a hunted caribou limping through the snow, a thousand other moving and nomadic things, and countless birds gliding in the sky. Not to forget a woman's pudenda, stared at by the camera, in close-up, which says a whole lot about the desire to give and the travels it spawns. Not a word and certainly no music on the soundtrack; nothing but a drum beat underlining the editing. We are being offered fragments of reality in the rough, caught in flight, beginning- and endless, and mind-blowingly beautiful if we let go. The shoulder-held camera calls to mind the aesthetics of *cinéma-vérité*, except we don't know what truth this particular cinema is serving. The series of shots don't form sequences, nor sequences scenes, nor scenes a narrative, nor the narrative a film. The meaning of the whole is a mystery. Two thousand little gems of pure visuality threaded together like beads on a necklace—the world offered in bits, in motion, in the present, without the weight of the world to cope with. A true present, indeed.

The critics slammed *Presents*. Those in the know about experimental film and those best-versed in the "structuralist" deconstruction (all the rage in film magazines in the 1970s) were those most thrown into confusion by the last part of the film. Yet they were the best-placed to call themselves wised-up. They had seen—or rather, read—the first two parts as a critique of film representation and had declared themselves delighted. Like most intellectuals in the artworld of the times, they were convinced that "critic" rhymed with "skeptic," and they thought Snow was on their side. Once again, the filmmaker of *Wavelength* and *Rameau's Nephew* had subjected one or two Hollywood film conventions to his scathing irony. The narrative offered was no longer believable, the couple in the story came across like the actors they were, the set like a set, the image like an image, the framing like a contrivance, the synchronized background music like a convention that is shattered. And the camera work made its presence known *a contrario* in the busy labor that its immobility forced all around it. Cinema was given a theory lesson by *experimental* cinema, with an artist-*cum*-semiologist having shown it that it is no more than a language confined within itself. You can't get away from representation; thinking you can is the most naïve of illusions; nipping this belief in the bud is Snow's salutary lesson in the first two parts of *Presents*. Thus ran the argument of the critics best informed about "structural" film and up-to-date film theories. They had trouble including the third part of the film in their agenda, and declared it tedious. The idea that an artist might seek to resurrect *presentation* out of the reduplications of *representation* did not even cross their minds, and even less the idea that the camera's revolt could be motivated by the fact that it no longer tolerates being confined in the boundaries of "film language," whereas it feels called on to open up a window onto the world. They completely missed the fact that Snow was attacking the conventions of experimental film becoming academicized every bit as much as the conventions of Hollywood cinema. They also missed the non-strategic reversal—the *revolution*, in the literal sense—set forth by the camera's incoherent "acting out." They picked up on the irony in the title's wordplay. They read it, but not out loud, refusing to hear in it the words "present" (gift) and "presence" which it nevertheless contains. That an artist as aware as Snow of film conventions could sincerely believe that the task of the presentational device was to present—this was more than they could bear. In the editing cuts leaping from drum beat to drum beat, all they saw was the cut and all they heard was the repetition, without wondering whether the filmmaker's obsession was not a sign of his obstinate desire for fresh starts, despite the taboo. In the huge number of shots, they read an endless inventory of bits and pieces of the world mapped onto the inventory of editing procedures, without narrative unity and synthesis, nonsensical—all of which was to their liking because these were negative qualities. They remained impervious to the breakaways of the hand-held camera, the smoothness of its movement, the musical rhythm of the editing, and the rhyming effects brought about by the recurrence of similar images. Or, if they were not altogether impervious to them, they didn't know what to make of them beyond their deconstructive reading. It should be said that Snow had done nothing to break them out of their habits in the first two parts of the film, and that not a clue was given that might provide a reading for the camera's revolt at the juncture of the second and third parts. And with good reason: his film is a diatribe against *reading* and a plea for *looking*. But the critics made a point of not looking beyond their self-referential readings. "When the wise man points his finger at the moon, the fool looks at the finger," as a Chinese proverb has it. When a camera films a bird in flight, the film critic looks at the camera work and speculates about film language; and fails to see the free-flying bird, the moon at the fingertip, reality offered, the *present*; and shuts himself off from the meaning of the film. He doesn't want to see that the recurrent caribou hunt, which he can't help thinking makes the metaphor of image hunting a literal one, is filmed with such an

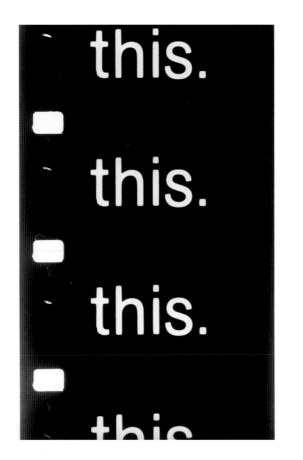

Michael Snow
So Is This, 1982, film 16 mm,
color, silent, 43 minutes

empathy for the creature that it says a whole lot about the image hunter's feelings for his medium. He doesn't want to see that it is poignant and not merely "critical" to castrate the camera's enthusiasm. Above all, he refuses to see that in these abruptly cut flights of the image there are, all the same, birds soaring languidly, borne along by the wind and their whims, and that the flight of a bird has always been the most wonderful symbol of freedom there is. In *Presents* he has read everything, but seen nothing. This critic and his theorist colleagues put a great deal of energy into their skepticism. Armed with abstruse semiotics and suspecting all presence of only ever being an illusionist effect of representation, they end up doubting the fact that images show something other than their own techniques. They only conceive of their experience of experimental film as confined within a laboratory on whose door is written: "Here we make films about film!" without even being aware of the prison they have built for themselves. Obsessed by their radical lack of faith in images, they are in fact true believers, no matter how skeptical they say they may be. So converted are they to the religion of "This is not a Pipe" that they very nearly wouldn't see the pipe in Magritte's *La Trahison des Images*. For them, the word "this" can refer only to itself.

Spurred on by the disappointing critical response *Presents* received, Snow straightaway dug out a script that had been collecting dust since 1975, and made *So Is This*.

(The literal French translation would be: *Voici ceci*.) Since the most in-the-know critics don't want to see, but only to read, let's quite literally give them a film to read. Since they persist in not picking up on the moral revolt of the presentational device, factoring it, rather, into the theoretical critique of representation, let's confront them with the most universal of presentational devices, the word "this" (re)presented. And since they like self-reference more than anything else, let's rest assured that they are in no doubt that the word "this" refers to itself more often than not. *So Is This* is a silent, 16 mm, 43 minute film, made in 1982, and consisting solely of words. As for pictures, there are none: no female pudenda, no wounded caribou, no bird gliding in the sky. No visible bit of the world, only legible signs. Nothing other than words being presented one by one, typed white on black in Helvetica, the type size varying in such a way that each word, be it short or long, has the same screen width. The words stay on screen for a second or two, sometimes more sometimes less, with one word driving out the other, just as in *Presents* a shot filmed at arm's length drove out the previous shot. The viewers don't scan the wording with their eyes, the way you do when you read a book, and they can't select their reading speed. They're riveted to their seat, just like the camera in the first part of *Presents*. Sovereign, that's going a bit far. Hostage might be more accurate. Indeed, unless you shut your eyes or leave, you're forced to read. Nothing is less an act of will than reading, when you know how to read, and nothing is stronger than the sensation of the authority of writing when it's flung at viewers who have gone to the movies expecting that the screen will open up a window onto the world for them. So they read. And laugh, a more infectious laughter than at the best of Buster Keaton. The words play with hilarious wit on the ambiguities of reference and self-reference inherent in the deictic "this." Here's the first sentence: "This is the title of this film. The rest of this film will look just like this." And a little further on: "This film will be about an hour long. Does that look like a frightening prospect? Well, look at it this way: how do you know this isn't lying?" And further on still: "In some respects, this is a first. Obviously this is not the first time that this has been used for the first time. This belongs to everybody!" Thanks to the artist for his generous understanding of Duchamp. Words are ready-mades belonging to everybody, and presentational words are pedestals on which other words are put, the way art objects in museums are things presented by means of other things. We don't get any further away from the prison of language when all there is on the screen is words than we do from the prison of the museum when anything and everything is art. But with the layman as judge of the "this is art," there's no question of letting *So Is This* run the circle of self-reference, which is only of interest to the artworld: "In case you're getting restless this film won't discuss itself all the time. It's going to get into some real stuff that will make you laugh and cry and change society." Which is of course what the film—we're laughing indeed—carefully avoids doing. At a particular moment, Michael Snow, who knows all about the problems bilingualism poses in Canada and who, at the time, had planned a French version of the film, shifts to the other national language: "Just for now though : en français le titre de ce film sera : ceci est le titre de ce film. Ça fait penser l'auteur au tableau bien connu de Magritte : Ceci n'est pas une pipe. C'est vrai ici aussi. L'auteur aime beaucoup le mot 'ceci'." ("Just for now though: in French the title of this film will be: this is the title of this film. This makes the author think of a well-known Magritte painting: This is not a pipe. It's true here too. The author is very fond of the word 'this'.") Thanks to the artist for his timely mention of Magritte (Broodthaers would have appreciated that) and for the word "*aimer*"—to be fond of. Being fond of deictics, what a weird idea. At the very end of the film, a flashback is announced which surprises by the precision of the philosophical allusion: "You know Phaedrus that's the strange thing about writing which makes it truly analogous to painting. The painter's products stand before us as though they were alive, but if you question them, they maintain a most majestic silence. This film will seem to stop"

There is no period after "to stop." The film is open-ended. The philosophical allusion was a quotation from Plato's *Phaedrus* (in a mediocre translation), the Socratic dialog where the philosopher denounces writing on the grounds that it doesn't answer when questioned. Writing is mute and as such resembles portrait painting (Plato says *zoographia*, or drawing of the living), which is incapable of *presenting* the life that it *represents*. Writing is merely the dangerous substitute for the living word, as deceptive and seductive as painting, and, like it, a *pharmakon*, at the same time poison and cure. Let's not rush to make Snow a Platonist. Plato wanted to expel poets from the Republic and entrust the reins of power to philosophers alone. Snow quotes him as a poet and visual artist, and *So Is This* is his riposte to the "philosophers" of experimental film who slammed *Presents*. Yes, writing is like painting—or like film, as it so happens—and vice versa. So, is it inevitable that we can't break away from language and representation? *This remains to be seen.* Let's be prepared for some kind of reflexive reversal giving presentation back its rights—vaccine strategy *oblige*. Vaccine strategy? The interest of the allusion to the *pharmakon* is to show that the limits of the vaccine strategy have been reached. Not just as a strategy but as a vaccine, too. Broodthaers had already worked out that when art appropriates the art of war, it always ends up waging war on art, even if it conceives its strategy like a vaccine, and all the more so since vaccinating is a strategy. We go round and round in circles, and art is in danger. There was something vicious from the outset in the vaccine metaphor. It presupposes that it's possible to heal evil by evil, to be done with it. Root it out, as we have rooted out smallpox. The *pharmakon*, for its part, is forever ambivalent by nature. It vaccinates against both evil and good. Plato must have known as much, he who mistrusted writing because it kills the living word, yet set down the word of Socrates in writing. The *pharmakon* is a dangerous medicine, bearing death to the very heart of life and reminding us at every turn that we have to live with that. Heidegger said that man is a "being-for-death," but you don't have to be Heideggerian—you can be a biologist, for example, or just human, for all humans have an awareness of death—to know that life kicks off again with every generation harboring death. Confusing the *pharmakon* with the vaccine leads to the illusion of a life delivered from death, an illusion so well refuted by reality that it runs the philosophical risk of considering that death is the real life. This risk is called nihilism. No philosophical century has been closer to giving in to nihilism than the 19th (witness Hegel, Schopenhauer, Nietzsche), the century which took note of the "death of

God" and saw the emergence of the artistic avant-gardes. But no political century has succumbed more to the *acting out* of philosophical nihilism than the 20th, the century of the Shoah and Hiroshima—the century, too, that saw avant-garde art find its way into the museum, never again to be flushed out (witness Duchamp).

So, for more than a century the avant-garde has tried to cure evil by evil. Giving itself doubt as the antidote to loss of faith. It called painting, writing, and all the arts into question, taking nothing for granted: no style, no technology, no convention, not even art's right to existence. From its plunges into doubt, it has often hoped for a rebirth of a new art, not to say a new man. Many artists have made up for their anxiety by falling headlong into the utopian and ideological creeds which boosted their morale. They are rarely the best. Or else their work belies their beliefs, when it really is good. The greatest have always known they were struggling for the survival of their tradition *by destroying it*. How far can we push the paradox? To what degree are the logic of the vaccine, the positivity of the negative, and the famous "less is more" of modernism tenable? The answer is that there is no limit, if we stick with this strategy: painting did not die with the monochrome, nor sculpture with the readymade. The art of these past thirty years shows, over and over again, that artists have not been at a loss for invention once it was a matter of producing new forms of negativity. It also, and too frequently, demonstrates that negativity has lost its corrosive power once a consensus has been reached on it, which is the case in the post-Duchamp artworld. If it's in the museum, it's got to be art. And then: either it's art *because* it's in the museum—and there are indeed strategists for their own career that have understood the advantage they might derive from this tautology—or, alternatively—as is thought and wished by the vaccine strategists committed to the escalation of negativity—it's art *because* it's non-art or anti-art (dated words), or *because* it fosters the *informe* and the *abject* (recent words). Structuralist film criticism is not alone in having turned its skepticism into a religion. It reigns everywhere; it is the *doxa*. Set up as methodical suspicion, doubt has so effectively vaccinated against loss of faith that it has become the new creed. A church has been formed based on Duchamp's reception in the 1960s; periodically it gives way to nihilistic drifts—understandable, since the god of tautology, who has taken up residence in the post-Duchamp museum, is a nihilist. When it is a given that one can make art out of anything whatever, all that remains to do for artists keen to stand up to the god of tautology is to feed suspicion. They actually take no risks. "There is no escape from representation" means: there is no escape from art as an institution. How different is Duchamp's reception in the work of Broodthaers and Snow. Never did Snow beg the art institution for permission to turn against the institution his prodigious understanding of the conditions in which artists work from now on. Whether a painter, photographer, sculptor, musician, or filmmaker, what concerns him when he moves from one medium to the next, always highly aware of the medium he is using, is questions having to do with art in general. Art *tout court*, the *pharmakon*, that medicine which heals but does not deliver us from death. Like all great artists, Snow is struggling with mystery. He asks himself questions about the relationship between art and life, time and eternity, death and mortality, the hereafter and the unknowable, questions that are too big for us humans, but which concern us all, and not just the artworld. Existential and metaphysical questions, in a nutshell. Snow has never turned his back on them, causing discomfort for critics happier thinking that his films raise questions about film conventions and slate Hollywood ideology. With modesty and a keen understanding of his time, he disguises his "existentialism" beneath the "materialism" of his approach to the medium. But when pressed about his metaphysical persuasions—these embarrassing and strictly private things—he ends up admitting, with Kierkegaardian wit: "Out of facetious humility, I'm 'religious'." "Religious" in quotation marks, to be taken with a grain of salt, and deadpan. Whatever, the word is out.

Do we have to go to church on Sunday or the synagogue on Saturday or the mosque on Friday to be "religious" these days? Or not go? It's irrelevant; faith in God has become a private matter settled according to individual conscience. On the other hand, are we not more religious (and the quotation marks vanish, dangerously) when, beer and pennant in hand, we get excited at a World Cup football match, knowing that the globalized "cathodic" Church communes in the same ritual? (Ditto for a Wimbeldon final, a Formula 1 race, a golf championship; it is with religions and mores as with sports: class-based, all of them.) Tackier: when, with Lady Di's timely sacrifice on the altar of the media, we join with the chorus of mourners steeped in popular catharsis? Younger: when, high on *ecstasy*, we play at shedding our individuality in the collective trance of a rave? More scary: when, ecstasy for ecstasy, we let ourselves be carried away by the words of a political leader who has the knack of spellbinding the masses? Or even, more inoffensive, when we make our pilgrimage to the Venice Biennale or the Kassel Documenta with those who commune in contemporary art? "God is dead" means that there is no longer any Father, up there, around whom the social order is organized. This doesn't mean that the collectivity shouldn't organize itself around Absence. Humankind has too short an experience of life without God to have learned to call this Absence by another name and give up filling it with the sound and fury of the society of the spectacle. We can be sure of one thing: art and religion have been in league since the palaeolithic period. From the day the first humans started to bury their dead, they deified them *and* they venerated them in effigies. Since humans clearly have not become immortal, it is hard to see how these two interwoven impulses might cease to trigger one another. We can wager that tomorrow's art will be every bit as in league with the "religious" as the art of yesterday and the day before yesterday. Here, however, quotation marks are a must. They are imposed by the very lengthy history which swept up humans—with the West leading them, for better and for worse—and gradually prompted them to do without gods, and then without God, finally bringing them face to face with Absence as such. For art to march explicitly on the path toward the *presentation* of Absence, it took the spectacular secularization of minds brought about by the rationalism of the Enlightenment, and then the sudden waning of religious practice in the 19th century, in a word, what Max Weber has called the disenchantment of the world. The advent of the Museum, that cemetery haunted by a dead God, resulted in art's progress on this path being experienced in the negative, like a permanent crisis in *representation*. This crisis is one of the names of a God-less world. Manet was the first painter to have glimpsed the positive consequences of this, but for all time, even the time when the religious alibi was the common creed, the greatest artists knew that the function of art was to fit Absence with a void *at the heart of the social* and to display the void to those willing to look. Yet this metaphysical void is not displayable as such. It cannot be put on a stand and presented. Nobody can say that he or she has seen death itself, which is its sign here on earth. It is only negatively displayable, which is an unfathomable paradox, given that, for us, death is absolute negation. Now art—and visual art especially—has an irrepressible desire to show that can and should go as far as the desire to show what is not showable. This is why art is condemned to resurrection.

Resurrection doesn't mean denial of death. It doesn't mean immortality. You have to be mortal and you have to die in order to rise from the dead. Looking for religions of immortality these days, you'd rather find them in cloning and in the *cyborg* myth, or in the prophecies about the "post-human." Resurrection doesn't mean Renaissance, either. The spirit of Erasmus will not come and save us from the post-human. The problem with the idea of Renaissance is not that it is humanist but that it presupposes ushering in a new golden age: whether *Jerusalem Delivered* or *Utopia*, or still, Revolution, or the End of History. Evil rooted out. The idea of resurrection presupposes nothing of the kind. It only presupposes faith in life, which itself presupposes nothing more than that elementary act of faith: life will go on without me. There's nothing grandiloquent about this; it's even rather banal. Anyone who has children makes this act of faith every day by loving them. The same goes for anyone who gives birth to art—which, incidentally, doesn't erase the difference between life and art: life can be experienced without having to show itself, art cannot. We do not vaccinate ourselves more surely against death by leaving behind a work of art rather than offspring, but "in life" we may die in peace, if we've had a good life, and leave our offspring to live their lives in their turn; "in art" we cannot leave this earth without having produced—in both senses of the word, manufactured and shown—a duplicate of life which attests the "without me." If possible, a living duplicate, embodied not in a child but in a thing. If possible? Impossible! Unless you believe, superstitiously, that things are living beings. Things are not living because they are not mortal. The sign of this is that we throw them away when they are worn out, we don't bury them. Works of art are an exception to this rule: we keep them, we embalm them, we venerate them—which seems to be self-evident as long as they resemble us, but should be startling when they are explicitly reduced to mere things. The idea that in five hundred years Duchamp's urinal will, if all goes well, be next to the *Victory of Samothrace* in the Louvre should leave us totally perplexed. This observation offers two avenues: either thinking, like Plato and almost the whole philosophical tradition, that art is doomed to *mimesis*, to representation; or, on the contrary, like poets and artists, that it is doomed to resurrection. The artist's task is to turn a thing into a living being so that it can be mortal. Only then can it "really" be called living, and deserve receiving the esteem due to living beings. Aesthetic creation only gives birth to a work of art if it first of all resurrects its raw materials.

It took a painter who was outstandingly attuned to his times, a painter who had registered the "death of God" (with or without Renan and whatever his personal religious persuasions may have been), a painter who catapulted modern art along the path towards abstraction—it took Manet for us to realize that resurrection is, in the final analysis, the only subject matter of art, a subject matter that it perforce betrays if it treats it as a "subject," that is to say, as belief and representation, or as belief in representation. A Christ who rises from the dead because the painter has *represented* him caught at the precise moment when he travels back along the road leading from life to death is not "really" rising from the dead. He only "really" rises from the dead if he is *presented* to us rising from the dead. And he is only presented to us rising from the dead if he presents himself on his own initiative. Manet was the first to realize this. He also doubted whether his Christ could present himself without the help of a presentational device. Then along came Duchamp and took note of the doubt. He put a simple thing on a pedestal in place of Christ, and attention was shifted. From Christ, who had to be looked at looking at us with his dead eye in order for us to be touched by him, our attention strayed toward the pedestal, and from there toward the word designating the *thing*, and affixing to it the name "art" resulting from a judgment: I have been touched, *this* is art. Broodthaers arrived and summoned Magritte to separate the word from the thing: *this* is no more art than a pipe, if "this" is a word. Last of all, by appropriating the word, Snow turned it into the subject of *So Is This*. We might say, in shorthand, that Snow reduced Manet's Christ to the word "this." Will it rise again from the dead?

The answer lies in the countless interplays of reference and self-reference which inform *So Is This*. Viewing the film, with each occurence of the word "this"—and God knows there are many—we catch ourselves asking what "this" refers to, this time around. The referent is ever-shifting. Sometimes it is mentioned before, sometimes after "this" in the sentence given to us to read, one word at a time. Sometimes "this" designates itself, as a word, at others it refers to the fact of its appearance on the screen, as if it were an image. And more often than not, it refers to the whole film: to the work titled *So Is This*, which starts off with "This is the title of this film." But never, ever, does it point to an element of the visible world beyond the screen. The pleasure we get in viewing the film is mixed with an odd little stab of pain, and a dash of joy that is stranger still. Its irresistible funniness has to do with the slight delay with which we discover what word in the sentence was being referred to by such and such a "this." Laughter breaks out over the punch line of a joke, and *So Is This* seems to string punch lines together. But the laughter mingles with frustration at never seeing the words land beyond language. Like all deictics, "this" is a presentational device, a designator, an index finger pointed at some element of the real: the moon, a woman's pudenda, an eagle soaring in the sky, a urinal, a Christ. It does not represent anything, it shows. Its task is to open in the wall of language a window onto the world. But if it is not accompanied by another index finger, already situated in the world, the window it opens gives onto a void and an uncertainty, or as in that famous Matisse painting *Fenêtre à Collioure*, onto the dark absence of the visible. It takes two deictics to establish the reference and escape from language. Hearing your interlocutor utter the word "this," you don't know what he's talking about if he does not, at the same time, designate something with his finger—or with a nod of the chin, or a glance of the eye. The word "this" needs a second sign to be "activated." To be living, we might say. Otherwise it remains a dead letter. In *So Is This*, the second sign is missing: no image, no opening onto the visible, nothing but letters and words endlessly circulating in the maze of an overall self-reference. Now, and this is what is surprising, this missing is a source of joy, as if the word "this" were sharing with us its freedom to thus move about in the prison of language. It gambols like a lamb from one word to another in Snow's text, and we enjoy watching it gambol. Our joy reaches its peak when "this" takes itself for referent, which happens now and then and causes brief outbursts of intellectual pleasure, precisely the same as when you "crack" the riddle of "Nebuchadnezzar, king of Babylon, write that for me in four letters." *That* or *this*, four letters deemed to remain a dead letter if what they present is not additionally supported by a second presentational device, but four letters which, here, work this little miracle of presenting themselves on their own. While self-reference is, for most post-Duchamp artists, a sign of their confinement within representation and the art institution, for Snow it is the instrument of resurrection. As he admits in *So Is This*: "The author is very fond of the word 'this'." Quite understandable: nobody can prevent "this" from referring to itself occasionally, it is one of its mischievous liberties. When "this" is its own referent, it is a presentational device which, in presenting itself, consequently amounts to: "Here I am—*Me voici*." Resurrection wasn't any more magical than that. Nothing very religious, or very glorious. We have the resurrections and the enchantments we can get, in a world which it doesn't pay to want to re-enchant. By all means not.

Manet

On the interpretation of *Le Christ aux anges* and the question of whether it represents a *Dead Christ* or a *Christ Rising from the Dead*, see:

Baudelaire's letter to Chennevières, quoted by Michael Fried, *Manet's Modernism or: The Face of Painting in the 1860s* (Chicago: The University of Chicago Press, 1996), p. 494, n. 161.

Eric Darragon, *Manet* (Paris: Citadelles, 1991), pp. 142–146, and Fried's commentary in *Manet's Modernism*, pp. 517–518, n. 76.

Jane Mayo Roos, 'Edouard Manet's *Angels at the Tomb of Christ*: A Matter of Interpretation,' *Arts Magazine*, 58, April 1984.

The notice on *Le Christ mort et les anges*, as well as those on the watercolor and etching of the same title in Françoise Cachin and Charles S. Moffet, *Manet*, exhib. cat. (Paris: Grand Palais, 1983), pp. 199–207, where the comment by Théophile Gautier in the *Moniteur universel* is quoted. Engl. transl. of Gautier's comment in George Heard Hamilton, *Manet and His Critics* (New York: Norton, 1969), p. 57.

Baudelaire's letter to Manet of April 1864 about the spear blow, in Pierre Courthion, *Manet raconté par lui-même et ses amis*, vol. 1 (Geneva: Pierre Cailler, 1953), p. 110. The fact that the spear blow has found its correct placement in the watercolor is due to the mirror-reversed composition, probably executed in preparation for the etching.

The article by Thoré-Bürger in *L'Indépendance belge* of 15 May 1864, *ibid.*, pp. 111–112. Engl. transl. in *Manet and His Critics*, p. 61.

On Renan, his possible importance for Manet, and Manet's relationship to the religious, see:

Ernest Renan, *Vie de Jesus* (Paris: June 1863); transl. *The Life of Jesus* (Prometheus Books, 1991). See in particular the end of Chapter 16, where Renan winds up his agnostic reflections on the myth of Christ's resurrection by the words: 'Divine power of love! Sacred moments when the passion of a hallucinated woman gave the world a resurrected God.' See also the Appendix.

Fried's above mentioned commentary on Darragon's pages on the subject, where there is also mention of the Abbé Augustin Hurel, a friend of Manet (who painted his portrait in 1875) and author of *L'art religieux contemporain: Étude critique* (Paris, 1868): 'What does this artist propose? What is his idea? What's the tendency of his work? An anti-social or anti-religious theory is doubtless concealed in the depths of this talent.'

Alain de Leiris, 'Manet's *Christ Scourged* and the Problem of His Religious Paintings,' *The Art Bulletin*, 41, June 1959.

We should bear in mind that shortly before his death, Manet confided to Antonin Proust: 'There is one thing I always had the ambition to do. I'd like to paint a Christ on the Cross. [...] What a symbol! You could go on looking until the end of time, but you'd never find anything like that. A Minerva, that's allright, a Venus, that's allright. But neither the heroic nor the amorous image will ever match the image of suffering. It's the ground of humanity, its poem.' Antonin Proust, *Edouard Manet, Souvenirs* (Paris: L'Échoppe, 1996), p. 64.

Duchamp

On 'The Richard Mutt Case,' title of the editorial of the magazine *The Blind Man*, 2, New York, May 1917, see:

William Camfield, 'Marcel Duchamp's *Fountain*: Its History and Aesthetics in the Context of 1917,' *Dada/Surrealism*, 16, 1987. For a fleshed out version, see William Camfield, *Marcel Duchamp, Fountain* (Houston: The Menil Foundation and Houston Fine Arts Press, 1989).

Thierry de Duve, 'Given the Richard Mutt Case,' chapter 2 of *Kant after Duchamp* (Cambridge, Mass.: MIT Press, 1996).

On the controversies of the Salon in the 19th century, the birth of the *Salon des Indépendants* and its American namesake, see:

Patricia Mainardi, *The End of the Salon, Art and the State in the Early Third Republic* (Cambridge: Cambridge University Press, 1993).

W. Hauptman, 'Juries, Protests and Counter-Exhibitions before 1850,' *The Art Bulletin*, 67:1, March 1985.

Albert Boime, 'The Salon des Refusés and the Evolution of Modern Art,' *Art Quarterly*, 32:4, 1969.

G. Wildenstein, 'Le Salon des Refusés de 1863,'

Gazette des Beaux-Arts, 66, 1965.

Martha Ward, 'Impressionist Installations and Private Exhibitions,' *The Art Bulletin*, December 1991.

René Huyghe, *Un siècle d'art moderne: L'histoire du Salon des Indépendants, 1884–1984* (Paris: Denoël, 1984).

Clark S. Marlor, *The Society of Independent Artists, The Exhibition Record 1917–1944* (Park Ridge, NJ: Noyes Press, 1984).

The article by Mallarmé publised in *La Renaissance* of 12 April 1874, where the poet declares: 'the jury has nothing else to say but: this is a painting, or that is not a painting,' is reproduced in *Manet raconté par lui-même et ses amis*, vol. 1, pp. 167–169. Engl. transl. in *Manet and His Critics*, p. 185.

Broodthaers

Broodthaers' invitation card to his 1964 exhibition at the Saint Laurent Gallery has been often reproduced, sometimes even on the cover or flyleaves of the catalogs of his major retrospectives. See:

Marge Goldwater and Michael Compton, eds., *Marcel Broodthaers*, exhib. cat. (Minneapolis: Walker Art Center, 1989), flyleaves.

Catherine David and Véronique Dabin, eds., *Marcel Broodthaers*, exhib. cat. (Paris: Galerie nationale du Jeu de Paume, 1991), cover.

Engl. transl. in Benjamin H. D. Buchloh, 'Open Letters, Industrial Poems,' *October*, 42, Fall 1987.

On the Düsseldorf exhibition, see:

Museum, two volume catalog of the exhibition *Der Adler vom Oligozän bis heute*, subtitled *Marcel Broodthaers zeigt eine experimentelle Ausstellung seines Musée d'Art Moderne, Département des Aigles, Section des Figures* (Düsseldorf: Städtische Kunsthalle, 1972).

'Dix mille francs de récompense' (interview with Irmeline Lebeer), in *Marcel Broodthaers, Catalogue / Catalogus* (Brussels: Palais des Beaux-Arts, 1974). Engl. transl. Paul Schmidt, 'Ten Thousand Francs Reward,' *October*, 42. The interview recorded was considerably rewritten by Broodthaers. Both the questions and the answers, which cannot be told apart in the typescript, are by him.

Douglas Crimp, 'This is Not a Museum of Art,' in the Minneapolis cat., reproduced in *On the Museum's Ruins* (Cambridge, Mass.: MIT Press, 1993).

Thierry de Duve, 'Artefact,' chapter 1 of *Résonances du readymade, Marcel Duchamp entre avant-garde et tradition* (Nîmes: Jacqueline Chambon, 1989); 'Echoes of the readymade: Critique of Pure Modernism,' *October*, 70, Autumn 1994; and 'Archaeology of Pure Modernism,' chapter 7 of *Kant after Duchamp*.

On Magritte, Broodthaers' relationship with Magritte and Duchamp, and the 'theory of figures' that he derived therefrom, see:

René Magritte, 'Les mots et les images,' illustrated text published in *La révolution surréaliste* in 1929, and reproduced in René Magritte, *Ecrits complets* (Paris: Flammarion, 1979), pp. 60–61.

Michel Foucault, *Ceci n'est pas une pipe* (Paris: Fata Morgana, 1973); transl. James Harkness, *This is Not a Pipe* (Berkeley: University of California Press, 1983).

Thierry de Duve, 'Ceci ne serait pas une pipe (Magritte et Broodthaers),' in *Magritte en compagnie*, exhib. cat. (Brussels: Labor, 1997).

Dirk Snauwaert, 'The Figures,' *October*, 42.

Snow

On Michael Snow's films in general, and on *Presents* and *So Is This* in particular, see:

Regina Cornwell, *Snow Seen* (Toronto: PMA Books, 1980).

Bart Testa, 'An Axiomatic Cinema: Michael Snow's Films,' in Jim Shedden, ed., *The Michael Snow Project, Presence and Absence* (Toronto: Art Gallery of Ontario, 1995)

Bruce Elder, 'Michael Snow's Presence,'

Thierry de Duve, 'Michael Snow: The Deictics of Experience, and Beyond,' *Parachute*, 78, April–May–June 1995. Michael Snow's response appeared in the same number.

The contrast between the respective conceptions of Snow and Brakhage to do with the camera is examined by Regina Cornwell in *Snow Seen*, pp. 60–62. See also p. 76.

The handwritten script of *So Is This* is reproduced in facsimile, followed by a typed transcript, in *The Michael Snow Project, The Collected Writings of Michael Snow* (Waterloo, Ont.: Wilfred Laurier University Press, 1994), pp. 209–220.

On Michael Snow's 'religious inklings,' see:

The artist's statement about *Wavelength* at the Knokke-le-Zoute festival: '*Wavelength* was shot in one week Dec. '66 preceded by a year of notes, thoughts, mutterings. It was edited and first print seen in May '67. I wanted to make a summation of my nervous system, religious inklings, and aesthetic ideas. I was thinking of planning for a time monument in which the beauty and sadness of equivalence would be celebrated, thinking of trying to make a definitive statement of pure Film space and time, a balancing of "illusion" and "fact," all about seeing. [...] the film is a crescendo and a dispersed spectrum which attempts to utilize the gifts of both prophecy and memory which only film and music have to offer.' Michael Snow, 'A Statement on *Wavelength* for the Experimental Film Festival of Knokke-le-Zoute,' *Film Culture*, 46, p. 1, quoted by Regina Cornwell, *Snow Seen*, pp. 66–67, and by Philip Monk, 'Around Wavelength,' *The Michael Snow Project, Visual Art*, exhib. cat. (Toronto: Art Gallery of Ontario, 1994), p. 322.

'Michael Snow and Bruce Elder in Conversation,' in *The Michael Snow Project, The Collected Writings of Michael Snow*, p. 225: 'Out of facetious humility, I'm "religious".'

On Plato's *Phaedrus*, the joint condemnation of painting and writing, and the interpretation of the twofold nature, good and evil, of the *pharmakon* in Plato, see:

Jacques Derrida, 'La pharmacie de Platon', in *La dissémination* (Paris: Le Seuil, 1972); transl. Barbara Johnson, 'Plato's Pharmacy,' in *Dissemination*, (Chicago: University of Chicago Press, 1983).

Here I am

overture

To say: "Here I am" is to introduce oneself. Only a living
being endowed with language can do this; inanimate
things cannot. Works of art, however, are things. We lend
them human properties; we judge them to be alive, and
we call them eloquent when they are successful; we treat
them with the respect due human beings; and we deem it
barbaric to destroy them.

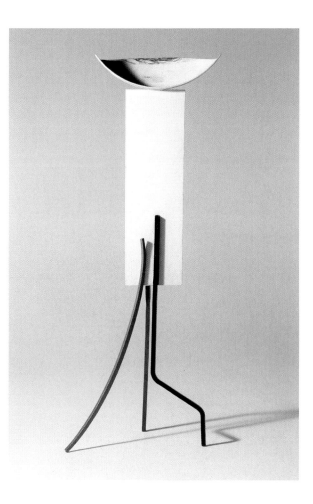

David Smith
Tanktotem IX, 1960

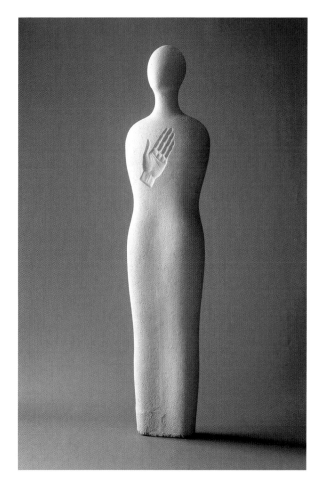

Fausto Melotti
Costante uomo, 1936

But none of all this is self-evident. As long as works of art resembled us, it wasn't too difficult to lend them life and the capacity to speak, as is still so, despite its marked stylization, with this statue by Melotti greeting us, hand on heart.

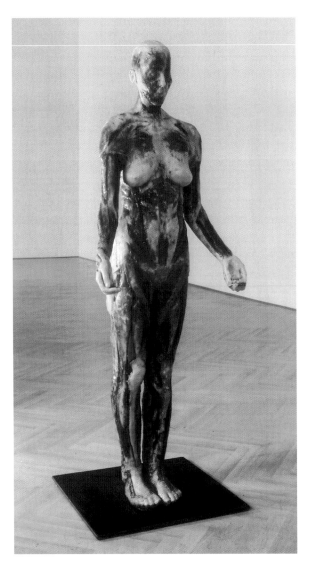

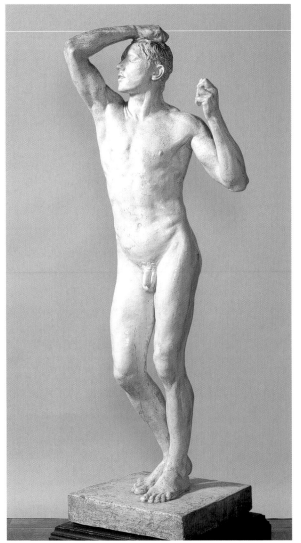

Kiki Smith

Virgin Mary, 1992

Auguste Rodin

L'Âge d'airain, 1875–1876

introductions

Things are no longer so easy with abstract art. In one
century, we have proceeded from *The Age of Bronze*,
over which Rodin was accused of having cast his statue
on the body of his model, so life-like did it seem,

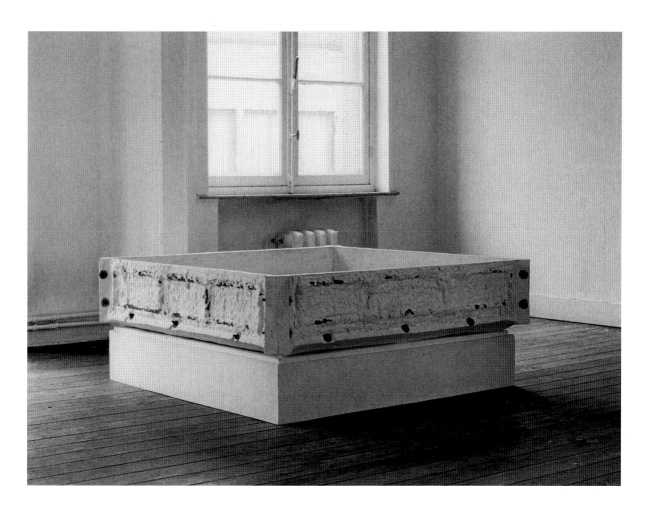

Didier Vermeiren
Le Baiser, 1984

to the casting of the base of Rodin's *Kiss*, on which
Didier Vermeiren has placed the mold of the cast base.
The statue has vanished. Artists trained in abstraction
no longer take the human figure for granted.

Bernd Lohaus
Münster, 1991

With Brancusi, you never know where the base stops and
the sculpture begins, but there's one thing he never turned
his back on—the vertical thrust of the upright position. Artists
such as Carl André, Richard Nonas, and Bernd Lohaus have
laid Brancusi's *Endless Column* flat, and made it run hori-
zontally on the ground. Sculpture has learned to be humble.

Constantin Brancusi
Socle, after 1928

Gerhard Richter
Kugel, 1989

Roni Horn
Pair Objects VI c : For Two Locations in One Place, 1988

There is a Pieter Claesz still life, painted circa 1660,
which depicts, on a table, a glass ball in which the painter
is reflected. Gerhard Richter, *painter*, has certainly not
forgotten this. But his ball is on the floor, like Roni Horn's
matching cones.

Louise Bourgeois
Single I, 1996

All the while, Louise Bourgeois' headless but gendered
doll is hanging from the ceiling. Has art been turned
upside down, or inside out? The fact is that the 20th
century has challenged every form of humanism.

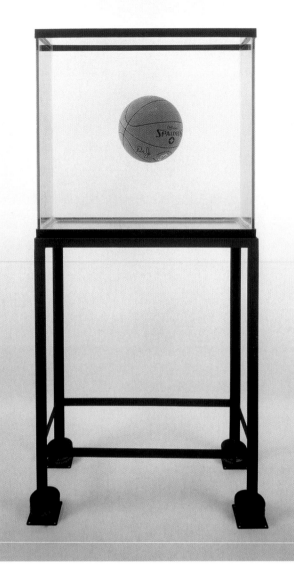

Jeff Koons
One Ball Total Equilibrium Tank, 1985

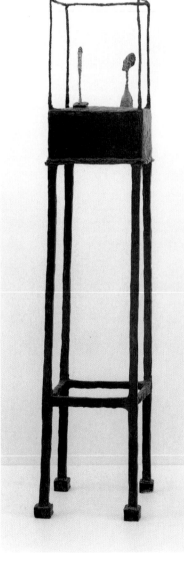

Alberto Giacometti
La Cage, 1950

What on earth can Giacometti's *Cage* and Jeff Koons'
"aquarium" have in common? Nothing except their
surprising formal similarity, which is certainly something.
The two works embrace the issue of the presentation
device—whether pedestal or frame or display case. In
both instances, a virtual cube is placed on a strongly
emphasized base.

Didier Vermeiren
Untitled (commonly called *Chariot*), 1986

In his miniature theater, Giacometti represents the relationship between the viewer and a statue that is not on
his scale. Koons hangs a basket ball in his display case,
floating there as if by magic. The human figure has made
way for the thing.

Piero Manzoni
Base Magica, 1961

Marcel Duchamp
Roue de Bicyclette, 1913 ; 6th version, 1964

Anyone who climbs onto Manzoni's *Magic Base* turns
into a work of art, and stops being one when he or she
gets off the stand. Things have come full circle with the
scandal stirred up by Rodin and his statue, deemed too
life-like. Meanwhile, Duchamp had done his thing. The
result: even a bicycle wheel fixed to a stool was–and is–
acknowledged as art.

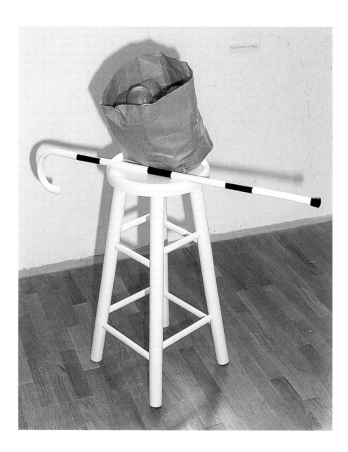

George Brecht
Untitled, 1962–1986

Robert Filliou
Le Siège des idées, 1976

Because ideas are invisible, they can't be shown. You can't put them on a stand or in a display case. *Fluxus* and the best of Conceptual Art nevertheless found ways of *presentifying* them.

Marcel Broodthaers
Section des figures
(Der Adler vom Oligozän bis heute),
1972 (detail)

Marcel Broodthaers
Section des figures
(Der Adler vom Oligozän bis heute),
1972 (detail)

Anything and everything can be given the "this-is-a-work-of-art" label, as long as it's in a museum, so said Broodthaers to himself, dissatisfied with this state of things. So he appointed himself director of a fictitious museum of his own invention, the *Musée d'art moderne, Département des aigles,* and thus came up with a riposte to Duchamp. The eagle, universal symbol of power...

Marcel Broodthaers
Section des figures (Der Adler vom Oligozän bis heute), 1972 (detail)

Marcel Broodthaers
Section des figures (Der Adler vom Oligozän bis heute), 1972 : double page from the catalog

artist's project 1 : this

Michael Snow
That / Cela / Dat, 2000

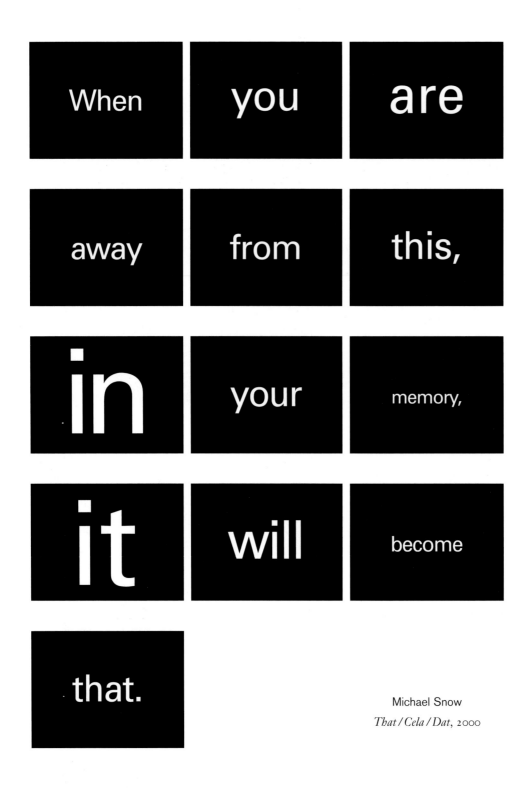

When you are away from this, in your memory, it will become that.

Michael Snow
That / Cela / Dat, 2000

Words belong to everyone, and the word "this" is free to designate what it wants as long as nothing is pointed at. Including itself.

Joseph Beuys
Wirtschaftswerte, 1980

still lifes

East German consumer goods on shelves, a block of fat smelling of rancid butter, with paintings from the time of Karl Marx surrounding the piece—replaced in *Voici* by still lifes with skulls by Picasso and Richter—such are the *Economic Values* according to Beuys.

Gerhard Richter
Blumen, 1994

Pablo Picasso
Nature morte au crâne et au pichet, 1943

Two thousand years before Duchamp, the invention of the
still-life—a genre already familiar to the Greeks, who decorated their dining rooms with pictures of food—marked the
moment when simple perishable *things* took on the dignity of works of art. As long as it's in pictures, these things
are represented. But modern artists have shifted the
emphasis from representation to presentation.

Gerhard Richter
Schädel, 1983

In the wonderful little Cubist canvas on the next page, Picasso has his whole picture rest on the molding of the table running along the bottom. The table itself is turned up into the plane of the painting. What is the presentation device of these objects: the table or the *tableau*?

Pablo Picasso

Nature Morte : bouteille, cartes et verre de vin, 1914

Jean Fautrier

Le Bouquet de violettes, 1924

Peter Fischli & David Weiss
Untitled (Equilibrium Series), 1985

Peter Fischli & David Weiss
Uomo Intimo, 1987

Is it ridiculous to get the century's most metaphysical
painter of still-lifes in dialog with Duchamp's grand-
children? Fake readymades made of black rubber, Italian
light gnawing at the outline of objects: are these two
worlds, or just one?

Giorgio Morandi

Natura morta, 1951

Giorgio Morandi

Natura morta, 1960

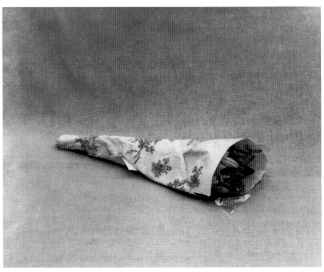

Jacques Vilet

Deux sacs galbés, 1996

Cinq abricots, 1993

Deux pommes, 1992

Jacques Vilet

Deux poires, 1996

Bouquet emballé, 1996

Deux sardines et un merlan, 1994

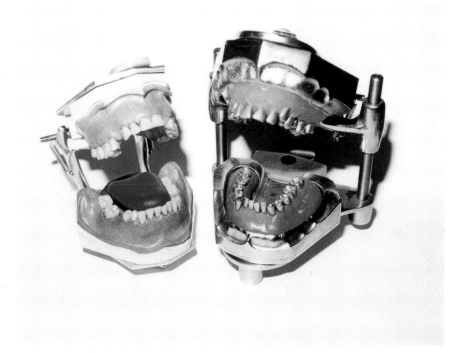

Andy Warhol
False Teeth, 1982–1983

Photography was fit to take up the meditation on the *real* and on death, which has always been the distinctive feature of the still-life. Vilet is close to Morandi, and, once again, Warhol shows himself to be a most formidable artist of death of the second half of the century.

Jaroslav Rössler

Untitled, 1933–1934

Jaroslav Rössler

Untitled, 1934–1935

Jaroslav Rössler

Cérès, 1935–1939

Jaroslav Rössler

Thymolin, 1935–1939

James Welling
Gilded Frame (93) – July 13 1981, 1981

James Welling
Untitled 61, 1981

The real is the enigma of all enigmas, which eludes the imaginary and the symbolic, but which art nevertheless makes presentable. Welling is seeking it in the interstices of matter, or in the corner of a frame–this presentation device. Rössler makes it emerge from the everyday products, which his profession as an advertising photographer prompted him to stage, subverting the commission and turning it into a exercise on form.

René Zuber
Sèvres, tasses en porcelaine,
1937

François Kollar
Lunettes, ca. 1920

Piet Zwart
Untitled, ca. 1934

Wols
Loupes et centimètre, 1951

Walker Evans
Trash # 4, 1962

Walker Evans
Trash # 3, 1962

William Henry Fox Talbot

Lace, 1839–1840

This piece of lace is one of the very first photos in the history of photography—which Fox Talbot called "photogenic drawing," and which he also described as the "Pencil of Nature." Walker Evans must have thought that nothing was unworthy of the pencil in question, and that even the *Trash* on the edge of a sidewalk was not devoid of photogenic quality.

Raymond Hains
Untitled, 1976

helter skelter things

We may well wonder if making art isn't withdrawing
things from the world rather than adding them to it. The
amazing thing is that we carefully preserve the products
of this removal, whereas we throw away our used objects.

Wols

Canaille sur la palissade, 1951

Kurt Schwitters
Untitled, 1939–1944

Isn't this Arman violin, destroyed, burnt as if in a cremato-
rium, and embalmed in resin, the poignant reminder of our
own mortality–a *memento mori*?

Arman

Diabelli, 1971

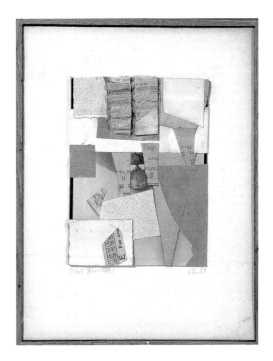

Kurt Schwitters
Collage # 47-22, 1920

Kurt Schwitters
Weisser Kreis, 1922

Richard Artschwager
Hair Sculpture-Shallow Recess Box, 1969

You can make art with anything whatever: scraps of paper, train tickets, bits of colored cardboard, as in these wonderful little Schwitters collages; or with pieces of driftwood, as in Hans Arp's *La Trousse du naufragé*; or, still, with marzipan fruit, as in Duchamp's delicious *Sculpture morte*, winking at Arcimboldo's 16th-century portraits composed of fruit.

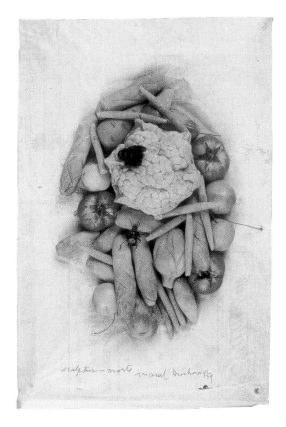

Marcel Duchamp
Sculpture morte, 1959

Hans Arp
La Trousse du naufragé, 1921

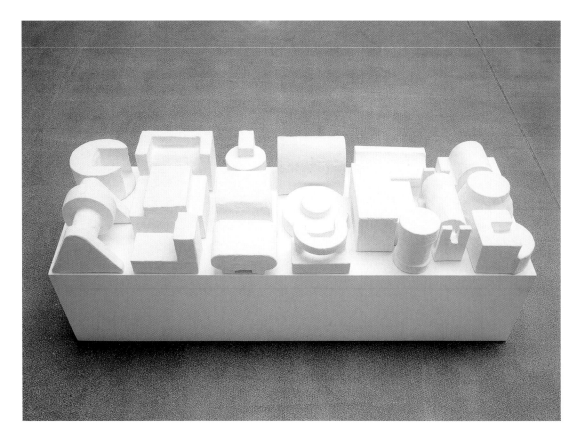

Absalon
Proposition d'objets quotidiens, 1990

Giovanni Anselmo
Verso l'Infinito, 1969

American *Minimal Art* and Italian *Arte povera*, which are often associated as the two twin art movements of the 1960s, share a certain asceticism. But their roots are quite different. Minimal Art stems from the feeling of American painters of no longer being able to carry on along the path of Abstract Expressionism, once the informed public declared itself ready to accept any flat object affixed to the wall—even a blank canvas!—as a picture. They leaped into the third dimension and, like Donald Judd here, hung on the wall objects of uncertain status, neither really painting nor really sculpture.

Donald Judd
Untitled, 1967

Donald Judd
Untitled, 1965

Richard Artschwager
Blp, 1969

Arte povera, for its part, has its immediate sources in
Fontana and Manzoni, but also much more ancient
sources, in the complex relationship between Catholicism
and art. We might say that it is a "Franciscan" reaction to
the Baroque tradition.

Mario Merz
Salamino, 1966

Eric Cameron
Chloé's Brown Sugar, 1992–

Eric Cameron
Exposed-Concealed: Laura Baird II, III, V, VI, 1994/4/6/6

Eric Cameron

Exposed-Concealed: Salima Halladj, 1993–

Eric Cameron is not, as one might think, a sculptor; he's
a painter. He paints objects, like a painter of still-lifes,
actually. But with just this difference: he paints *on* objects.
A coat of white a day. It's a ritual, the way some people
exercise or pray. At the core of *Chloé's Brown Sugar*
there's a little packet of sugar, and at the core of *Sonnets
from the Portuguese* there's a book. It's covered with 828
coats of white. The artist calls the result a *Thick Painting*.

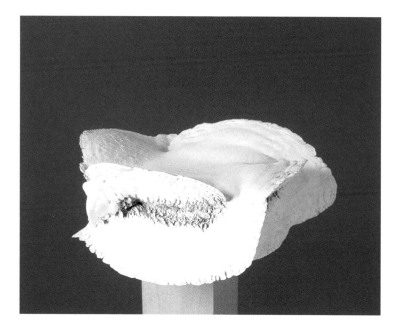

Eric Cameron

Sonnets from the Portuguese (1656) – for Margaret, 1992–

Thick indeed. We can consider each one of these works as a tomb for the object in the middle. But what really gets Cameron going is seeing how the object has its own life. As it swells under the successive coats of paint, its shape changes in an unforseeable way. For a thing to be living, it has to be mortal; it must also manifest its own freedom.

Anthony Caro
Table Piece XXII, 1967

Constantin Brancusi

Sculpture pour aveugles;
« Le Commencement du Monde »,
1914

Caro's *Table Sculptures* deal with the problem raised by
the presentation of small-scale sculpture, which is always
in danger of being taken for a *bibelot*. The novel solution
consists of "dropping" a part of the piece lower than the
plane of the table.

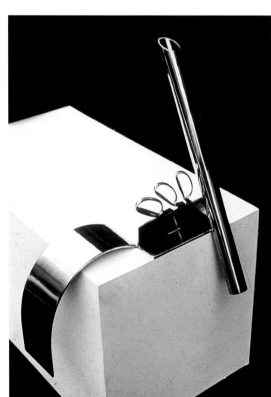

Anthony Caro

Table Piece VIII, 1966

The result is that there's only one way of installing them. Although the presentation device is independent of the sculpture, it is taken into consideration. Note, too, the incorporation of handles into the pieces. These indicate the scale, as well as inviting our grasp *abstractly*.

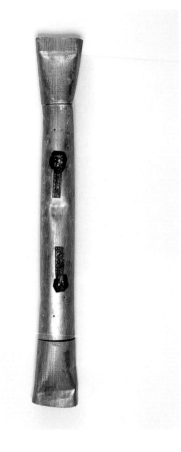

Denis Castellas
Untitled, 1991
Untitled, 1987

Denis Castellas
Untitled, 1986
Untitled, 1998

Denis Castellas
Untitled, 1987

Linda Benglis
Pour Daum # 2, 1979

Linda Benglis
Untitled, 1979

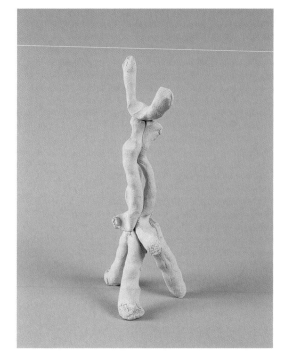

Barry Flanagan
Untitled, 1985–1986

With caustic wit veiling real humility, Manzoni devised
Body of Air in two versions. This one is a balloon you
blow up yourself, sold in its little box with its folding stand
for the meager sum of 30,000 lire. The "de luxe" version,
titled *Artist's breath,* was blown up by Manzoni himself,
presented on a mahogany base adorned with a copper
plaque bearing the artist's name, and sold for 200 lire
per litre of air thus authenticated.

Piero Manzoni
Corpo d'Aria, 1959–1960

The price, though, never amounted to more than twice
the "do-it-yourself" version. The "authentic" balloons lost
their air a long time ago and are just relics today. The
ones he entrusted to us are alive with our breath. So it
is with any work of art. They are all the emanation of a
unique personality, but for the work to really be saying
"Here I am," the artist still has to withdraw and let the
spectator enter.

Here you are

Gerhard Richter
Spiegel, (619), 1987

Action and speech are so closely related because the primordial and specifically human act must at the same time contain the answer to the question asked of every newcomer: "Who are you?"

Hannah Arendt

Mirrors

Let's imagine an object, but an object that's alive, has the power of speech, and can present itself without the help of any presentational device, and say: "Here I am." It would be saying this to someone, obviously. It would be *presenting itself* to someone and *addressing itself* to that someone. Let's imagine, too, that its function is to greet the person coming up to it with an: "Ah! so here you are," and deal with the introductions. No doubt about it, this object has to be a mirror. Lastly, let's imagine that it is a work of art. It might be Gerhard Richter's *Spiegel*, 1987, 200 x 180 cm. This isn't a painting of a mirror, nor is it an abstract canvas with the metaphorical title of *Mirror*. It's just a plain mirror, a ready-made thing straight from the mirror factory. This mirror looks like a Dadaist joke in Richter's work, a footnote or a slap in the face of those critics who can't bear anyone being as intelligent, as conceptual as Richter and yet also being *a painter*—the mere fact that the first example of a mirror-work-of-art which comes to mind should be by one of the best living painters sets the tone.

The interesting thing is that mirrors are indeed objects, and that you don't have to think of them as alive and endowed with speech to realize that they are actually very good at their job, provided they are facing a living, talking being. Their intelligence derives from the fact that they have the ability to reflect, and to induce reflection in, whoever is facing them. The play on words doesn't come out of the blue: the history of philosophy amply demonstrates the potential for reflection, not to say speculation, that lies in the reflecting properties of those *things* called mirrors. But a play on words is just a play on words, and mirrors don't think. Like any object, they are no more capable of talking to someone (here you are) than of saying "I" (here I am). Suggesting a talking mirror by means of a play on words is one thing, but reckoning that a mirror speaks the way you'd judge that a work of art speaks to you—that is a different matter altogether. *Spiegel* isn't a mirror that has miraculously become eloquent because it is a work of art, it is a work of art if it succeeds in working the miracle of making an irreversible relationship between a *thing* and a human being reversible. What is this relationship? That between "I" and "you." In any conversation between living, talking beings, the first and second person pronouns shift with the interlocutors each time they exchange a word. But how can you hold a conversation with things? As a general rule, things aren't given to us either in the first or second person, but in the third. They don't talk, and we don't talk to them—we talk about them. For a thing to be a work of art, it would have to escape from the third person and access the first. Hence the interest of approaching art via mirrors: they short-circuit the third person. We pay little attention to their thing-like existence because we don't look at them, we look into them—as we might look into an Old Master painting to see the scene it represents. Unless of course the way we look has been "distorted" by having been around modern art too much, in which case we see the composition, the forms, the handling of paint, the flatness of the painting, before we delve into the spectacle and read the story it tells us. The surface of a mirror is really transparent, the way the surface of an Old Master painting is, conventionally. In both cases, the surface is invisible, like a window behind which a duplicate of the world we live in unfolds before us. Moreover, we thinking beings see ourselves in a mirror. *Cogito ergo sum.* In front of any mirror there's a man or a woman asking questions about themselves, and addressing their image; human beings seeing and sensing themselves in the second person in order to get to know themselves in the first. Exit the third. This doesn't happen to us every morning when we shave or put on make-up, but it does happen to us. Narcissus gazing at himself in the water is no less of a philosopher than Hamlet meditating on Yorick's skull, which should act as a warning. The pictorial tradition of the *Vanitas* got it right: it contains almost as many girls at mirrors as it does still lifes with skulls. The fact is that mirrors speak to us if we speak to them. They do so not because they are alive and talking, but because they bounce our image back to us, and because we are so made that our image speaks to us. Narcissus wouldn't have drowned, otherwise: Echo was his loss. Richter's *Spiegel* confronts us with narcissism, for the sake of both our embarrassment and our reflection. His ready-made mirror would have been no more than a joke, had the artist not pounced on the ability mirrors have to reverse our address to them, and to make us ponder the consequences. And what consequences! Speech rendered unto things because we talked to them first, such is the miracle of their resurrection, seen from the beholder's vantage point.

But hold your horses. If the matter were that simple, all mirrors would be works of art and all works of art mirrors. And speech rendered unto things on the simple understanding that those things reflect our image would just be Echo's voice again, bouncing our own voice back to us. A fatal decoy. We would hear mirrors telling us what we want them to tell us, and we might soon end up drowned in our own image. What's more, Narcissus is a mediocre philosopher. He found nothing better to address to the reflecting surface of the spring than the most desperate demand for love. The spring replies, Narcissus dies. He hadn't read Freud, poor guy. It's true that Freud only wrote his *Introduction to Narcissism* in 1914, which offers some kind of excuse for Descartes—even though he's an infinitely better philosopher than Narcissus—in also failing to understand that the fact of reflecting about yourself in the mirror of consciousness doesn't give the thinking subject see-through access to itself. We do have an unconscious. It—the *id*—thinks in my stead, therein, and the *cogito* is no longer what it used to be. Philosophical mirrors have become a tad opaque since Freud, and the reflectiveness of real mirrors has also become clouded if you use them to reflect. The only privilege mirrors have over ordinary things is that they are objects which look at us more clearly than other objects. Thinking henceforth that in mirrors "I" and "you" are reversible simply because the gaze goes back and forth, is to make the mirror as object vanish, and to believe that you're done with the fact that things look at us. This would be confusing the specularity of the gaze with the reversibility of speech. Richter is not this naïve, he whose entire work consists in getting us to lay down our gaze before his pictures the way you lay down arms, so the picture becomes "a reality facing me, confronting me, something incomprehensible and autonomous." Something *else*, and not the mirage of the self in love with itself.

Even if *Spiegel* is neither a Dadaist joke nor a footnote in Richter's œuvre as a painter, it is all the same one heck of an exception in the history of painting. The first painter to put a real sliver of a mirror in a picture was Juan Gris in his 1912 *Le Lavabo*. "You want to know why I had to stick on a piece of mirror? Well, surfaces can be re-created and volumes reinterpreted in a picture, but what is one to do about a mirror whose surface is always changing and which should reflect even the spectator? There is nothing else to do but stick on a real piece." Maybe. But painters didn't hang about until Cubism, either, to make the mirrors painted in their pictures signify that they are the viewer's presentational devices, or to invite reflection. The history of painting is every bit as rich in mirrors as the history of philosophy. They are all the more intriguing because they almost all cheat with the laws of optics, even though we rarely realize as much. Let's take the equalness of the angle of incidence and the angle of reflection, that law which says that light rays bounce on the surfaces reflecting them like billiard balls on their cushions. And let's take a close look at the mirror which a winged cupid holds up to the goddess of love so that she may admire herself in Velázquez's *Rokeby Venus*. Since we're lucky enough to see her face reflected in the mirror, we must conclude that she can't see herself in it. What she sees is us.

Diego Vélasquez
Rokeby Venus, 1650

But who thinks of this in front of the painting? Looking into the mirror on the far wall in yet another Velázquez, his *Las Meninas*, who imagines that King Philip IV and his wife, whose glowing reflection gleams in the surrounding half-light, are not the royal personages whose place we believe we occupy in front of the picture, but rather their portrait painted on the large upright canvas that we see from behind? Velázquez has so cleverly plunged the painting's vanishing lines in shadow that you have to lay a ruler on a reproduction to discover that the vanishing point is in the doorway at the back, just beneath the elbow of the *aposentador* drawing the curtain, and not in the middle of the mirror. There are countless examples of painted mirrors, but these two provided by Velázquez suffice to singularly complicate their status as the viewer's presentational devices. The mirror in the *Rokeby Venus* is perpendicular neither to Venus' gaze nor to ours. The one in *Las Meninas* is central and parallel to the picture plane, but this time we are off-centered in relation to the scene, and our gaze into the mirror is oblique, despite the obvious frontality of the mirror. The potential for philosophical reflection of painted mirrors is on a par with the perverse ease with which they cheat with the most elementary laws of optics. Even Michel Foucault (though a philosopher) tumbled into their trap in his famous analysis of *Las Meninas*.

Diego Velázquez
Las Meninas, 1656

Not that he was in the wrong, philosophically speaking, in seeing the viewer taking the king's place, or ushering in, by way of his analysis, a major book (*The Order of Things*), where we realize, once the final page is turned, that it is the farewell to representation and humanism of a present day philosopher turned "archaeologist" of the classical age and, more surreptitiously, of modernity. He simply forgot to be as "stupid as a painter" when he looked at the painting. Painters, and modern painters in particular, are concrete people, empiricists, technicians, observers who, to borrow Cézanne's expression, have their "eye glued to the clod," pragmatists who see in their colleague Velázquez a realist, a virtuoso when it comes to light, who wields the brush like no other, a Spanish Franz Hals who abbreviates and paints true. Foucault's Velázquez is tempting, but Manet's may be preferable—Manet who wrote enthusiastically from Madrid to Fantin Latour that all the painters clustered about the master at the Prado seemed to him like "tobacco chewers" in comparison: "He's the painter of painters. He didn't amaze me, but he delighted me."

Manet in five paintings

Manet—once again. Manet and presentational devices, Manet and mirrors, Manet the best guide there is to tackling the question of *the other* to whom works of art are presented and addressed. He certainly looked at Velázquez as a painter, not as a philosopher. "He's the painter of painters" may mean: "He's the pick of the bunch," but also, and above all: "He's a painter's painter." Like Velázquez, Manet passes for a partisan of painting true, a master of spontaneity, an Impressionist, the very opposite of a speculative painter. But he knew better than anyone that painted mirrors are capable of all manner of spells and that they can fruitfully be put to work to stimulate reflection. Manet was the first modern, or modernist, painter, and what we call modernism in painting has everything to do with the reflexive withdrawal of painting into itself, and of painters into a public made up mainly of the painters coming after them. Whence the utmost importance of Manet's legacy for all subsequent interpretation: among so many other wonders, a mirror at the same time more perverse and more honest than the one in *Las Meninas*, a painted mirror where the reflections are clearly not in their right place, a mirror that plays on the equalness of the angle of incidence and the angle of reflection, not to enclose the viewer in the orb of Representation and the order of the Same (like *Las Meninas* did for Foucault), but, on the contrary, to confront the picture/viewer duo with their reciprocal otherness. We are in January 1882. Manet is only just fifty, but he's seriously ill, and can feel death closing in on him. He does his most to deny it, and works night and day on the painting he has planned for the upcoming Salon, which will finally, or so he hopes, earn him the public's recognition. It is a large, ambitious painting which would soon truly become his testament, but which, for the time being, is no more than the *ébauche* for one of those scenes from modern life that have made him both famous and controversial. What he has in mind would transport the Salon visitor to the Folies-Bergère, the latest fashionable *café concert*. We'll spend a while with *A Bar at the Folies-Bergère*, for there is no more disconcerting, misleading, complex, enigmatic, and, when all is said and done, luminous painting than this, when we question it as the viewer's presentational device; nor is there any painting richer in lessons to be learned for anyone thinking about the challenges of today's art. But it calls for a certain amount of preparation. It wouldn't be Manet's testament if it didn't sum up the endeavor of an entire lifetime. So we have no option but to review this life, albeit very cursorily. Let's do this with four pictures which we'll rename *Farewell to the Gaze, Suzanne, The Proof is in the Cat*, and *Do Redheads Blush?*, their official titles being: *L'Enfant à l'épée [Boy with a Sword]* (1861), *Nymphe surprise [Surprised Nymph]* (1859–1861), *Olympia* (1863), and *Le Chemin de fer [The Railroad]* (1872–73), also called *La Gare Saint Lazare*.

Farewell to the Gaze. We are first brought up short by the child's gaze. The half-brown, half-green eyes are dark yet transparent water, innocent but solemn beneath the rather heavy lids, wet as from a pinch of kohl but without Murillo's mawkishness; neither wide open nor round with wonder but receptive and expectant, open onto the future and projected ahead in space. When we take our leave of the picture, we have to bid our farewells to that gaze. We may well have seen everything in the picture except it, because what looks at us cannot necessarily be looked at. Yet it was this child's gaze that held our attention for a minute, or a quarter of an hour, or an hour in the room at the New York Metropolitan where *Boy with a Sword* is on view (right beside *Christ Rising from the Dead*). It's this gaze which gives the face its solemnness, lends determination to the shape of the mouth, belies the deliciously

Édouard Manet
L'Enfant à l'épée, 1861

juvenile texture of the skin without detracting from it, and delicately separates the oval of the face from the helmet of fine flaxen hair framing it, enough for us to see it floating like a mask in front of the picture, or, on the contrary, emerging, the only living flesh, from the hole for the head in a fairground backdrop all arranged for the photograph. The cheek stands out so distinctly against the white of the collar that the ear seems to be part of the decor. The other cheek is so quickly plunged in shadow that it seems to be cast upon the cardboard just behind. The blonde bangs, laid down in three just vigorous-enough brush strokes, suffice to attach the gold of the hair to the porcelain of the face, pinning both to the same picture plane, and refashions from a floating mask a real and beautiful flesh-and-blood child's face, which "holds" thanks to its gaze—the open door to meaning, reading, and interpretation. Our gaze may then leave the child's, leap the dazzling barrier of the white ruffle, rebound on the huge sword in the lad's hands, slide along the sheath, then, like a toboggan, run down the broad leather harness hanging below his knees, finally leap a new, if more discreet, color barrier, and land on the common ground. The child walks. He moves in the direction of the narrative, from left to right, like writing, parallel to the rear wall. The shadow of his steps draws him on: he'll soon leave the frame by the right, leaving us facing a latter day Rothko.

Suzanne. But no, the boy with a sword hasn't budged, and he won't. A painting able to arrest us with its gaze represents a boy stopped short in his walk by the gaze directed at him. The narrative gets suspended just when we arrive on the scene. All Manet is there, potentially. He hasn't forgotten that great painting is history painting, which is defined by two dictates: that it edify us by telling stories, and that these should be edifying because they are taken either from the epic History of the worldly great, or from mythology, the fabulous history of the gods which all men of breeding should know, or, still, from the Scriptures, familiar not only to the well-educated but also to any ordinary good Christian. In all three cases, the viewer is supposed to be familiar already with the story told by the picture. Aware of these dictates and ambitious, young Manet has launched into a masterly *Moses Saved from the Waters*, composed à la Giorgione, with the central subject (the maidservant carrying the infant Moses in his basket) reduced to anecdote, and the secondary subject (the Pharaoh's daughter bathing naked in the river) thrust onto the foreground. There still exists a sketch of the projected work, but all that's left of the definitive painting is the woman bathing. This is *Surprised Nymph*. The rest has been cut away and destroyed. The pose, rich in scholarly allusions to Bathshebas and Susannahs by Rembrandt, Rubens, Van Dyck, and Giulio Romano, is held by Suzanne Leenhoff, the artist's mistress. Her full, round body is all surface given tension by two contradictory desires: ours at seeing her offering us her charms and opening herself to the caress of eye or hand, and hers at curling into a ball like the cloth bound around her knee, shielding her modesty and her shame, and turning her back to us. But the painter was ruthless: there is not a hint of chiaroscuro here offering her shadows in which to hide, and giving us some secrecy to entertain our desire. Not much modeling; harsh lighting; a hand emerging from the cloth and protruding from the picture, and pulling backwards a shoulder painted without the slightest foreshortening; and this huge back, unfurled

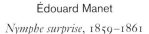

Édouard Manet

Nymphe surprise, 1859–1861

beyond any verisimilitude in the plane of the canvas; and lastly, this surprised look that we're not quite sure what to do with! A *Susannah and the Elders*, called Suzanne in real life, turns her head toward the viewer and finds herself being watched. Of all the sources claimed for this picture, the one with the closest resemblance is Vostermann's engraving after a *Susannah and the Elders* by Rubens, now lost, with which Manet was acquainted through Charles Blanc's *Histoire des peintres*. It must have had quite an effect on him, for Rubens pulls the alibi rug of our own voyeurism out from under us. Tradition has it that by turning her back on the elders' lecherous gaze, which invariably comes from the back of the painting (and the Rubens is no exception), Susannah turns inadvertently toward us, which prompted Diderot's disingenuous remark on a Susannah by Lagrenée: "When Susannah exposes herself naked to my eye, withstanding the elders' gaze with all the veils swathing her, Susannah is chaste, and so is the painter, for neither of them knew I was there." Rubens' Susannah does know we are there. She is as much startled by our look at her as she protects herself from the elders' gaze by turning away from them. Manet was even less hypocritical: he did away with the elders. We are the peeping Toms. (There are serious objections to this interpretation, but none of them decisive. They are mentioned in the references at the end of the chapter.)

The modernist reading of *Surprised Nymph* has Susannah's body standing for the canvas' surface, and reflects on voyeurism as metaphorizing the act of looking at pictures. It's not a false reading, it is even very fruitful, and boils down to this: the real

Vosterman, after Rubens

Susannah and the Elders

(here mirror-reversed)

Édouard Manet

Study for *Nymphe surprise*

(*Moïse sauvé des eaux*), 1860–1861

or the prime subject of the picture is the presence of the beholder in front of it. The picture is the viewer's presentational device, and "here you are" is the first message it addresses to him, or her. In other words, the picture "knows" it is being beheld, and lets this be known to the beholder. The voyeur is himself being seen, caught red-handed, as it were. Everything is frozen in this split-second of pure reciprocity in shame, when Susannah and her peeping Tom can say to each other: "I know you know I know." There is no possible narrative left. In *Boy with a Sword*, the boy's gaze was the open-door to the flow of meaning and time. Susannah's gaze is their lock-and-bolt. And to think that this picture had started out as a history painting, complete with movement, anecdote, water flowing in the foreground, and dwindling clouds being blown to the rear by the wind! Once completed and severed from its biblical reference, its apparent aim was to get painting to admit that it is an art with no access to time. And with time, speech, and with speech, the possibility of telling stories, and with that, the possibility of relating History. *Surprised Nymph*, with its vaguely mythological title but no reference to any known narrative, was the first painting in Manet's career where he sensed the path he'd have to follow given his intution that he'd have to give up history painting and become a painter of the contemporary. But he wasn't ready, for all that, to give up on the narrative ambition of his art. For a while, everything would hinge on the figure of the beholder beheld: if the picture is explicit enough to show, through the entangled eyes of the figure in the picture and the viewer in front of it, that the beholder has become a protagonist in the story being told by the picture, then not all narrative possibility is lost. However, there is a consequence to this: from the moment the viewer becomes part of the narrative, he also becomes its narrator. The price to pay is an unprecedented shift of authority which—and did Manet realize as much?—would capsize tradition and usher in modernism, because from now on, painting would no longer receive its legitimacy from the past, but instead from the future.

The Proof is in the Cat. The elders have left the picture and become incarnate in the viewer. Does the latter realize as much? Has he understood that he's part of a narrative that stops at the precise moment when the figure in the picture recognizes the presence of a *vis-à-vis* outside the picture, and that the narrative's sequel will depend on him? The nymph is surprised, and surprises are instantaneous. Contemplating a picture, on the other hand, takes time. How are you to extract time from the gaze if it is condensed into the *Augenblick* of mutual surprise? But how to avoid doing this if you spend a while in the company of the picture? It is impossible to sustain Susannah's gaze without betraying Manet's intent. Not that it is frightening or unbearable; it simply doesn't have any existence in duration. As soon as you dwell on it, it loses its astonishment and changes meaning. It becomes shrouded in melancholy, meditativeness, private thoughts, and interiority, the very opposite of the surprise that Manet intended it to signify—and which a weakness had him mention in the title, a concession to intelligibility that he would never again allow himself. So the nude's gaze in *Le Déjeuner sur l'herbe*—and even more Olympia's gaze—has qualities quite different from that of the *Surprised Nymph*. It is, precisely, a sustained gaze—steady, unflinching. We put up with it because it puts up with ours. Or else we have trouble putting up with it for the very same reason. The hysterical laughter triggered by *Olympia* at the 1865 Salon was a defensive reaction on the part of the male visitors, embarrassed by the fact that a woman should stare back at them so unabashedly. Even today, Olympia's eyes exude the insolent certainty of her equality with the so-called stronger sex. If the picture hasn't dated one iota, being as exciting today as it was troubling back then, it is also thanks to the personality of Victorine Meurent, Manet's favorite model from 1862 to 1875, who is featured in *La Chanteuse*

Édouard Manet
Olympia, 1863

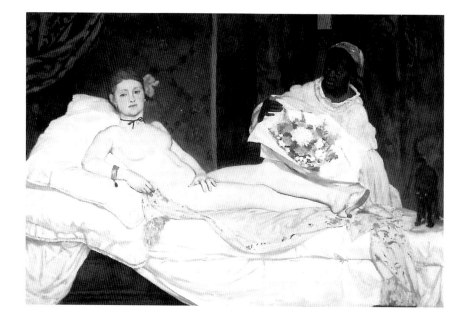

des rues, L'Espada, Le Déjeuner sur l'herbe, Olympia, La Femme au perroquet, Le Chemin de fer and that exquisite one and only little portrait in the Boston museum where Victorine appears as Victorine. We know precious little about the human relations that must have come into play between painter and model in the studio. Manet was a discreet person, and his biographers have not been very talkative either in this respect. All we can say is that what emanates from *Olympia* and the other paintings for which Victorine sat is a sensation of amity and equality, which makes any speculation about their relationship "in life"—Pygmalion-like or in the style of Raphael and la *Fornarina*—a cheap shot. Victorine felt at ease in her body, which was shapely but rather ordinary, with breasts set well apart, knock-knees and bony ankles, lightyears away from the phoney perfect beauties with which the likes of Cabanel, Baudry, and Clésinger filled the Salon. She had the milkwhite, light-absorbing skin of a redhead and a superb head of hair, of which, oddly enough, Manet never really made the most. Her face must have been extraordinarily mobile and changing, to judge from the range of her features in her various appearances. She was a chatterbox, and the painter, who loved bantering with his models while he worked, enjoyed her scamp's cheekiness. In the end she herself started painting in the 1870s. A *Self portrait* earned her a place at the 1876 Salon, from which Manet himself was barred. Everything suggests that she was treated as a human being in her own right, as a real flesh-and-blood woman, and as a peer, something that wasn't that common in 19th-century studios, where the borderline between female model posing naked and harlot was anything but clearcut. Nowhere is this equality more visible than in *Olympia*. The sustained, unflinching gaze she offers us—or aims at us—is the outcome of this equality of relations, the deposit on the canvas of the calm self-assurance with which Victorine engaged the painter's gaze throughout their modelling sessions, and addressed her gaze to him, just as she now addresses it to us.

Supposing that the real subject—the modernist, reflexive subject—of *Surprised Nymph* is the no-holds-barred assertion of the viewer's presence in front of the picture, and that Manet realized that the nymph's gaze failed to get across because, in contemplating it, we make it lose the instantaneousness of surprise, then Olympia's sustained gaze is a solution to this problem. Is it satisfactory? Not really. It may sound strange, given the scandal surrounding its reception at the time and the provocative vigor it still broadcasts in our own day and age, but *Olympia* is a picture which too easily re-incorporates the tradition of *la grande peinture* for its reflexive meaning to be immediately perceptible. The idea that its primary message to the viewer is "here you are" may very well not spring to mind, so numerous are the other layers of meaning. Yet Manet makes it a point to let the viewer know that the picture "knows" it is being looked at, not because this is its true, primary, or only subject-matter (this is where the modernist reading is much too simplistic), but because it is on this proviso that rests his hope to give speech back to the art of painting so that it might tell stories even when the end of the story is unknown—which is clearly the case when you paint contemporary life. Olympia's addressed gaze inhibits rather than encourages this. It isn't innocent enough; it is too aware of the conventions it borrows from *la grande peinture* to be able to indicate to the beholder that his presence is not simply the tacit requisite presupposed by any painting, but that it is a *fact*, incorporated into the picture. No painter paints so that his or her painting won't be looked at; this is so obvious that it will take extraordinary measures to get the picture to say as much explicitly—and all the more so because the convention dominating classical painting (further bolstered from the last three decades of the 18th century on) is to smother this obvious fact. A good picture acts as if the beholder weren't there. When Diderot said that "Susannah is chaste and so is the painter, for neither one of them knew I was there," he was subtle enough not to delve on the so-called chasteness of the viewer, knowing very well under what alibi the "male gaze," as we would put it now, had free rein in the Salon of his day. By requiring that no exhibitionism on Susannah's part should come to meet the beholder's voyeurism, his concern was not to observe the proprieties but rather to respect what was for him an absolute convention of painting—that the picture should feature a story which unfolds of its own accord, whether the viewer is in attendance or not. Much more than any hypocrisy of voyeurism, it was this particular convention that Manet broke by signifying to the beholder not only that his presence was called for if the narrative were to be "activated," but also that it be taken for granted. The extraordinary thing is that he did this without breaching the essential demand of *la grande peinture*, according to Diderot and his tradition: not merely that it should edify us but above all that it should touch us.

Manet would probably have been hard-pressed to explain what he did in *Surprised Nymph*, and ditto regarding what he would be doing differently in *Olympia*. He was in the process of inventing a new picture/beholder relationship which was to have consequences for art history to come as enormous as the fact of making the viewer part of the narrative, so that he becomes both one of its protagonists and its narrator. Needless to add, he wasn't aware of any of this. But he did seem to have had the following intuition: although the gaze of *Surprised Nymph* had the drawback of losing its instantaneousness as soon as it was lingered on, it had the advantage over the gaze of *Olympia* of not being addressed to us—or to anyone, for that matter. The last thing we can say about a woman discovering that she is being observed in the nude is that she reciprocates when she stares back at the man sneaking a glimpse of her. The split-second of astonishment when their eyes meet is a split-second of sheer reciprocity, because the voyeur is himself seen, but the reciprocity here is asymmetrical. The voyeur's gaze is intensely addressed to the object of his desire. The gaze of the *Surprised Nymph* is anything but addressed. The nymph is no less chaste than the *Susannah* by Lagrenée about which Diderot so enthused, but not at all for the same reasons. Her innocence doesn't stem from her ignorance, but from the fact that her surprised gaze doesn't intentionally meet the eye catching her unawares. Olympia doesn't have this innocence, so another eye, guaranteed to be natural, has to show the beholder that the picture "knows" it is being looked at. This eye would be that of the black cat at the foot of the bed. Animalness is summoned as a proof of innocence, and the subject of *Surprised Nymph* splits into two: Olympia incarnates the nymph and the cat the surprise. Standing stiffly, fur bristling, eyes staring, everything about the cat points to the brothel customer's—and Salon visitor's—sudden appearance on the scene. The cat is the cue for the viewer to enter the narrative, and the snapshot around which the story revolves. Just a moment ago, it was still languidly curled up at Olympia's feet, like the little dog in Titian's *Venus of Urbino*, the main source of the picture; the customer rang the door bell; the maid went to take his coat and the bunch of flowers he brought to wrap the venal nature of his visit in amorous gallantry; she's just opened the bedroom door to him. He is right now making his entrance; Olympia turns her head in his direction, in no way surprised—she'd been expecting him—while the attentive maid presents her mistress with the gentleman's floral offering; and from sheer reflex, the cat, roused from its slumbers, shows its disapproval. It is up to each one of us to imagine the next step in the narrative, based on our desire, our morality, and the figure we identify with. But in the brief moment "snapped" by Manet, nobody had any choice. Even women saw themselves incarnated in this role of the gallant gent, just long enough to take over the function of narrator from this character, absent from the painting but so crucial to the tale it tells. Strange incarnation.

Do Redheads Blush? The way an artist's intelligence works is the most intriguing of mysteries, and Manet was devilishly intelligent. There are two things about him that cannot be overestimated: an intuitiveness that instinctively prompted him never to satisfy the demands of the audience of the day, if he felt that they were dragging him downwards; and a fierce, relentless, and even obsessive wish to be understood. Understood by all and sundry, that is, by the crowd that was flocking to the Salon just like it went to the theater in droves, a crowd infuriated rather than moved by the feats of arms of the high and mighty of this world, a crowd with neither Pliny nor Virgil—at the most its catechism—on its shelves. Throughout his life, Manet was driven by the desire to be understood and, throughout his life, he suffered from not

Édouard Manet
Olympia, 1863, detail

being understood. All the while—as we have already seen with regard to his *Christ Rising from the Dead*—he was incapable, wonderfully, genuinely, and viscerally incapable, of giving in to the conventions which would have made his painting understandable to his contemporaries. Hence the ongoing impression we get that he simultaneously hands over and refuses us the clues to his work, that he is alternately or both luminous and murky, the most realistic of observers and the most intellectual of allegorists. Certainly, Courbet's lesson wasn't lost on him. No painting is more consciously reflexive than Manet's: it always speaks to us of painting. And no painting is more transitive than his, either: nobody better than he has opened his eyes to the city life of his time, to the fleeting modernity sung by Baudelaire, to the thousand and one ways in which "the age, fashion, morality, and passion" affect human commerce, relations between men and women, their stride, their body movement, and their facial bearing. His gift of observation was extraordinary, but he was unaware of it to such a point that today he appears to us as an artist blessed with not having understood why he was not understood. "So what's more naïve than Olympia? There are tough things there, I'm told. They were there. I've seen them. I painted what I saw." Yes, but he saw like nobody else and, more than a century after his death, we are not through with learning to see what he saw.

Olympia attracted every manner of incomprehension, and Manet was deeply depressed by this. The next time he would attempt to measure up to the dictates of history painting, it would be with a real piece of contemporary political history and not with a modern Venus, whose allusions to Titian didn't suffice to make it palatable, and where the presence of the bristling cat merely prompted sardonic and amused comments, but no awareness of the new narrator's role handed to the viewer. Like many of his compatriots with Republican sympathies, Manet had been outraged by the Mexican tragedy. Napoleon III had ditched emperor Maximilian of Austria after setting him on the throne of Mexico, and Maximilian was executed by the Juarists on 19 June 1867. Shortly afterwards, Manet set to work on *The Execution of the Emperor Maximilian of Mexico*, for which, in addition to the picture finished in 1868, there are two sketches and a large composition cut into pieces. He was informed that the picture would be refused by the Salon, so he didn't even bother to submit it, so disgusted was he. This time he would have been understood, though: he had painted a real history picture whose story was well known and whose last line had been written. As with *Surprised Nymph* and *Olympia*, he had boiled down the narrative to a snapshot—the salvo from the firing squad—but a snapshot leaving the beholder outside the event. He had read what the press had to say and gathered photographic documentation together, and he had gleaned information about the uniforms like any old Meissonier. He had also pledged his allegiance to tradition, since his composition was directly inspired by Goya's *Tres de Mayo*. And now political censorship robbed him of his reconciliation with the public. He withdrew into portraits, countryside landscapes, and scenes from bourgeois life, like the admirable *Balcony*, until political history—real and immediate history, namely, the siege of Paris by the Prussian army—caught up with him again. Among the rare pages dating from that period, there is a wash drawing titled *The Barricade* which repeats, line for line,

Maximilian's firing squad. He enlisted in the National Guard after dispatching his family to the region of Arcachon, rejoining them in February 1871 when the war was over. He was not in Paris during the Commune, leaving that old socialist Courbet to be jailed for having knocked down the Vendôme column. He felt made for the painting of modern life, Baudelaire-style, but not for ongoing history and its tragedies. You can't be involved and detached at once. Well-removed from current events, his palette grew lighter. He let himself be influenced by the young Monet and Renoir, not yet called Impressionists, who would before long, and more or less in spite of him, regard him as their *chef de file*.

   In 1874 he was ready to return to the Salon in full force, with a watercolor and three paintings, including *The Railroad*, which is now in the National Gallery in Washington. It is worth noting in passing that it was as a result of the refusal of the other two paintings, *Swallows* and *Masquerade at the Opera*, that Mallarmé took up his pen to enjoin the jury to content itself with "choosing, from among the pictures presented in a frame, those that truly exist as paintings, in order to put them before our eyes." For *The Railroad*, Manet returned to Victorine, fresh from a storybook love affair in the United States. It is pointless trying to describe the painting when you can see it with your own eyes, even if the reproduction betrays what really matters. Let's tell its story instead, for Manet had gone back to the *Olympia* method: the viewer is at once the character missing from the picture, without whom the narrative is not complete, and the narrator. Let's pass him the mike, because he lived through the story and is thus in a position to tell it in the first person. Dressed to the nines, I am this Parisian dandy, this conceited *flâneur* confident in his charms who has just glimpsed this young "provincially" dressed governess and the little girl in her charge.

Édouard Manet
Le Chemin de fer,
1872–1873

She hasn't noticed me drawing close to her, absorbed as she is in her book. Strange that she has her finger marking a page that she's not reading! Maybe she's studying. Fine, a serious girl whose upward mobility doesn't rely solely on her looks. All the more exciting. Oh dear, the little girl's already got the whole picture. She's seen me coming and turned her back on me, terse and sulky, and pretending that the passing trains are a much more interesting sight than this fellow about to snatch her nanny's attention from her. Ah, women … "Good afternoon, Miss, lovely day, isn't it?" Have I surprised her, disturbed her? The time she takes to look up from her book! And how she stares at me! Not shy for a bit, but then not easy either. Heavens, not a word from her, not even a good day back. Ah! Am I mistaken or is she blushing? It would seem I've touched her …

Let's stop this stream of consciousness right here, a stream we've had to invest with as much sexism as possible to get the picture's intensity across, once we seriously assume that the viewer is part of the tale it tells. You may reject this interpretation and think that Manet sketched a little cameo of city life, in which nothing is missing. But what then about Victorine's gaze that steps out of the picture and greets us? It is so visibly addressed to someone facing her and so unflinching that you'd reckon that Victorine was giving us the once over, registering our appearance, and right away pigeonholing us in the category of people you would—or wouldn't—want to be seen with. Someone is standing in front of the picture—there is no other way of explaining this gaze. That someone might of course have more honest intentions than our *flâneur* looking for adventure. That someone could be a woman, although … There are definitely many other plausible scenarios. The little girl could very well not have turned her back just the moment before; she could have been there getting bored stiff for half an hour while her governess read and was neglecting her, or she might really have been having fun watching the trains passing. And why couldn't the governess be the little girl's mother? It doesn't really matter. One of the undoubted charms of *The Railroad* is that it is open to a whole host of narratives which we can all add to or leave suspended according to our own sensibility. The narrative here proposed leads to the fact that Victorine, or rather the character she plays, is blushing. This opens the door to many other amusing speculations about the rest of the story: the dandy thinks he's chalked up a point, but the governess' blush possibly doesn't in any way suggest that she's prey to his charms. It may convey shyness or, more likely, anger, an anger contained by her smart city dweller's composure, one who's been through all this before. Alternatively, we might imagine that our handsome gentleman is being more coarsely direct in his approach, or a tad exhibitionistic, and thus read Victorine's crimson cheeks as a mark on her face of the affront to her propriety to which she has just been subjected. Herein lies the rub: the blush is an acknowledgement of receipt.

Blushing is an involuntary phenomenon; it betrays some inner feeling but it wouldn't be quite right to say that it expresses it, for blushing is neither deliberate nor addressed; in people who tend to blush, it often appears when they are interpellated or addressed, as a result of having been spoken to. The blush thus acts as a kind of seesaw movement: the reversal of an addressed message sent back to the sender without being addressed to him or her. And this reversal does not rely on the gaze but rather on the complexion. This much can be said about any real blush. But when it is painted? The painter knew what he was up to. He wanted to paint a person blushing. And he addressed this blush fairly and squarely to us. Let's applaud this stroke of genius: Manet found a way to send us a message whose essential purport is that it is not being addressed, and to associate it, in the very same character, with a message that is being addressed. The governess looks at us and blushes. Olympia looked at us and the cat's hair stood on end, which, for a cat, amounts to more or less the same thing. As to the surprised nymph, she has seen us unwittingly. In *The Railroad*, the combination of an addressed message whose vehicle is the gaze—like Olympia's sustained gaze—and an unaddressed and unintentional message—like the surprised expression in Suzanne's eye—but whose vehicle, this time, is the skin and not the gaze, helps to solve the problem posed by duration in the gaze of the *Surprised Nymph*, without having to resort to the makeshift represented by Olympia's cat. Brilliant. Needless to say, Manet was totally unaware of the consequences. It remains that what would later come to be called modernist—let's say, abstract—painting would issue directly from them.

We still must see Victorine blushing—which we're not bound to do—and this, it goes without saying, in the original painting. Once we have seen that, the impression is irresistible and lasting. It is enhanced when we get a chance to examine the painting up close, fades when we look at it too long, and comes back when, having left the picture, we do a quick about-face. The x-ray and photos taken in raking light show that Victorine's face in *The Railroad* is one of the most worked-up Manet ever painted. The paint is thick and powdery, applied with a dry brush in successive touch-ups, which explains why the initial impression fades when the eye lingers long on the painting. It is almost impossible to distinguish between complexion and make-up

Édouard Manet

Le Chemin de fer, 1872–1873

(detail)

Édouard Manet

Portrait de Victorine Meurent, 1862

(detail)

Édouard Manet

Un bar aux Folies-Bergère, 1881–1882

(detail)

when dealing with painting. Has Victorine put rouge on her cheeks? Doesn't her skin tend to be naturally blotchy, anyway? Is she reacting to the cold? The little girl's summer dress clearly answers this last question negatively. To try and answer the first two, we should consult the Boston portrait, the sole image of Victorine that depicts her not playing a part: no blushing, no blotchiness, just this diaphanous redhead's complexion with its milky skin. And then get back to the Washington picture: the redness of Victorine's cheeks has a triangular shape which follows the salience of her cheekbones. Nobody puts on make up like that. It also has a hue tending to brown. Brunettes, as a rule, don't blush much; blondes often do, but not like this. When a redhead blushes, she tends to do so exactly like Victorine in this picture. There's no way of proving this. We engage our subjectivity when we respond thusly to Manet's trust in his gift of observation. This is a risk we have to run.

So here we are, primed, now, to broach Manet's testament, and broach it from the same angle (and with the same risk), for it sticks out a mile: the barmaid in *A Bar at the Folies-Bergère* is also blushing. She blushes the way certain blondes blush, all over her face, and even behind the ears, while her neck and breast remain as white as snow. Instant question: who's making her blush? Equally as instant a reply: the top hatted gentleman standing opposite her in the mirror's reflection. Who is he? We are sufficiently primed to recognize in him our acquaintance, the sexist *flâneur*, or his twin brother. What's more, we no longer need to take on his role and dream in his stead; he is in the picture this time. It is almost painfully clear that he represents us in it. The mirror reflects the space we are in, in front of the picture. It looks as if Manet, beside himself at never being understood and desperately eager to be understood at least posthumously, decided to be didactic just for once. This isn't wrong.

Édouard Manet
Un bar aux Folies-Bergère,
1881–1882
(COLOR PLATE P. 218)

But what narrow terms for a testament! Things are a whole lot more complex, as we soon realize. What is the reflection of the couple doing in the right hand corner of the picture? Shouldn't they be right behind the barmaid, given that the mirror's gilt frame runs parallel to the bar, which is itself parallel with the picture plane? This reflection is not in its proper place, so we can't trust it. Yet if, despite the evidence, we did trust it, shouldn't the gentleman in the top hat insert himself between the barmaid and us? We sense him there, so conspicuous is his absence. Unless we incarnate him? Questions tumble forth, too numerous not to keep some of them waiting, and too pressing for at least the one to which the blush offers a tentative answer not to afford to wait: incarnation, oh yes. A major thing, and no more or less "religious" (note quotation marks) than resurrection. No one with a Christian culture should be surprised. Without a God incarnate, there's no need for resurrection. Whole religions are founded on metempsychosis, reincarnation, and the immortality of the soul, without the motif ever appearing of the resurrection of the flesh on judgment day—a consequence of the fact that God consented to become incarnate among men. Painters—western painters at any rate—can't dodge the enormity of the matter, even when they don't engage in metaphysics. Their excuse is that incarnation presents itself to them as a technical problem, and they think it is sorted out when their work lands in the museum, as if judgment day had taken place there. Manet must have relieved them of all their illusions, he who painted indifferently for the Museum and the Salon. His genius—and his relevance today—have to do with the fact that incarnation presented itself to him as something neither religious nor technical, but ethical. As a matter of relationship to the other—to the other being addressed, that is—in other words, to the "you."

Since *Surprised Nymph*, we have seen Manet concerned to let the viewer know that he must incarnate the missing character in the picture, if the story being told by the picture is to be complete. This is a strange incarnation, which takes place outside the picture, and one to which a real human being, made of flesh and blood, lends his body and his voice. His body, because the picture only comes to life with the physical presence of the beholder in front of it; and his voice, because at the moment when the character he's about to incarnate steps out of the picture, he enters the narrative and becomes its narrator. This is not how the problem of incarnation traditionally translates to the painter. It is rather with the technical and *conventional* problem of rendering flesh. For example, the flesh of Titian's *Venus of Urbino* is made of oil on canvas, yet we feel how it quivers with life. Does it suffice to congratulate the artist and credit his legendary talent for *sprezzatura* for the miracle? Maybe not. Titian is a fabulous painter, a better one than, say, Cima da Conegliano, and more modern and a bit more recent in that milestoned art history first described by Vasari (and last by Gombrich) as the progress of illusionism. But the very idea of confining painting to illusion is a convention, identical whether for Cima or Titian. A complex and refined fabric of conventions, as it happens, which are at once technical and aesthetic. They prescribe what painters should paint, and how, and what viewers should see, and how they should appraise what they are seeing. A pact, in a nutshell, something like a religion, a shared belief that unites the painters' guild and the viewers' society. Not a superstition: nobody is lured by Titian's power of illusion—his art is not *trompe-l'oeil*. The pact is based on suspension of disbelief. We look at Venus the way we might look at a thing—the thing she actually is, since she is a picture. Let's remember that things don't speak; neither do we speak to them; we talk about them. Venus' body is in the third person. She comes to life under our gaze, ready to speak to us and thus shift from the "she" to the "I," as long as we acquiesce to the powers of semblance, act *as if*, and suspend our disbelief. Titian is more persuasive than Cima, but the pact is a prerequiste valid for the whole culture the two painters share. It is this particular pact that modernity has broken. We are heathens. When it was common currency, those things called works of art could expect to leap from the third person to the first without any transit through the second. This is no longer the case. Either what we call art has completely changed meanings with modernity, and we are suffering from schizophrenia when we claim to appreciate modern art in continuity with the art of the past, or the pact has been reconstructed differently. Hypothesis: the new pact is Manet's invention; it shifts those *things* called works of art from the third to the first person, by way of the second; it is henceforth based on the "you," the pronoun of the recipient or addressee. As naïvely referred to in relation to Richter's *Spiegel*, speech rendered unto things because we spoke to them first, such is the miracle of their resurrection, seen from the beholder's vantage point.

Of course, there is no miracle. No more so in *A Bar at the Folies-Bergère* than in *Christ Rising from the Dead*. It was the spectator's gaze which brought Christ back to life, tantamount to an act of faith. Not quite the same thing as belief in miracles, or, for that matter, suspension of disbelief. If speech is to have a chance of being given back to things, the prodigious seesaw represented by the barmaid's blush must first be activated, that seesaw which returns to the sender an addressed message in the shape of a non-addressed acknowledgement of receipt. And to activate it, get the girl to blush, address her—touch her, move her, or even hurt her if need be—in such a way that the involuntary reaction of her body shows me that I am indeed in front of her. Just as with our *flâneur* trying to pick up the governess, for the time being, the use of the first person is the privilege of the gentleman in the top hat, alias the viewer, the one difference being that the viewer no longer has to get into the man's skin to take up the narrative himself, for the mirror has repatriated this particular narrative back into the picture. So, I went to the Courtauld Institute in London to pay a visit to Suzon—this being the first name of the barmaid in the *Bar at the Folies-Bergère*. The absence of my *alter ego*, the man in the top hat, had such a presence that it drew me in like a magnet. I was unable to resist the idea of walking straight up to the picture with my eyes shut, and only opening them when I was close enough to order a drink from the barmaid. The first thing that struck me, and considerably irked me, was that the picture was hung too high to enable me to enjoy the dreamed of face-to-face with my dear Suzon. And the second thing that struck me, like a flash of lightning, quite unexpectedly, was that Suzon is blushing. I'd never noticed this in reproductions: she's blushing! I know this is a personal impression, to be treated with caution. Suzon might well be made-up, and with Baudelaire's blessing, to boot, who sang the praises of make-up in *Le Peintre de la vie moderne*. But I couldn't help it. After all, the picture is addressed to ordinary museum visitors, something even an art historian may be from time to time. And ordinary museum visitors are entitled to their subjective impressions. I didn't waste much time speculating about the issue of knowing why Suzon was blushing. Being acquainted with the literature, I didn't really care. The most plausible scenario was that I, the (male) viewer, or my stand-in, the man in the top hat, had just propositioned her. Was she blushing out of emotion, shyness, shame, or anger? I didn't really care about that either. The literature has credited her with such a wide gamut of expressions—from professional amiability to unruffled indifference, from modesty to boredom, from absentmindedness to melancholy, from flirtatiousness to disgust—that at the end of the day, any of the above might be the one. Why does a woman blush, anyway? Some women blush at next to nothing, others never do. And there are men too … Forget the literature. After all, I was there, and that was enough. Suzon was blushing because it was I making her blush. By which I mean, obviously, that she was blushing because I felt she was blushing—and there's nothing else to prove her redness than my sensation. For me to have this sensation, something in the painting must have touched me. And what had touched me was the awareness—not even that, but the sensation, here, too—that something must have touched her, and made her blush. All I could be sure of was that this something wasn't me. There was nothing directly reciprocal between her and me when I stood in front of her in that room at the Courtauld. I could see her, she couldn't see me. She was just a picture, looking at me, yes, but not seeing me. The something or someone who must have touched her and made her blush was the man in the top hat whom I could see in the mirror occupying the very place where I found myself trying to engage Suzon in conversation. I could watch him, even spy on him out of the corner of my eye, and see him as clearly as anything talking to the barmaid. It was his address to Suzon which Suzon's redness, addressed to me by the painter, expressed. Independently of this, Suzon's redness betrayed the presence of someone in front of her who had just addressed her. It was as if her complexion—her carnation—were his incarnation, and his incarnation my own presence.

Crazy Folies-Bergère! Champagne, brass bands, music, electricity, trapeze artists in green shoes, worldly women with binoculars, demimondaines in yellow gloves, stiff-looking gentlemen slumming in top hats, English beer, scents of evil's flowers, and stench of tobacco … Spin the merry-go-round: Offenbach, a whirl round the boulevards, Parisian nights, the fair in the Place du Trône… And then slow down the whirligig and, in the midst of the hullabaloo, look—look at the unfathomable weariness of Suzon's face, the vacant eyes, the melancholy pout of the lips, the bangs too low on the forehead, tacky pearls pinned on the ears. Look how vulnerable she is, and how she is quickly moved, this country lass who hasn't had time to get accustomed to the city and still has to learn how to put up a mask. Go with the lyricism. Even if it means forcing the note, *first* be moved and touched. Then in slow motion follow the big dipper careering its way through your head, and repeat: *it was as if her carnation were his incarnation* … and pause here. In its immediacy, aesthetic judgment is a way of reasoning, reflecting. Manet painted Suzon's complexion. Granted, a picture is a thing, but a thing made by a human hand. We can talk about the rendering of flesh, and why not? This flesh was born from Manet's brush strokes, he has addressed it to us. It's not from addressing herself to us on her own behalf that Suzon blushes in her flesh. But nor is it from having been *represented* blushing by the painter. It's from having been *presented* by him as interpellated by the person facing her. The words spoken by the man in the top hat get incarnated in the reddening of the feminine other he has addressed. The painter has not been able to paint these words, for painting is an art without a soundtrack. We've seen Manet lamenting this ever since he decided to cut up *Surprised Nymph* in what was to be a *Moses Saved from the Waters* relying on prior knowledge of the biblical tale. And we've seen him going out of his way to shift the initiative of the soundtrack to the viewer-narrator, who refused to pick up the clue despite *Olympia*'s cat and Victorine's blush in *The Railroad*. For now, the gentleman is depicted in the picture and because the picture is a mirror, he should be in front of it. But he isn't, he still lacks flesh and blood. Proof by surprise, by the cat, and by the blush—wouldn't each have been to no avail? At the moment of signing *A Bar at the Folies-Bergère*, his testament, Manet reinforced the reflection of the man in the mirror with the conspicuousness of his absence before the mirror. Everything he has managed to teach us in four pictures leads, in the fifth, to the idea stronger than ever that it is up to us to embody the man in the top hat. Let's be done with the big dipper ride: ... *and his incarnation, my own presence*. With the arrival of the real viewer, incarnation has stepped out of the picture. It was a matter of the rendering of flesh, one last time, just long enough to activate the seesaw that will turn it into a question of address to *the other*. The red on Suzon's cheeks is the last touch to the painting.

As ever, the critics weren't in the least bit moved. Left incredulous by *Christ Rising from the Dead*, they still hadn't realized, eighteen years later, that Manet was requesting from them an act of faith of a quite different intensity than mere suspension of disbelief. "To adore the little blue salesgirl selling oranges at the Folies-Bergère, we must learn to cherish cardboard women," wrote the critic Paul Mantz after his visit to the 1882 Salon. Mantz was wont to dip his pen in fire and brimstone as soon as Manet loomed on the horizon—"a knave of diamonds pinned to a door," he said of *Le Fifre*; "figures stuck to wallpaper backdrops," about *La Serre* and *Jeanne*—but he was by no means the only person to express the horror inspired in him by the absence of flesh in Manet with metaphors revolving around the card game and the advertising billboard. "Silhouette and cutout glued on grey paper," said Joséphin Péladan about *The Fifer*, a picture which Zola, whom one might imagine inclined to greater indulgence, described as "a costumier's sign." Even Courbet saw in *Olympia* just "a queen of spades in a card game emerging from her bath." We might say that Mantz's wish was granted: we have learned how to cherish cardboard women, we whose eye has been exercised by the *papiers collés* of Braque and Picasso, Matisse's *La Danse*, Mirós of the 1920s, Malevich and Mondrian, Pollock and Newman, or even—since we're talking here about female flesh—by Warhol's *Marilyns* and Wesselmann's *Great American Nudes*. A whole, by now canonical, conception of modernism in painting rests on the reversal of judgment that turned the absence of depicted flesh into an assertion of the *flatness* of the picture, and this into a positive value. The cardboard women were converted into *Demoiselles d'Avignon*; the absence of flesh into literalness of the support; the lack of transparency of the picture plane into exalted opaqueness; the poverty of rendering into emancipation of the *facture*; the loss of represented reality into a gain in autonomy for the picture; the failure of figuration into abstraction; and the disbelieving refusal of the suspension of disbelief into critical consciousness. But this conception has now become a prisoner of the logic of its reversals. In the positiveness of its appreciations it is too easy to read the negativity of the initial judgements it has reversed, and with it the revenge of the likes of Paul Mantz, returned to haunt the "postmodern" scene under the guise of revisionist art historians. Manet deserves better than a reading which gives credit to what the critics of his day decried. Breaking pacts has no value *per se*. Only the new pact has any value.

Touch

New York, 1962. The day when barmaids, top hatted men, and yellow gloved *Parisiennes* started to leave paintings was already quite remote. It had been decades since cabaret decors, painted mirrors, bottles of Bass, fruit bowls, and flower vases were no longer even pretexts for painting, and decades since the human figure had beaten a retreat from painting just as the gods had beaten a retreat from the disenchanted world ushered in by the Prometheuses of modern times. In 1962, the most advanced painting was abstract, and had been so for almost fifty years. It might be thought that the new pact had consciously become the common rule, but nothing could be less sure. What *is* sure, on the other hand, is that the *tradition of the new* had taken over from the old, and that it was in full swing, as if by chance, in the new World, less cluttered by history than old Europe. The American Babylon had stolen the avant-garde torch from Paris, even if Paris hadn't yet quite realized as much. The influence of one man dominated the New York art scene, and that man was not an artist but a critic. He declared: "By now it has been established, it would seem, that the irreducible essence of pictorial art consists in but two constitutive conventions or norms: flatness and the delimitation of flatness; and that the observance of merely these two norms is enough to create an object which can be experienced as a picture: thus a stretched or tacked up canvas already exists as a picture—though not necessarily as a successful one." Thus spoke Clement Greenberg. He had discovered Pollock in the 1940s, backed Rothko, Newman, and Still in the 1950s, and was then currently paying close attention to Louis, Noland, and Olitski. What all these painters had in common was that they were abstract, that they had abandoned composition for the all-over surface of the picture, and that they had emancipated color. They were painting in the euphoria of the *Color-field* and their art was buttressed by the considerable theoretical clout that Greenberg's support lent it. It should be said that, in 1962, any self-respecting young New York artist was touring the galleries with *Art and Culture* in his pocket (the book Greenberg published in 1961), ears ringing with an article that had appeared that same year, and which is still making waves today, titled "Modernist Painting." In it, Greenberg put forward a forcefully synthetic vision of the history of abstract painting—or rather, as he called it, modernist painting—which in his view started with Manet. Abstraction is not its essential feature; above all, it is not a criterion of quality; at most a secondary, contingent effect, probably not definitive but quite constraining all the same, of the ever-growing tendency, since Manet, to assert the flatness of the picture. Flatness itself is a somewhat flat term, still reeking of those "cardboard women" who greeted Manet in his day. All of modern painting has not surrendered to this tendency, as Greenberg was well aware. Only the best painting surrendered to it—the best according to his eye, of course—and it is this painting which he called modernist. Surrendering is the right word, for Greenberg was altogether indifferent to the various manifestos and declarations of intent that abounded in the 20th century, and explained that the tendency toward flatness was never an intentional program, but rather something akin to a capitulation by the best painters to the basic physical feature of their medium: it is a plane. All that is available to painters is the two dimensions of their canvas, unlike sculptors, whose medium is three-dimensional. Why have the best among them been gradually prompted to confine themselves to them, or rather—for all painters are by definition confined to two-dimensionality—prompted to show their medium a regard verging on moral respect? Greenberg doesn't put forward the slightest ethical argument. He defines modernism as "a kind of bias or tropism toward aesthetic value." Just as sunflowers turn toward the sun, so modernist painters turned to flatness as if it were *per se* an aesthetic quality. Greenberg obviously knew very well that it wasn't any such thing. If it were, a monochrome would have to be the most beautiful picture in the world, Mondrian as good, no more, no less, as his epigones Fritz Glarner and Jean Gorin, Gauguin always better than Van Gogh, and Piero della Francesca automatically a greater painter than Raphael. Greenberg meant that throughout the history of modernist painting, those painters who revealed themselves, in hindsight, as the best of their generation were those whose taste veered toward an increasing flatness, following the example of the best painters of the previous generation, and that the pressure thus applied would steer the next generation in the same direction. After a hundred years of this history, Greenberg reckoned he was in a position to ascertain as much.

We won't concern ourselves here with the reasons Greenberg put forward to explain why tendency toward flatness and tropism toward aesthetic value *had* to go hand-in-hand. The main thing is that the inexorable logic he saw at work in the best painting since Manet forces the beholder to talk about it, in retrospect, in terms of a string of relinquishments of a whole number of conventions which might be thought vital to the art of painting, but which turn out actually not to belong to it and, thus, prove "expendable." Once Manet had renounced the use of modeling and chiaroscuro for hewing out the picture, these processes showed themselves as imitating the tactile sensations of sculpture, which the Impressionists further abandoned, without robbing their art of anything essential, either. Monet, Renoir, Seurat, and Van Gogh managed to do without value contrasts, Cézanne and Gauguin without linear perspective, Matisse without the dash of illusion of depth that remained, and painting was none the poorer. Rather, it became all the "purer." Cubism would speed up the process of abandonment, when Euclidean space was broken into smithereens and the collage technique returned illusionism to the picture's actual surface. Figuration vanished with the earliest abstracts, centred composition with the all-over treatment of the canvas, and figure-ground contrast with the monochrome. The result was that, in 1962, if we are to believe Greenberg, color itself could fade away: "…thus a stretched or tacked up canvas already exists as a picture—though not necessarily as a successful one." You have to pinch yourself to make sure you're not dreaming. Here we have one of the century's best art critics seriously saying, and in a tone a long way from parody, that he is prepared to admit that an untouched canvas—a readymade bought in an art supplies shop!—can be perceived as a finished, albeit mediocre, picture. "Modernist Painting" has been the object of so many rigged trials, prompted however by very good reasons, that it possibly deserves being protected from itself. For Greenberg, there was definitely an historical determinism at work in the history of modernist painting, but what kind of determinism is it that *orients* painting toward purism, not through programs and projects but through *a kind of bias or tropism*? There is likewise a logical determinism in the claim that an art keeps itself pure from any confusion with a neighboring art by emphasizing the physical nature of its support; but it is not logic (perhaps it is the art of warfare) that explains why an art asserts its identity through *willing acceptance* of the limitations of its medium, or why modernist painting preserves its integrity through *surrender to the resistance* of the picture plane. Such expressions, taken from "Modernist Painting" and elsewhere, suggest a duel between the artist and his medium, a struggle as much in the nature of love as of war, and which results in a capitulation, an abandonment, or an acquiescence. Be it in the chord of war or love, the artist finds himself in the position of the conquered and not the conqueror; the least one can say is that these are not the connotations most commonly attached to the word avant-garde. *Surrender* is the keyword in Greenberg's entire aesthetics and, more importantly still, it is the word that enables us to see the ethical question of the relationship to the other emerging from painting's famous reduction to the flatness of its medium.

So in 1962 Greenberg surrendered to the blank canvas. In theory. In practice, he resisted it with all his might. He who had admitted in "Modernist Painting" that the "limiting conditions" of painting "can be pushed back indefinitely before a picture stops being a picture and turns into an arbitrary object," now bumps into an object he sees as respecting the two conventions which, in his view, define "the irreducible essence of pictorial art," but which is barely more than a *thing*. A flat and bounded surface totally without *flesh*. One of the most significant art movements of the 1960s, Minimal Art, emerged almost directly from this contradiction between practice and theory. A whole generation of artists, painters at the outset, and influenced by "Modernist Painting" to the point of reading it literally, had to take the opposite tack to come into their own. They abandoned painting and espoused an art of objects using machined materials and supposedly finding appreciation without the judgment of taste having to surrender to the quality of the works. As Donald Judd put it: "A work needs only to be interesting." This discharge of aesthetics in turn gave rise to Conceptual Art. From that moment on, and for more than twenty years, the most up-to-date artists and critics took issue with Greenberg in an attempt to take the monopoly of the real avant-garde away from him, without realizing what they owed him, despite themselves—and himself. For his part, Greenberg took a hard line on the residual illusionism that he had experienced in the "atmospheric" quasi-mono-chromes of Louis and Olitski, to grapple with the excess of literalness—we should say: of *thingness*—of Minimal Art. He had already observed in "Modernist Painting": "The flatness toward which modernist painting orients itself can never be an utter flatness. The heightened sensitivity of the picture plane may not permit sculptural illusion, or *trompe-l'oeil*, but it does and must permit optical illusion." For the rest of his life, *opticality* became his fetish-word, leading him to deny any entitlement to tactility in the best of contemporary painting. An interesting repression. If Greenberg had said that it was impossible for him to be *touched* by a painting which the painter's brush had never *touched*, instead of surrendering in theory to the virgin—untouched, intact—canvas and resisting it in practice, history would possibly have taken another course.

Past history can't be changed but it is constantly being rewritten, and there's nothing to stop us speculating if not about the artistic posterity then at least about the critical reception a work such as, for example, Dan Flavin's *Icon V (Coran's Broadway Flesh)*, might have enjoyed if Greenberg's surrender had been interpreted, by him or by others, in terms of the seesaw movement between "touching" and "being touched." The word flesh appears in the title of this pivotal 1962 work, and the problem of incarnation is part of its subject-matter. It was one of the very last paintings produced by Flavin before he switched to the neon tubes that made him famous, and also a harbinger of the neon works, since it consists of a square masonite panel evenly painted a *flesh* color and framed by a frieze of lit light bulbs. Past history doesn't get changed, but it gets reassessed when it is rewritten. Flavin, LeWitt, Morris, and Judd (the main representatives of Minimal Art) certainly deserve their propulsion to centerstage in the 1960s, and their having remained there. Louis, Noland, and Olitski will remain, too, but these days their slot in art history is far from being as secure as Greenberg had hoped. The minimalism *of the object* triumphed over late modernism *in painting*. But who, today, would still dare make the claim—common currency until the late 1980s—that painting was rendered obsolete once and for all by Minimal and Conceptual Art? In the 1960s, in New York, there were abstract painters who, without further ado, took up a stance elsewhere than in the thick of the crossfire between Greenbergian modernists and minimalists. Not one of them, not even Frank Stella, has had the good fortune to find favor with Greenberg, not to mention Brice Marden and Robert Ryman, who have never even been entitled to a line on his part. Ryman, however—considering the quality of the work he managed to build up over the years, and which he still pursues with the same rigor—proves to be one of the best living painters worldwide, and one of the most authentically modernist.

There are critical misapprehensions that are not easily undone. Ryman came to notice in the latter half of the 1960s in the context of minimalism and process art, which doesn't make sense. For those championing these movements, painting was only tolerated provided it was an exclusively reflexive, or self-referential, practice, and it was for this very reason that Ryman found favor with them. Painting could

Dan Flavin
Icon V (Coran's Broadway Flesh),
1962

escape anathema provided that pictures showed reflection on the medium's basic components—format, surface, pigment, brush stroke, mode of presentation, and the like—and could be construed as a kind of commentary on painting made in painting, whose meaning is more conceptual than pictorial. Ryman's work lends itself easily to this kind of reading, even if it gets betrayed and drained of its human content and its ethical dimension in the process. The work's subject-matter seems to consist in the countless variations the physical features of the medium assume when read against the backdrop of one deliberate invariant: Ryman only paints in white. It is as if he had inherited the responsibility for taking care of painting at the very moment when Greenberg ascertained that the starting point for every painter—the blank canvas—had become his point of arrival; as if he had taken upon himself the state of extreme dereliction to which the long succession of surrenders consented to by the history of modernist painting had abandoned the medium; as if he were camping this side of the monochrome, in the "zero degree" of painting drained of color, something like Manzoni's *Achromes.* In one sense, nothing could be further from the truth. For Ryman, white is a color, just like red and green. In another sense, nothing could be apter. Ryman has been called the last of the modernist painters, which should be understood with Baudelaire's famous remark to Manet ringing in the ear: "You are but the first in the decrepitude of your art." This was an ambiguous compliment from Baudelaire's pen, but it was a compliment, and it still should be if we applied it to Ryman, after replacing "first" by "last." Manet was blessed with not having understood why he was not understood. Ryman is blessed with not having understood that modernist painting, in Greenberg's sense, should logically be over. When an untouched canvas is a finished picture, the sublime spills over into the ridiculous. Has modernism been just a reprieve for an out of date, comatose art? Since Manet, has painting been a patient "in intensive care," the announcement of whose clinical death had to wait until the 1960s? There is some good reason to fear as much, but none to decree it without further trial. Ryman as guardian of modernism's grave, tactfully mourning for painting in painting, is a portrait that has its own lucidity, from whose fascination however we should tear ourselves free in order to see that in the tact with which Ryman paints, there are, without the slightest theological connotation, myriad minute incarnations and minute resurrections at work *on the scale of touch*. Ryman's state of grace is an object lesson. At the two ends of the history of modernist painting, Manet and he are both painters practising incarnation in the second person. Ryman's sustained practice over now more than forty years shows that incarnation in the second person is the stuff of the new pact introduced by Manet, and that the pact is effective, even though it still needs interpreting.

Against or despite Greenberg, first. The main parameters that Ryman varies have to do with the Greenbergian repressed, tactility. Variable tactility of the support: linen or cotton canvas, fibre glass or wax paper, grain of the wall or watercolor paper, polished coldness of mylar or metal. Amorous tactility of the stroke: spreading out the pigment or piling it up, sensing the smoothness of the oil or the stickiness of the enamel, painting from top to bottom, left to right, diagonally, rotating, in one or more coats. Tactility visible on the surface or layered in depth; adherent tactility of the works executed directly on the wall or, conversely, detached tactility of the works set some way from the wall on small metal braces; tactility of the edge in the unframed/reframed works, and so on. Tact, in the literal sense, is one of Ryman's ongoing concerns, which forty years of extraordinarily consistent practice have lent a range of mood all the more dazzling that the field of painting, according to Ryman,

Robert Ryman
Untitled, 1961
(COLOR PLATE P. 201)

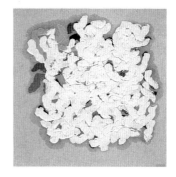

Robert Ryman
12″square, 1965

is restricted. But in order to be touched by this tactile quality, there is nothing like the early works, most of which remained in the artist's collection, for they share the fact of being small format and highlighting the work of touch and coating. Many of these works are made on a piece of coarse-grained, unstretched, linen canvas, subsequently mounted on a framed background. Several—but by no means all—seem to have been hastily cut out, with no respect for the weft of the canvas. Their outline retains signs of the tension caused by their being pinned to the wall, table, or easel acting as their workbench. You get the impression that the painter has haphazardly grabbed offcuts of fabric lying about the studio to test the flexibility and strength of his brush on them, check the smoothness or liquidness of the pigment, and try out his stroke to make sure he's in control of it before seriously getting down to work on a more ambitious canvas, and that some scruple had him hang on to these test bits rather than chuck them out once the real work is complete. This impression is immediately belied by the individualized care with which every scrap of canvas has been chosen, stretched or otherwise, snipped or torn, cut clean or jagged; the care with which the pigment marks on the canvas do or don't impregnate the fabric, stand out on the background, do or don't veil the underlying colours; the care with which the "image" is centered or off-centered, laid down flat or thickly modeled, densely built-up or hemstitched; the care with which the canvas is possibly signed, in some cases several times over. The two impressions are not consecutive, the second gradually replacing the first as we discover that there is no large picture for which these are the test pieces, but that it is they which are the works. They are actually simultaneous, lasting, and mixed together, even if one tarries for hours gazing upon these poor, pathetic things demanding attention—but so tactfully.

Care on the part of the artist, attention on the part of the viewer—let's be clear about these words. The last thing Ryman offers is *peinture soignée*—carefully crafted painting. He takes care of painting, but that's quite different. He takes care of it, the

Robert Ryman
Untitled painting #10, 1963

Robert Ryman
Untitled, ca. 1964

way you'd talk about taking care of somebody sick, or your elderly parents, or your-self. And rather than saying that his paintings demand attention, it might be more to the point to say that they demand attentiveness. Without an attentive look, the care Ryman gives painting would go unnoticed. Taking care of painting means first and foremost addressing it. And giving it an attentive look means lending it the proper-ty of incarnating an Other addressed by the painter. These things can't be explained, they are felt. If they really had to be explained, it would have to be negatively, by say-ing, for example, that a painter who makes carefully crafted painting has his sights set on the taste of the audience he's addressing and hopes to touch through his paint-ing; further, that the attention he claims is the acknowledgement of his talent or, fail-ing that, the effort he's made to please his audience. A painter, on the other hand, who takes care of painting never thinks about the public's taste while he's painting, and knows that he shouldn't expect acknowledgement from his viewers. He hands the finished picture over to them. The precarious unfinishedness of these small Ryman canvases makes this act a poignant abandonment. It is easy but simplistic to read them as a reflexive commentary on the touch made by means of the touch. For this reading, the at once offhand and systematic variety of the brush strokes has no raison d'être other than to make the load of pigment on the brush, the pressure or restraint of the stroke, the act of coating the surface, and, above all, the covering of the colors which the white smothers in differing degrees, both explicit and autonomous. It is as if Van Gogh had taken the expressive power of his colorful commas as subject-matter, detached from what the picture represents and expresses, and, to make it quite clear to us that he was no longer an Expressionist, had resolved to censure himself before our very eyes by covering up the *Sunflowers* with white paint. This image is a caricature, but only barely, to such an extent did the phobic desire to stay aloof from the Abstract Expressionism of the previous generation hold sway over the minimalist discourse on painting in the 1960s and 1970s. Anyone who has given the small canvases of the young Ryman enough regard and attention will see what interpretation has lost by yielding to the modernist dictate of self-reference. Saying that Ryman makes paintings about painting, or, as here, that he works the touch to get it speaking about the touch, is tantamount to saying nothing. We must put tautology to one side.

Care and attention are names of love, and love—including the love of painting—is something addressed and something physical. Anyone who has had sex with and without love knows, from experience, that it's love that makes body contact touching and that it's sex that addresses love to the body. Anyone who has known passionate love knows in his or her flesh that all declarations of love host a demand for love. Happy is the passion if the demand is reciprocal; awful if there is no demand from the other party. And anyone who has thought a little bit about these things knows that a demand is always addressed, and even more, that there is no address that is not beseeching. Here, and nowhere else, lies the enigma of the pictorial touch, an enig-ma whose name is reversal and transfer of the address. Let's imagine Ryman at work, *in process*, not quite as far from Van Gogh as the end result would have us believe. Each touch of his brush is a caress addressed to the canvas, as if the canvas were a liv-

Robert Ryman
Two Paintings (A), ca. 1964

ing body capable of an erotic response. The painter feels the canvas quivering with life, and if he feels that it is dead, he remedies things with the next touch, just as lovers adjust their caresses to their partner's desires. Here he is putting a first brush stroke on the surface, then a second and a third, breaking off now and then to step back and let the canvas address him. In other words, to make an aesthetic judgment, and check whether he has been touched. Then he resumes his work, engrossed in his intercourse with the canvas, and always listening to its answer. Clearly, the canvas doesn't answer. It is Ryman who experiences his own touch as if it were addressed in return by the canvas. He is or is not touched by his touch. Likewise for the next touch, and so on and so forth until the picture is finished or, rather, left to its unfinishedness. This is the crucial moment when the painter makes way for the viewer. Now it is up to this viewer to say whether he or she is touched or not. In these early Rymans, it's palpable how the final touch (in *Two Paintings(A)*, 1964, we can almost tell which one it is) brings out the absence of the extra touch—or the one touch too many—that the painter has not allowed himself, and that it's this absence that makes room for the viewer. The final touch addresses the picture to him or her. None of the previous touches are addressed to the viewer. They're addressed to the picture, or rather, to the medium, for in its individuality the picture is an occurrence of "painting" in general. If this weren't so, we couldn't say that Ryman cares about painting, but only about his picture. But then he'd be making *peinture soignée*. The painter who makes carefully crafted painting doesn't work like Ryman. Technically speaking, he also addresses each one of his brush strokes to the canvas. He, too, is all ears for the canvas' answer, an answer that proceeds by way of being or not being touched by his own touch. But he indulges in the narcissism of this process. Because the canvas doesn't incarnate the *other* he addresses, it risks being the mirror in which he tries to recognize his talent. The painter who makes carefully crafted painting addresses his slightest brush stroke to his audience, be it real or imaginary. As a result, he isn't touched by his touch, but by the effect he imagines his touch will have on the audience. For him, putting the final touch to his picture is to declare his satisfaction with the anticipated overall effect. We can see that *peinture soignée* is a shorthand definition of academic painting, and that it doesn't necessarily spare abstract painting, or monochrome painting. We can also see in what sense Ryman is a modernist painter—the last one? certainly not—just as Manet was the first one. In the sense that modernism is painting *in the second person*. The pact that shifted a Titian Venus from "she" to "I," based on rendering of flesh and suspension of disbelief, has been broken. Because it has been broken, because the painters' guild and the viewers' society no longer share this common mediation, it is no longer possible to see in the painter's *métier* a means of communication between artists and public. Rather than addressing their public through their medium, modernist painters at work address themselves to the medium and address their finished picture to the viewer. We can see, last of all, in what sense Suzon's blush is the final touch given to the *Bar at the Folies-Bergère*. Like the final touch of white in the Rymans, the touch of red to Suzon's cheeks brings out the absence of the extra touch—or the touch too many—that the painter hasn't allowed himself: the touch incorporating within the picture the man in the top hat, alias the viewer, for whom Manet got a man named … Gaston La Touche, a painter by trade, to pose.

Either coincidences such as this are too good to be true, or else they are not coincidences. What chance is there that the *personification* of the final touch by a painter-viewer called La Touche, *incarnated* in Suzon's complexion without being *incorporated* in the picture (he's in it, but only as a reflection, a virtual, bodyless image), is anything but sheer coincidence? What do we know that might tip the scales in favor of a conscious choice? Manet was keen to have a real *Folies-Bergère* barmaid play her own part. In the sketch for the Courtauld picture, Suzon was preceded by another young woman, whose name has not gone down in history, but whom we know to have been a real barmaid at the *Folies-Bergère* as well. In this sketch, just as in the *ébauche* beneath the final painting, revealed by the x-ray, the role of the man in the top hat was played by Henri Dupray, painter of military subjects, who had his studio not far from Manet's on rue d'Amsterdam. He would be replaced by La Touche at a later stage in the execution of the work. The choice of a painter for the man in the top hat thus seems just as intentional as the choice of a real barmaid playing her own part. Was the name of La Touche a factor in Manet's decision to have him replace Dupray? We shall never know, except that Manet was a witty man, and that he was well-aware of the flattering wordplay on his own name—*Manet et manebit* (He remains and he will remain)—with which Poulet-Malassis had paid him tribute and which Bracquemond had etched on an *ex-libris*. It is pretty unlikely that he would not have noticed the uncanny name of his colleague, and been amused by it. *A Bar at the Folies-Bergère* is still far from having said everything it had to say about modernism as painting in the second person. For the time being, the fact that the first and the "last" of the modernist painters join forces over the issue of the final touch, as an address to the beholder, highlights above all what separates them. Manet is figurative and Ryman is abstract.

It might well be that the essential difference between abstraction and figuration—the touchstone of their difference, to put it as literally as possible—is not either the absence or presence of a figure in the picture, but rather the absence or presence of a model in the studio. Abstract painters are alone with their canvas. Their risk of drowning in the narcissistic mirror set on their easel is greater than it ever was in the past, for they are, physically speaking, facing no other interlocutor but their canvas. Painting to indulge yourself is an even more frequent form of academicism in abstract painting than painting to please the public. This is why it is vital that otherness bursts into the studio and that the canvas imposes itself on the abstract painter like the other in the second person, the other to whom to address eye and brush, the other incarnated in this particular other, here—the canvas—in the same way that humanity is incarnated in a particular human individual. For a figurative painter, who paints from nature, the act of painting constitutes a triangle: the painter, the model, and the canvas. The beholders will in due course position themselves at the tip occupied by the painter. The moment of the final touch is the moment when the painter is the first beholder of his finished picture, then steps back and makes way for the public. The picture will be positioned at the tip of the triangle occupied by the model. The beholder looks at the picture the way the painter looked at his model. And the tip occupied by the picture, for the painter, is, for the beholder, the place of the enigma embodied by the touched surface that touches him or her. The rotation of the triangular relationship between painter, model, and picture is the process in which the enigma of touch reveals itself in its nature as transference. Transference in the sense of transposition—the image of the model transferred onto the canvas—but also and above all, transference in the psychoanalytical sense of love shifted from one "object" to another. We modernists tend to think as if all painting were abstract painting, or at least as if painters had always worked as we imagine the abstract painter works. We should do the opposite: think as if the model hadn't ever vanished from the studio. We would then perceive the triangulation and the transference hidden in the face-to-face within even the most abstract of paintings. Let's return for a moment to Olympia's gaze. Who knows who is addressing what or whom in this disconcerting look! What does it mean to paint a gaze, to begin with? Eyes, yes, but a gaze? What does it mean to cast your gaze on someone else's in order to put it down on a canvas? What part of the outcome should be attributed to the painter's gaze, what part to the model's, and what part to our own? Although this is not an answer, we can say that even though a painted gaze is experienced as face-to-face, it is invariably triangulated. Painter-model-canvas at the start, viewer-canvas-X at the finish. The X is always an unknown quantity. It is very rare for you to have the sensation of the third tip of the triangle when you stand looking at a picture which confronts you with a direct gaze. This almost never happens in a portrait, because the law of the genre is to fold the "canvas" tip of the triangle over onto the "model" tip—except with Goya and Manet, and who examined Goya better than Manet? In the small Boston portrait, Victorine seems either not to see us as she looks at us, or to be looking elsewhere when she sees us, who knows? This is even more palpable in *Mlle V. in the Costume of an Espada*, where the two halves of the face look at us neither in the same place nor from the same place, as if divided by a slight wall-eyedness. This gaze is undecided; it goes looking for a point beyond our eyes, behind us, it seems, in our future. In *The Street Singer*, and more particularly in *Woman with a Parrot*, it is the opposite: Victorine seems to be engrossed in the contemplation of an invisible point situated between the picture and us. Victorine's gaze—and Olympia's more strongly and clearly than any other—is laden both with the memory of Manet's eye cast upon her, and with a request for a return gaze cast ahead of itself. This is the picture's address to posterity. The best abstract painting, from Mondrian to Ryman, is the acknowledgement of receipt of this address. Greenberg was right about the following, at least: the frontality of the best abstract paintings, their flatness, was not an "absolute flatness." He just got it wrong when he thought he could contrast the opticality of the painting which he deemed to be the best with the tactility of the painting which he deemed to be bad because it flirted too closely with the thing that is the medium. He would have been better off recognizing the triangulation at work in the best abstract painting, because it is there. Even the flattest and most literal of monochromes, if it touches us, opens up within it a space which triangulates it and makes way for the other, giving it the thickness, depth, and *flesh* of a face. Facingness is the word Greenberg should have chosen to say flatness, for it is the other name of painting in the second person. Its essential feature is not abstraction—let us repeat—at a time when the great struggle of the century, pitting abstraction against figuration, seems to have wound down, for lack of combatants. It hasn't really stopped, though. It is the terms that have changed. It should be renamed: the struggle between art in the second and third persons.

Struggle

Here's an amazing photo, trace and witness of the tremendous if brief struggle waged, at a precise moment, between painting in the second and third person in the practice of that 20th-century superstar, Picasso. The photo gives form to the triangle: on the left, the model; on the right, the picture; and straight ahead, where we are, the painter-photographer. The model is neither Fernande nor Eva, Picasso's lovers in the Cubist years, but Marie Laurencin—a painter colleague, a female Gaston La Touche. The canvas is unfinished, and in a very odd way. The upper part is virtually completed and the lower part virtually untouched, giving the—false—impression that Picasso used to fill in his canvases from top to bottom, without pentimento, according to a preconceived plan. Actually, the whole lower part of the canvas has been added, sewn to the upper part to solve a visual problem which couldn't have been remedied by retouches to the existing format. It's quite likely that Picasso never thought the graft to be a success, because the picture remained in his hands all his life, clearly unfinished. It is currently in the Picasso Museum in Paris. At a given moment, it went by the title *Man with Mandolin*, a sex change that obviously can't be checked in the painting and that casts doubt over the photo, or exacerbates it, since the photo is a joke. There is nothing to show that Marie Laurencin, or anybody else for that matter, ever posed for the upper part of the picture. Picasso often did with-

Pablo Picasso
Photo of Marie Laurencin in
Picasso's studio, 1911 or 1912

Pablo Picasso
L'Homme à la mandoline, 1911–1912

out models and didn't draw his inspiration from his face-to-face with the other; he identified with the other. Perhaps the only constant factor throughout his work was his empathy for the subjects of his pictures, a devouring, cannibalistic empathy, which appropriated the model in the very fervor with which the artist merged with it. Picasso was possessed by his subjects, and painted in order to possess them. This applies to the women in his life, as well as to the *saltimbanques* of the blue and pink periods, gazing lovingly and jealously at their women; it even applies to objects. There is no fruit bowl, guitar, pipe, or newspaper that isn't a sign in which he managed to project himself, inasmuch as he incorporated them as part and parcel of his daily world. With Picasso, humanity always, to some extent, takes on the figure of the *thing* or monstrous *beast* that he suspected everyone, men and women alike, of harboring within them, because it was natural for him to identify with it. So any living being who might act as a model for him was, in advance, promised the status of a still-life and then re-awakened by his formidable vitality. Without this deeply human and deeply monstrous character trait, Picasso may well not have been what he was—the only artist of the century to have given (at this level of quality) a definition of modernism in painting which was diametrically opposed to the one proffered by Manet; the only person to have clung on to painting in the third person, while having systematically destroyed its traditional bases.

Painting in the third person is classical representation. As we have seen, it was based on a complex fabric of conventions, the two main ones being, on the one hand, illusionism—perspective, chiaroscuro, rendering, and the whole technical mastery inducing credibility in the reality of images—and, on the other, the famous suspension of disbelief, where people know that images are not "for real" yet treat them as if they were. The latter convention is crucial to the success of the former. When you are taken in by an illusion, you are dealing with *trompe-l'oeil*, not with representation. Is it sheer coincidence that it was *trompe-l'oeil* that reconciled Picasso with flatness? And that he himself hadn't had the idea? It is well known that he got it from Braque (the *trompe-l'oeil* nails in *Nature morte au pichet* of 1910, the three letters "BAL" stenciled on *Le Portugais* of 1911, the scrap of mock-wood wallpaper bought in Avignon in August 1912 and incorporated into the first *papier collé* in history, *Compotier et verre*, produced that September—all of them were innovations due to Braque). The piece of oilcloth glued on by Picasso in *Nature morte à la chaise cannée*, dated May 1912, undoubtedly predates Braque's first *papier collé*, but at that moment Picasso hadn't completely grasped its *trompe-l'oeil* nature. He used it in an illusionist way, like a witty ready-made makeshift for rendering texture. He would subsequently catch up with things, making infinitely more refined, complex and perverse use than Braque of the resources of *trompe-l'oeil* in his own *papiers collés* done in 1913–1914. The Synthetic Cubism that issued from them would mark his reconciliation with flatness, not because, thanks to them, he had given in to its ethical meaning of facingness, but because, by using *trompe-l'oeil* as *de-trompe-l'oeil*, and vice versa, he had found the way of putting pressure on the suspension of disbelief, in a way nobody had ever done before him.

Together with Matisse, Picasso was one of the only two great—truly great—20th-century painters never to have been tempted by abstraction. We might even go so far as to say that he resisted abstraction with all his might, and that he never stopped trying to prove that painting in the third person was still viable, despite the broken pact that had grounded it in illusionism and suspension of disbelief. When Picasso had his "*art nègre*" revelation in 1907, he discovered that it was possible for a major art to put the suspension of disbelief to the test, well beyond everything that a civilization which had always linked it with illusionism had ever imagined. Children, caricaturists and gestalt psychologists all know only too well that you can push the features of a face or a silhouette to extreme stylization, without endangering the reflex that allows us to recognize in them a fellow creature. It doesn't take much at all to trigger the suspension of disbelief—this isn't where the discovery lies. But the fact that a major art—and Picasso instantly saw a major art in African sculpture—could make do with so little is where the revelation lies. There is no doubt that Picasso needed a Westerner's eye, a colonizing and appropriating eye, ignoring the others' culture, in order to allow himself to reduce Africans' belief in magic to mere

Pablo Picasso
Femme aux poires, 1909

suspension of disbelief. But he would also have needed an eye that was *aesthetically* sensitive to the magic power of African art, in order to feel authorized to embark on the violent task of destruction that he was getting ready to undertake. He had just realized that the illusion of the third dimension could be separated from suspension of disbelief. In this sense, there is no "*art nègre*" in the *Demoiselles d'Avignon*. There is an appropriation of "*art nègre*" which simplifies it and then reverses its terms: "*art nègre*," as Picasso perceived it, was the suspension of disbelief without illusionism; his own art would be illusionism without the suspension of disbelief. In a nutshell, such would be the definition of painting in the third person according to Picasso, and also be the substance of the pact on which he tried to ground his painting, a pact as innovative as painting in the second person, but which in no way had the same ethical and aesthetic implications. Not only does the facingness of painting in the second person—which would lead to the flatness of abstract painting—not at all emerge straight from Cubism, and certainly not from the *papiers collés*, but, further, Picasso was essentially fighting it, before his borrowing of *trompe-l'oeil* from Braque reconciled him with the plane. Let's take a look, by way of example, at the way he fought against flatness and frontality in the 1909 portrait of Fernande called *Woman with Pears*: he brought the nape of her neck into the foreground and stuck a reversible cube in the middle of her forehead! We should add to this that Fernande has no gaze: the weird diamond-shaped shutters standing in for her eyeballs are blind. It would be hard to go any further in the invention of visual means which challenge the face-to-face between beholder and picture in favor of a prehensile vision of the world—a world that we handle and speak about in the third person, but that we do not address.

It has often been observed that in the busiest inventive period of Cubism—the so-called hermetic period wedged between the working holidays of the summer of 1911 in Céret and the summer of 1912 in Sorgues—Braque's and Picasso's paintings can barely be told apart. The two men formed a couple about which Picasso would say at a later date, with a certain macho cruelty, that Braque was the woman. It might be comforting, but it would be deceptive, to explain the twinned nature of their painting by the fact that both artists identified with each other. This could be true for Braque, but it certainly wasn't for Picasso. He didn't identify with Braque; he'd found someone to talk to. An interlocutor. Such exchanges, even in a real couple, don't last a lifetime, at least at this degree of intensity. The Braque/Picasso couple would come to an end when Picasso accompanied his drafted friend to the railway station in 1914. After that, he only saw him occasionally, much later, when their friendship had cooled and their careers had gone their separate ways. The fact is that the period when Picasso had someone to whom he could address his painting, and someone who could address his painting to him, coincided with the period when he was absolutely engrossed in the exacerbation of this pictorial world in the third person. He could make endless use of the illusionistic resources of *chiaroscuro*, and titillate every which way the viewer's readiness to suspend disbelief, because (along with his dealer, Kahnweiler) Braque was the sole addressee of the canvases produced in that period. The issue of addressing was temporarily sorted out by Braque's presence, painting alongside him, to whom he didn't merely address the finished painting, but to whom he also addressed himself while painting. He didn't have to worry about transferring his passion to the beholder, so he had no truck with rotating the triangular relationship between painter, model, and canvas.

Yet it is this triangular relationship that is staged by the photo of Marie Laurencin. Picasso lets us witness one of the rare moments in those years when his conviction faltered. Needless to say, the photo is a joke, but the joke is in turns ironic, parodic, pathetic, sinister, and, in the end, moving. For—especially in its hermetic phase, to which the unfinished picture on the easel belongs—Analytical Cubism has definitely been a matter of triangulation, but of triangulation within the space of the picture. This way of thrusting wedges into the frontal surface of the canvas, cutting the bodies into facets, multiplying front-back reversibilities, and using a pointillist shading to create oblique planes generating illusion, what are all these procedures aimed at? Getting the triangle, whose three tips are the picture, the painter, and the model, incorporated in the picture with no way to wiggle out of it, and proliferating at every possible scale. Picasso couldn't stand his picture incarnating the other in the second person. The triangulation of the space *of* the picture was, for him, the antidote to the triangulation of the space *before* the picture. In other words, for Picasso, there was no room for the twofold face-to-face—the painter and the model, the painter and the canvas—triangulated by transference. And thus, no rotation of the triangular relationship allowing the beholder to be placed at the tip occupied by the painter. The beholders can only introduce themselves obliquely into the picture and, once they have entered into it, remain captive there. This is why the photo of Marie Laurencin parodying the model's pose—back straight, clutching a mandolin, knee pulling her skirt tight over her leg, her face blurred—has everything to suggest a pathetic and, finally, very moving joke. It stages the triangle which the pictures don't want to rotate. It is touching that, with this photo, Picasso has given us a chance to step into his shoes in the studio, because this is what he bars us from doing in the canvases of the period. The photo is an avowal. As much as the triangulation work in *Ma jolie*—the most accomplished of the canvases painted, like this one, during the winter of 1911–1912—is harmonious, ventilated, lit from within, and offset by a vertical grid which, in spite of everything, allows us to take up a position in front of the painting without going astray, so, in the finished part of *Man with Mandolin*, the triangulation is *tied up*. At almost each one of the intersections of the diagonals, an arc of a circle makes a knot in it. The eye doesn't wander, as if it had a cramp. The predominant coloring—steel gray—doesn't breathe. There is no vertical/horizontal grid to give the picture a sense of gravity and upright stance. Maybe it was precisely to give it this sense that Picasso had a square of canvas sewn on at the bottom of his picture, even if this meant giving it an unusually elongated format. This is what the unfinished lower part seems to confirm: frontality and upright stance go together, and also go together with address to the person opposite—but do we have to twist the knife in the wound? Probably yes, for this is what stopped Picasso from finishing his painting. Let's take a look at this part. We are not invited to visually work our way into the wedged openings such as offered by *Ma jolie*. The drawing is frontal, parallel to the picture plane. The shades of color are warm, the touch breathes. In the photographed picture we can make out an upside-down Y drawn with charcoal, whose vertical shaft alone can be clearly seen in the "finished" picture, shaded on its right. The inverted Y appears to represent the tripod legs of the tasseled pedestal table that we see in the photo, or rather, something akin to its spine. Picasso knew as well as any maker of pedestal tables that three points of support are better than two or four when it comes to securing an upright posture. What must have preoccupied him here was the link between upright posture, frontality, and address to the other. While there is only one in the photo, the "finished" picture shows no less than eleven more or less decisively sketched images of the casters of this pedestal table, as if Picasso had wanted to represent a rotating horizontal triangle. Isn't it odd that the triangulation of the space in front of the picture—in which the picture plays a part at one of the triangle's tips, the beholder at another, and the X at the third—should have here seen fit to be depicted at the level of the legs and crossbars of a *thing* rather than at the level of the face of a living being? Where Manet incarnated the X in the gaze or in the flesh of the model depicted, Picasso attempted to reify it. And failed. The picture remained unfinished. Did he really have to fail? As much as it is absurd to deduce from the photo that Picasso worked systematically from top to bottom, so it is tempting to imagine him re-working the picture from bottom to top, in the technique of the added part—lighten it, give it back some breathing space, undo the knots, warm up the palette, now that it is solidly resting on a revolving triangular support. But Picasso didn't do this. That would have been to take the path of painting in the second person—the Cadaquès path.

Pablo Picasso
Guitariste, summer 1910

The Cadaqués path? The working holidays at Sorgues in 1912 and Céret in 1911 had been preceded by the less productive sojourn in Cadaqués in 1910—and without Braque. Picasso rented a seaside house and settled in with Fernande in late June. They were soon joined by Derain and his wife, and he stayed there until early September. He produced very little, and what he did produce was, to his eye, unsatisfactory—Kahnweiler would talk of unfinished paintings. But his Cadaqués work stands distinctly apart from that of the previous summer at Horta de Ebro, where the most sculptural phase of Cubism was initiated, as it does from the output of the following summer spent in Céret, where the artist would perk up. In Cadaqués, he seemed to be bored by the middle-class life he was being nudged toward by Fernande, and Derain was no Braque; Kahnweiler was far away: Picasso had nobody to whom to address his painting. Is this why the plane imposed itself on him in a face-to-face relationship altogether rare in his work, and one that was novel as well? He painted more pictures of figures than of still-lifes, and if some of them, like the *Woman with Mandolin* (now in the Ludwig Museum in Cologne), retain signs of his violent struggle against the plane, others, like the admirable *Guitar Player* (in the Pompidou Center), show him giving in. As Greenberg might have said, Picasso admitted defeat at the hands of the physical resistance of the medium, and surrendered. He couldn't do anything but respect the integrity of the picture plane. Yet there is no dearth of triangles driving a wedge into the *Guitar Player*'s flatness. Their tips are shaded and bounded by a line that limits their aggressiveness and moves them behind the picture plane, while their third side is open and worked in gradation in such a way as to get them to join smoothly with the surface. The three main ones, themselves forming a triangle, are rotating in the plane. This interplay of triangles is overlaid by an intermittent grid of verticals and horizontals which reinforce the resulting sensation, associating upright stance, frontality, and address to the beholder. It would seem that in the span of one summer in Cadaqués, Picasso did what the best abstract painters would later do: in the absence of any definite recipient, he addressed "painting" while he was at work, and he addressed the finished picture to an unspecified viewer. Nothing better illustrates the choice thus presented to him between painting in the second or third person, than a comparison between the charcoal work titled *Standing Nude*, produced in Cadaqués, and the ink drawing enhanced by watercolors produced a few months before, titled simply *Nude*, which is also a standing nude figure. This latter alternates shaded wedges and sculptural curves in such a way that the whole is saliently outlined on the surface of the paper, and keeps a firm footing on the ground. This nude has bodily substance. It may be deformed, but it is represented. It is a nude in the third person. Besides, it is seen in profile. The Cadaqués *Standing Nude*, on the other hand, has no bodily substance. It's hard to say if it is seen head-on or in profile, so contorted is it, but facingness wins the day. The few curves it does contain don't conjure up any feminine roundness and they have no relief. It can't be said that the interplay of verticals and horizontals

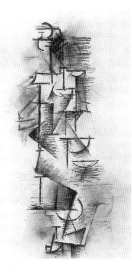

Pablo Picasso

Nu, spring 1910

Pablo Picasso

Nu debout, summer-fall 1910

Piet Mondrian

Tableau nº 1 (Composition avec lignes et couleur),

1913

provide it with a skeleton. The grid doesn't lean the nude on the ground, but affixes it to the surface of the paper. Likewise with the shadows: they weave a shallow space which alternately intertwines the front and the back of the sheet, but doesn't take off. This space no longer bears any resemblance to the prehensile space of the Horta pictures of the year before, or to the Céret paintings of the following year. When the eye is no longer a hand, the body threatens to fade away. Its flesh risks relying on an act of faith on the part of the beholder, like Manet's *Christ Rising From the Dead*. For a non-believer like Picasso, always ready to exacerbate suspension of disbelief provided there was illusion of depth in the picture so as to make a world, albeit a counterfeit one, this was tantamount to a self-betrayal. He would lose control of his art, and trust the viewer's gaze to incarnate it, putting himself into the hands of the public. This was not his calling. The Cadaqués experience left him depressed but sufficiently shaken up to attempt to sort out his dilemma by trying his hand at portraiture—a rare exercise in Cubism. So he finished the portraits of Ambroise Vollard and Wilhelm Uhde, both started in the spring, and executed the Kahnweiler portrait. Three art dealers: the world incarnated by painting and the world addressed by painting overlapped. With various twists and turns, Picasso stayed on the Cadaqués path until the spring of 1911, but that summer in Céret the choice was made: it would be incarnation in the third person. Yet Picasso had never brushed quite so close up against painting in the second person as in the drawing titled *Standing Nude*, from which Mondrian emerged.

Face-to-face

Why did modern art plunge headlong into abstraction? Why through painters and not through sculptors? Why through several painters independently of one another? Why at a precise moment? And why, as soon as it had gone abstract, did painting veer almost simultaneously toward those two extremes, the black and the white monochromes? The mood of the times, reciprocal influences, the desire to be done with tradition, the shock of modernity, the gust of freedom blowing over the avant-gardes since Impressionism, the mystical ubiquity of symbolism, the deafening anxiety welling-up in the world on the eve of the Great War—all this together still fails to explain why the year 1912–1913 abruptly saw the human figure drop out of the picture in the work of Delaunay, Kupka, Kandinsky, Picabia, Mondrian, Malevich, Léger, Herbin, Severini, Balla, Hartley, Dove, O'Keeffe, Larionov, Goncharova, Russell, Macdonald-Wright, Yakulov, Schoenberg (that's right, the composer), the list goes on and on. Nor does it explain why this renunciation—for that's what it was—was so imperative for the 20th century that every abstract work had to repeat it on its own. Birth and death of painting with every canvas. Black and white. We don't get much help from the utopian or apocalyptic prophecies about the "first" and the "last" painting. They tell us about the types of justification adduced by the painters who had taken the leap, but not about the challenge shared by one and all, which remained largely unconscious and, therefore, absolutely unique—for the greatest, anyway. And who among the creators of abstract art was greater than Mondrian?

Pablo Picasso

Les Jumelles, 1910

Piet Mondrian

Nature morte au pot de gingembre II, 1912

It is blatantly visible that Cubism worked its way into Mondrian's work between the two paintings known as *Still Life with Gingerpot I* and *II*, the former painted in autumn 1911, the latter a year later. However, this does little to unravel the enigmatic issue of the exact nature of his borrowing from Cubism and, more to the point, the most unexpected alteration he wrought on it. It was definitely not the handful of 1908 Braques and Picassos seen in the Moderne Kunst Kring in Amsterdam shortly after completing the first—vaguely Cézanne-like—of these still-lifes, that can explain the interplay of verticals and horizontals structuring the second, which seem to have been borrowed from the Picassos done in Cadaqués or a little later, such as *Les Jumelles*. Mondrian must have seen some of these at the time, at Kahnweiler's or Vollard's, and this was the Cubism with which he felt concerned. The discovery of Gleizes, Metzinger, Léger, and Le Fauconnier at the *Salon des Indépendants* of March 1912 certainly didn't come into the picture. As for his visit to the second Cubist exhibition at the Moderne Kunst Kring in October, this took place after he had finished the second still life. The fact that there he saw Picasso's *Le Joueur de mandoline* and *L'Homme à la pipe*, both painted in 1911, may be proven, yet there is little trace of either in Mondrian's subsequent work. The 1913 *Tableau n° 3* borrows the oval format of *Man with Pipe*, but that's about all. Mondrian's palette here was more akin to Braque's than to Picasso's. The painting didn't contain any of those schematic allusions to objects for which the Spanish painter had a soft spot. In particular, space in *Tableau n° 3* was made up of planes compartmentalized by a host of broken, faltering lines, completely alien to the decisiveness that informed the faceted space of *Man with Pipe*, but conversely very close to the linear compartmentalization of his own studies of trees, which was already a distinctive feature of the two bare trees in the

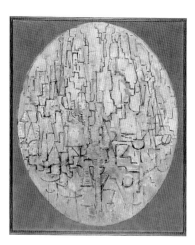

Piet Mondrian
Tableau n° 3 (Composition en ovale),
1913

Piet Mondrian
Le Grand Nu, 1912

foreground of his 1898 *Village Church*. Mondrian came to abstraction by way of land-scape—of all the traditional genres of painting, in 1911–1912, the least-practiced by the Cubists. But how did he come to it? The more we try to retrace, picture by picture, the route he followed, in the period from 1911 to 1915, the less we unearth any logical or linear development to the shift. Nothing could be more deceptive than the comforting image of a Mondrian "abstracting" from reality by means of progressive stylization, based on tree motifs, followed a little later by façades, then, later still, pier and ocean. Why, firstly, these three particular motifs? Why invent abstraction three times over, as it were? It's quite fascinating to see Mondrian tease out an enigma that is so closely bound up with the *flesh* of painting—he who rarely painted nudes, had no models in his studio, and broached abstraction by way of landscape. Isn't this enigma the X brought about by the painter-model-canvas triangle, when it gets replaced by the canvas-beholder face-to-face? The selfsame X—at the juncture of upright stance, frontality, and address to the other—which titillated Picasso in *Man with Mandolin*? Isn't the tree the most deeply-rooted manifestation of upright posture? And isn't the façade—above all the "flayed" façades of the rue du Départ which Mondrian drew in 1914, and from which he derived several abstract compositions—the supreme architectural metaphor of the face, the *visage*? And didn't Mondrian's strange passage, via the motif of the pier plunging into the sea, have to do with the depth and distance implicit in the relationship to others, via the gaze? Let's track these three intertwined motifs, from whose braid emerged the most singular formula for painting incarnate in the second person.

The 1912 *Great Nude* isn't Mondrian at his best. It is an anomaly in his painting itinerary, and a picture with no direct posterity; yet it is the work whereby Mondrian explored the "Cadaquès path" even more clearly than in the contemporary *Still Life with Gingerpot II*. The picture is clumsy, naïve, and coy compared with Picasso's *Guitar Player*, and asexual when compared with any Picasso you care to mention, but it does have something that no Picasso of those years had, except the Uhde portrait: a gaze. A one-eyed gaze—not sure exactly where it's looking, but a gaze nonetheless; a line that starts out from the picture and heads toward the other, opposite. It is this line, perpendicular to the picture, which would materialize in the piers penetrating into the sea in the various versions of *Pier and Ocean* painted in 1914–1915. These paintings are all enclosed in an oval space which in no way hails from Braque and Picasso, but rather conveys a perceptive experience already glaringly evident in the seascapes and the *Dunes* of 1909–1910: the curvature of the sea's horizon and the feeling that the sea is welling up. The ocean may well be a slack surface running away to the horizon, but it also advances toward the observer, tide-like, and makes space convex. Looking at the sea, Mondrian experienced what Cézanne had experienced facing the Montagne Sainte-Victoire. When Mondrian discovered Cézanne, he was on familiar ground, because Cézanne is the missing link between Manet and Picasso, and *the* painter in whom painting in the second person and painting in the third person vied with each other throughout his life. Like a mandorla, a similar but vertical oval surrounds the façades of the church at Domburg drawn and painted by Mondrian in 1914, and in some of the rue du Départ façades, painted that same year. In these works, the Cézannian motif of spatial curvature and the more traditionally figurative motif of the facial oval—like the 1912 *Great Nude*, now expanded to the format of the picture—were conflated. It was also an oval—at times vertical, at others horizontal—that surrounded several of the compositions coming from the tree motif, produced between 1911 and 1913. The last of these, *Tableau n° 3*, visibly borrowed its oval from Braque and Picasso, but others cast the oval in a more dynamic role, by the way it asserts the frontality of the picture: the tree's branches sweep the surface like a windshield-wiper, while the trunk is implanted squarely in the ground. Lastly, in the tree motif, this way of joining frontality with upright stance contends with a reticulate, grid-like space which, far from making the tree stand out against the background of sky, pulls sky "cells" back into the picture plane, like in a piece of *cloisonné* enamel. So, over a four-year period and by way of three landscape themes with little to connect them to each other, something was being sought which would articulate deep distance (the sea) and its reversal (spatial curvature) around the see-saw movement of a gaze which is alternately penetrating, like the pier, and salient, like that of the *Great Nude*; something that confronts the facingness of the façades and pushes the outside of the "face" they form into peripheral vision; something that strives to contradict local figure-ground relationships, to culminate in compositions which take up the *cloisonné* quality of the trees with no further figurative allusions. The years 1915–1916 mark a period of latency. Then everything precipitates. The pier that materialized the perpendicular, penetrating gaze—already virtually imperceptible in *Composition 10 in Black and White* of 1915—vanishes altogether in the

Composition with Lines of 1916–1917, which is the abstract culmination of the *Pier and Ocean* paintings. In the works done in 1917–1918, the *cloisonné*, compartmentalized space of the compositions in brown and gray, blue, gray, and pink, and gray, and yellow of 1913–1914 bursts out in colored planes, on the one hand, and lined grids, on the other, after having been rendered masterfully dialectical, one last time, in *Composition 1916*. The six *Compositions with Color Planes* painted in 1917–1918 give each of the color planes an independence never seen before. Let's pause briefly on the most beautiful of these works, the one from the Boymans-van Beuningen Museum in Rotterdam. Rarely has any painter gone further in his rejection of composition, and rarely has a painter been more precise in the way he has committed his rejection to the canvas. The distribution of the planes is centrifugal, and yet strictly static; it seems random and yet it is never caught off balance; it is wilfully asserted as illogical, and yet comes across as natural and obvious. The longer we contemplate the canvas, the more we detect compositional slips, moments of incoherence, and things that elude explanation; and the more we end up by concluding that it is precisely these oddities which make this picture a pure masterpiece. Rather than balance the areas of color, Mondrian stacked three yellows in a column slightly left-of-center, at the risk of cutting the picture in two. The picture retains its unity. The three rectangles on the righthand side are cut by the frame, the lowest one on two sides, whereas, on the lefthand side, a small margin separates them from the edge. Logically, the painting should look off-center on the right, and truncated. Not a bit, though. The canvas isn't structured by any underlying grid; the gaps between planes aren't commensurable; their rhythm is neither regular nor syncopated, it is unpredictable; at top right, a pair of planes are touching, but they are the only two that are; no rectangle is aligned with any other, whether in columns or rows; the middle is

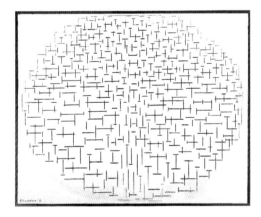

Piet Mondrian

Compositie 10 in zwart wit (Pier et océan), 1915

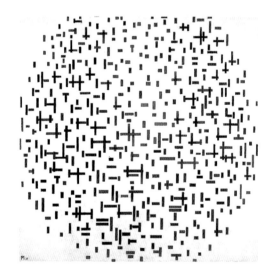

Piet Mondrian

Compositie in lijn, 1916–1917

taken up by a "hole," and there are two more "holes" off to the right. This should create something messy or untidy, but it doesn't. You get the feeling that all the elements are in their rightful spot, and that to budge any one by so much as a millimeter would destroy the whole. So you find yourself thinking that the picture is "held together" by the chromatic relations, in all their simplicity and nuance. This is undoubtedly so, but it defies analysis. The critical mind capitulates, the eye lays down its arms, and aesthetic judgment surrenders.

Or maybe not. Greenberg's word "surrender" is excessive, too brutal and too bellicose for a work of such delicacy. It suggests on the part of the artist a strategy with its sights on our subordination, whereas the sensation created by this picture is one of total detachment, its emotion one of extreme lightness, and its buoyancy one of absolute freedom. The only satisfactory description of this composition, doing its utmost not to be one, speaks about it as if the color planes, on their own, had placed themselves precisely where they are, freely, and with such respect for their neighbors that you end up giving in to the social order they have spontaneously chosen for themselves—and giving in doesn't mean surrendering. The color planes have an autonomy which Mondrian would later call their "egoism," yet which doesn't stop them from conversing with one another. How are we to imagine their "egoism" and their conversation simultaneously? Or their absence of concertedness and their free social life? How are we to conceive of their organization without referring it to the artist's authority? By referring it rather to the beholder's judgment—bearing in mind that the picture's author was its first viewer and that one could do worse to a painting's author than to call him the first person to whom his picture says: "Here you are." The artist must have withdrawn to ensure that two color planes had no relationship between them other than being triangulated by the eye cast upon them, and

Piet Mondrian

Composition 1916, 1916

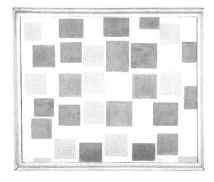

Piet Mondrian

Composition n° 3 avec plans colorés, 1917

<small>(COLOR PLATE P. 204)</small>

not by dint of his own will or his gift for composition. We all sense that words such as gift, talent, virtuosity, imagination, and self-expression have no bearing on Mondrian's art. His abstraction is not the projection of an imaginary world, as is the case with Kandinsky and Klee; his painting is completely devoid of technical virtuosity; Mondrian didn't express himself. He painted in the second person, not the first, addressing his medium in the singular face-to-face with the canvas, spending infinitely more time looking at it, his eye keenly set on the X, than on covering it with pigment. Striving for what is essential in painting in the second person, Mondrian sought to do away with the figure-ground contrast. Do away with it, period. Neither deny it, contradict it, thwart it, nor merge figure and ground. Abolish it. But why? Because as soon as a figure looms up against a background, it's in the third person. You're speaking to your beloved one, or you're conjuring up a deceased relative, or you're opening a door for somebody you've long been waiting for and were no longer expecting. Does their face loom up against a background? No—at the very moment when you address them, they make up the entirety of your perceptual field, figure and ground abolished by facingness. The real face-to-face excludes all contrast and all hierarchization between figure and ground, and this is why painting in the second person calls for their abolition. Mondrian wasn't the only artist to have intuitively sensed this. Malevich was concerned with the same issue, otherwise his *Black Square* wouldn't be an icon. When he theorized painting by way of the *Gegenstandlose Welt*—the "objectless world"—it was undoubtedly to rid himself of painting in the third person. The same thing applied to Sztreminski, when he invented Unism, the first historical incarnation of monochrome painting. And Pollock's all-overness—though with him things get complicated by the transfer of the canvas from the floor where it was worked on to the wall where it was hung—is another manifestation of this powerful tropism toward facingness that runs through the whole history of modernist painting. Poor Greenberg. Flatness is definitely a word too weak, flat, and technical for the facingness that he managed to see and appreciate aesthetically, but whose ethical *raison d'être* he failed to grasp. He was right when he overlooked the manifestos and legitimizing discourses espoused by the pioneers of abstraction—Mondrian in the lead—in favor of the unprogrammed chain of visual decisions taken by each generation's best modernist painters. He had realized that a great artist, while knowing very well what he's after, will give in to his aesthetic verdicts because it is part and parcel of aesthetic judgment to be unintentional and involuntary. Hence his word, surrender. The word is not a happy one, though. You don't surrender before a face, unless it's the mask of power. The same applies to the "capitulation" of the best modernist painters before the flatness of their surface, as it applied to "strategy" in Chapter One, albeit the vaccine strategy. No strategy will make a *thing* resurrect and receive the respect due human beings; no surrender before the flatness of a canvas will see that something human gets incarnated in it. Resurrection and incarnation do not require subordination to the victory of the other, but rather, an act of faith in his or her freedom.

Is the religious vocabulary bothersome? Only for those who confound faith with belief. Belief is a state, faith is an act. One is free to think that it is, essentially, a religious act, but it is more to the point to think that it is an ethical act, which stayed clad in the travesty of religion as long as the awareness of the disenchantment of the world hallmarking modernity had not moved sufficiently ahead. What is at issue in the act of faith? The other's freedom, precisely. I pledge an act of faith whenever I wager, in complete confidence, that you will make good use of your freedom. The act of faith is addressed. It presupposes another in the second person facing me. Were my own freedom to be won at the expense of the freedom of others, it would be devoid of any ethical dimension. The freedom of the other, in the third person, has only a diminished ethical dimension. What does *their* freedom cost me, as long it doesn't encroach upon mine? Only *your* freedom is thoroughly ethical. Mondrian invites us to deal with his color planes like this, by an act of faith in their freedom which addresses them and triggers the seesaw enabling them to address us. It is then that they incarnate the other, some other, and that they become the flesh of painting. Nothing to do with suspension of disbelief, which is merely a convention.

Richter

On the relationship of Gerhard Richter's painting with the gaze, desire, and the unconscious, see Birgit Pelzer's four essays:

Le désir tragique (Dijon: Les Presses du réel,
1993).

'The Elision of the Gaze', in *Gerhard Richter*,
exhib. cat. (Jerusalem: The Israel Museum,
1995).

'Il n'y a pas de là. Gerhard Richter au Carré
d'Art à Nîmes,' in *Gerhard Richter, 100 Bilder*,
exhib. cat. (Nîmes: Carré d'Art, Musée d'Art
Contemporain, 1996).

'Lines Escaping the Gaze', *Gerhard Richter,
Drawings 1964–1999*, catalogue raisonné com-
piled by Dieter Schwarz (Winterthur:
Kunstmuseum, 1999).

The Juan Gris quotation about the piece of mirror glued on in *Le lavabo* comes from a conversation with Michel Leiris recalled by
Daniel-Henry Kahnweiler in his *Juan Gris*
(London: 1947), pp. 87–88.

Velázquez

In his famous analysis of *Las Meninas*, which
introduces *Les mots et les choses*, Michel
Foucault assumes that the viewer is facing the
mirror at the rear, in which the king and
queen are reflected, and thus occupies their
place. Joel Snyder and Ted Cohen have shown
that the vanishing point is situated below the
elbow of the figure leaving the room through
the door in the background, and that the mirror is actually refecting the picture that
Velázquez is in the process of painting. This
demonstration doesn't invalidate Foucault's
reading insofar as the presence of the king
and queen in the beholder's space (but slightly
to his or her left) is nevertheless asserted by
the picture, and is required to bring the representation full circle. Among articles on
Las Meninas which may give a sense of the
philosophical and pictorial complexity of this
marvellous 'viewer's presentational device',
see:

Michel Foucault, 'Les suivantes,' chapter 1 of
Les Mots et les choses (Paris: Gallimard, 1966);
transl. *The Order of Things* (New York:
Vintage Books, 1973).

John Searle, '*Las Meninas* and the Paradoxes of
Pictorial Representation,' *Critical Inquiry*, 6:3,
Spring 1980.

Joel Snyder and Ted Cohen, 'Critical Response.
Reflexions on *Las Meninas*: Paradox Lost,'
Critical Inquiry, 7:2, winter 1980.

Leo Steinberg, 'Velázquez' *Las Meninas*,' *October*,
19, Winter 1981.

Svetlana Alpers, 'Interpetration without
Representation, or, The Viewing of *Las
Meninas*,' *Representations*, 1, February 1983.

Joel Snyder, '*Las Meninas* and the Mirror of the
Prince,' *Critical Inquiry*, 11, June 1985.

Manet

On *Surprised Nymph*: a mystery shrouds this
painting. Manet sent it to St. Petersburg in
1861 under the title *Nymph and Satyr*, which, at
first glance, wrecks the viewer-voyeur thesis.
The satyr is painted in so lightly in the branches at upper right that he doesn't show up in the
x-ray, even though he can be seen in the photo
taken by Lochard at the time of the inventory
after the artist's death. According to some com-
mentators, the painting was retouched by a
hand other than Manet's; according to others,
the date of the photo isn't reliable. The satyr
very definitely existed. He also very definitely
vanished from the title when Manet included
the painting in his 1867 retrospective at the
Pont de l'Alma, calling it *Surprised Nymph*—the
title that has stuck. Whether the satyr vanished
from the picture in Manet's lifetime or not is
still an open question. See:

Juan Corradini, 'La Nymphe surprise de Manet et
les rayons-x,' *Gazette des Beaux-Arts*, LIV:6, 1959.

Rosalind Krauss, 'Manet's *Nymph Surprised*,'
Burlington Magazine, November 1967.

Beatrice Farwell, 'Manet's "Nymphe Surprise"',
Burlington Magazine, April 1975.

Diderot's remark that 'Susannah is chaste, and
so is the painter,' occurs in:

Denis Diderot, *Pensées détachées sur la peinture*, in
Salons IV, Héros et martyrs (Paris: Hermann,
1995), p. 413.

It is discussed by Michel Fried on p. 96 of
*Absorption and Theatricality, Painting and
Beholder in the Age of Diderot* (Berkeley:
University of California Press, 1980).
See also p. 178 on the beholder as voyeur.

On the matter of blushing and make-up, the two most relevant articles of the day were:

Charles Baudelaire, 'Éloge du maquillage,' Section XI of *Le Peintre de la vie moderne*, published in *Le Figaro* in December 1863; transl. Jonathan Mayne, *The Painter of Modern Life and Other Essays* (London: Phaidon Press, 1995).

Stéphane Mallarmé, 'The Impressionists and Édouard Manet,' published in *The Art Monthly Review*, London, in September 1876; republished by, *int. al.*, Jean C. Harris, 'A Little-known Essay on Manet by Stéphane Mallarmé,' *The Art Bulletin*, December 1964. The original French essay has been lost. Mallarmé used the expression 'flesh-pollen' to describe the *natural* complexion of a woman. This term is discussed by:

Jean Clay, 'Onguents, Fards, Pollens,' in *Bonjour Monsieur Manet*, exhib. cat. (Paris: Georges Pompidou Center, 1983); transl. John Shepley, 'Ointments, Makeup, Pollen,' *October*, 27, Winter 1983.

And by Michael Fried in a footnote to *Manet's Modernism*, pp. 408–412, which dwells on the implications of 'flesh-pollen' with regard to the gendering of faciality in Manet's paintings being *at once feminine and masculine*.

Greenberg

There is an abundance of literature by and about Greenberg. For what concerns us here, see in particular:

Clement Greenberg, *Art and Culture* (Boston: Beacon Press, 1961).

John O'Brian, ed., *Clement Greenberg, The Collected Essays and Criticism* (Chicago and London: Chicago University Press). The first two volumes appeared in 1986, the following two volumes in 1993.

'Avant-Garde and Kitsch,' *Partisan Review*, Autumn 1939; *The Collected Essays I*.

'Towards a Newer Laocoon,' *Partisan Review*, July–August 1940; *The Collected Essays I*.

'Modernist Painting,' *Forum Lectures* (Voice of America, Washington), 1960; *The Collected Essays IV*.

Clement Greenberg, 'After Abstract Expressionism,' *Art International*, 6:8, October 1962, *The Collected Essays, IV*.

Clement Greenberg, 'Seminar One,' *Arts Magazine*, 48, November 1973; repr. in *Homemade Esthetics, Observations on Art and Taste* (Oxford: Oxford University Press, 1999).

Thierry de Duve, *Clement Greenberg Between the Lines*, transl. Brian Holmes (Paris: Dis Voir, 1996).

The Donald Judd quotation, 'A work needs only to be interesting' occurs in Donald Judd, 'Specific Objects,' *Arts Yearbook VIII*, 1965; repr. in D. Judd, *Complete Writings, 1959–1975* (Halifax: The Press of Nova Scotia College of Art and Design, 1975), p. 184.

Ryman

Yve-Alain Bois (by the way, one of the finest interpreters of Mondrian) is also the keenest observer of Ryman's work, and has been for many years now. In particular, we are indebted to him for the publication of a major 'Ryman File' in *Macula*, in 1978, with contributions from Naomi Spector, Barbara Reise, Stephen Rosenthal, Christian Bonnefoi and Jean Clay. The debate about just what, in the wake of Greenberg's writings, 'modernism' and the 'end of modernism' mean for painting, and monochrome painting especially, often revolves around the Ryman case. It has been more recently taken up again around the work of Marthe Wéry. On all this, it is interesting to read, in chronological order, the following essays, each for one reason or another, *dated*:

Barbara Reise, 'Robert Ryman: Unfinished II (procedures),' *Studio International*, March 1974.

Jean Clay, 'La peinture en charpie,' *Macula* 3/4, 1978.

Yve-Alain Bois, 'Le tact de Ryman,' in *Robert Ryman*, exhib. cat., (Paris: Georges Pompidou Center, 1981); transl. Thomas Repensek, 'Ryman's Tact,' *October*, 19, Winter 1981; repr. in *Painting as Model* (Cambridge, Mass.: MIT Press, 1990).

Thierry de Duve, 'Ryman irreproductible,' *Parachute*, 20, Autumn 1980; repr. in *Essais datés I, 1974–1986* (Paris: La Différence, 1987).

Thierry de Duve, 'Marthe Wéry, la peinture de près et de loin,' in *Marthe Wéry*, catalog of the 1982 Venice Biennale (Brussels: Lebeer-Hossmann, 1982); repr. with transl. Simon Pleasance, 'Marthe Wéry: Painting, Close To and From Afar,' in *Marthe Wéry, Penser en peinture* (Ghent: Ludion, 2001).

Thierry de Duve, 'The Monochrome and the Blank Canvas,' chapter 4 of *Kant after Duchamp*.

Yve-Alain Bois, 'Surprise and Equanimity,' in *Robert Ryman, New Paintings*, exhib. cat. (New York: The Pace Gallery, 1990).

Christian Debuyst, 'About Marthe Wéry's Work', transl. Kaatje Cusse, in *Marthe Wéry, Un débat en peinture / A Debate in Painting* (Brussels: La lettre volée, 1999).

Thierry de Duve, 'Marthe Wéry, or Freedom in Painting,' transl. Simon Pleasance & Fronza Woods, *ibid*.

Thierry de Duve, 'Taking Care of Painting', in *Robert Ryman, Paintings from the Sixties*, transl. Simon Pleasance, exhib. cat. (Brussels: Xavier Hufkens Gallery, 2000).

The issue of triangulation in painting is dealt with by several authors but in most instances—not quite by chance—from an angle. See in particular:

Leo Steinberg's comments in the article on *Las Meninas* mentioned earlier. Steinberg sees the nine figures in the painting arranged three by three on three equilateral triangles, based on what they are seeing.

Rosalind Krauss, 'On Frontality,' *Artforum*, May 1968. This article includes a discussion of the obliqueness of some of Kenneth Noland's 'chevron' paintings, and the way it affects the Greenbergian notion of flatness.

Hubert Damisch's remarks on braids and braiding (*la tresse, le tressage*) regarding François Rouan's painting, expressed in 'La peinture est un vrai trois', in *Fenêtre jaune cadmium* (Paris: Le Seuil, 1984).

Michael Fried's argument in *Manet's Modernism*, pp. 343–346, whereby, in Manet, 'the ternary relationship painter / painting / model takes ontological precedence over the binary relationship painting/beholder'. The present book is deeply indebted to Fried's pioneering work since *Absorption and Theatricality*. The difference, however, between Fried's notion of facingness and the notion put forward here has to do with Fried not perceiving that the painter / painting / model triangle is not replaced by a binary painting / beholder relationship when the painter withdraws in favour of the behold-

er, but that it undergoes a rotation which makes room for an enigma, an X. Yet the impression is strong that *Manet's Modernism* in its entirety revolves around this X.

The X in question has everything to do with *the object a*, as theorized by Jacques Lacan, especially in *The Four fundamental Concepts of Psychanalysis*, transl. Alan Sheridan (London: Hogarth Press, 1977).

Picasso

Although veering in quite another direction from his, the reflections sketched out here about painting 'in the third person' in relation to Picasso, around 1911–1912, owe a great deal to the thinking of T. J. Clark, whose entire work seems to be striving for the production of a 'third person' theory of modernism. Indeed, his materialist—i.e., monist—conception of representation leads him to such a theory. See in particular:

Timothy J. Clark, 'Cubism and Collectivity,' in *Farewell to an Idea, Episodes from a History of Modernism* (New Haven: Yale University Press, 1999).

See also William Rubin's introduction to *Picasso and Braque, Pioneering Cubism*, exhib. cat. (New York: The Museum of Modern Art, 1989).

Mondrian

In addition to the 'classics' by Michel Seuphor, Charmion von Wiegand, Joop Joosten, Carel Blotkamp and Robert Welsh, see the studies by Yve-Alain Bois:

'Du projet au procès', in *L'atelier de Mondrian*, ed. Yve-Alain Bois (Paris: Macula, 1982).

'Piet Mondrian, *New York City*,' in *Painting as Model*.

'The Iconoclast' in *Piet Mondrian*, exhib. cat. (Milan: Leonardo Arte, 1994).

Here you are

Gerhard Richter
Vier Glasscheiben, 1967

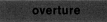

overture

Lee Friedlander
Colorado (Self Portrait), 1967

Michelangelo Pistoletto
L'uomo che pensa, 1962–1993

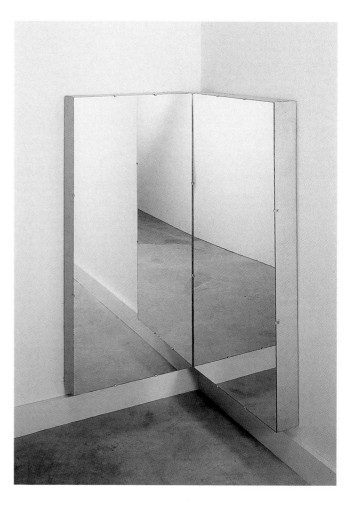

Art & Language
Untitled Painting, 1965

A mirror is a clever thing. It's an object capable of saying to the person standing in front of it: "Here you are. Here you are facing me." In Pistoletto's mirror, made of polished stainless steel, the image is slightly blurred. Furthermore, it already shows someone: a pensive man, seen in profile. In other Pistoletto mirrors, the man is seen from behind, never head-on. The face-to-face is reserved for you. Since Antiquity, painting has been compared to a mirror, and Leonardo da Vinci saw a picture as a window. The eye passes through windows, and rebounds from mirrors.

Michael Snow
Authorisation, 1969

Léon Spilliaert
Autoportrait au miroir, 1908

Richard Artschwager
Mirror and Wood Construction,
1962

Léon Spilliaert
Miroir, 1913

Florence Henri
Untitled, 1928

Luis Noronha da Costa
Objecto, 1967

Magritte represented the face-to-face between a human
being and a thing—flat, framed, and hanging on a wall—
which we call a picture. In his picture, all he did was represent the relationship you have with any picture, whether
a portrait or a black monochrome. Or a mirror.

René Magritte

L'Image parfaite, 1928

Raoul Hausmann

Regard dans le miroir, 1930

Roy Lichtenstein
Mirror, 1970

Günter Umberg
Untitled, 1999

A black monochrome absorbs all light, a cinema screen
reflects all of it, more or less like mirrors. Especially if, like
Sugimoto, the photographer has left the shutter open
throughout the projection. White is the sum of all colored
lights, black its subtraction.

Hiroshi Sugimoto
Marion Palace, 1980
Akron Civic Theatre, 1980

Eric Rondepierre
Le Voyeur, 1989

What happened to your reflection in Lichtenstein's black mirror? What became of that window opening onto the world that is the cinema?

Robert Smithson
Enantiomorphic Chambers, 1965

The *Enantiomorphic Chambers* are a strange device for "seeing one's own sight" and ... going blind. Mirrors are placed in such a way that, if you put yourself between them, your reflected image is cancelled out.

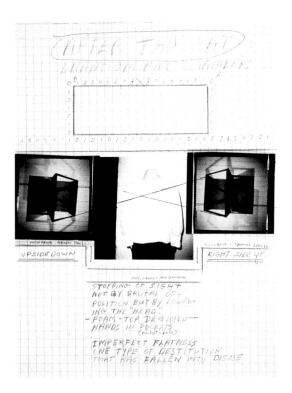

Robert Smithson
Afterthought Enantiomorphic Chambers, 1965

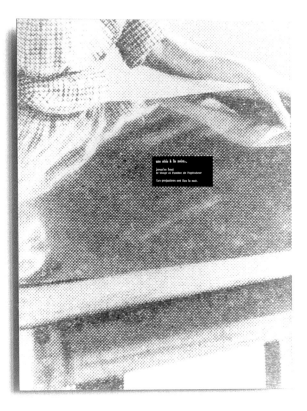

Sylvie Eyberg
1999, 29 x 21,5 cm, 1999

Sylvie Eyberg
1999, 29 x 22,5 cm, 1999

Sylvie Eyberg collects old magazine photos which she
then rephotographs, accompanied by poems made up of
found sentences. Words and images take years to meet
up. The theme of reflection recurs periodically.

Like all of Dan Graham's *Pavilions*, this one, designed
specially for the rotunda in the Palais des Beaux-Arts,
borrows its cool vocabulary from corporate architecture,
to which, however, it gives an intimate scale, inspired by
the "pleasure pavilions" of the Rococo period.

Dan Graham

Two Staggered Two-Way-Mirror Half-Cylinders, 2000

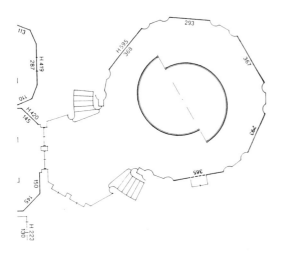

The curved glass pane is a two-way mirror, whose reflective power varies endlessly according to the changes in intensity of the natural light. You see your own image in it, in an anamorphosis, superimposed on that of the spectators on the other side of the glass.

Dan Graham

Two Staggered Two-Way-Mirror Half-Cylinders, 2000

Fabro's *Prisoners* are fettered to one another. For *Voici*,
they were freed and installed leaning on the rotunda's
balcony, overlooking the Dan Graham pavilion, the way
the *Voyeurs*—a piece similarly shaped but made of metal—
occasionally are.

Luciano Fabro
I prigioni, 1994

Jeff Koons
Christ and the Lamb, 1986

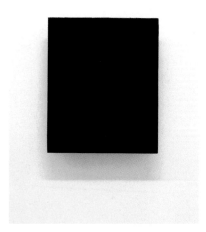

Günter Umberg
Untitled, 1999

reflections

Mirrors reflect... and make us reflect, among other things,
over what art historian Michael Fried has brilliantly analyzed:
the face-to-face between the work of art and the beholder is
tugged between the contrasting poles of absorption and
theatricality. In its day, the Rococo style was the last word in
theatricality, as well as the expression of the aristocracy's
disarray. Jeff Koons is *our* Rococo artist, and it is the

Gerhard Richter
Spiegel, grau (739-3), 1991

cultural disarray of the middle class in our "postmodern" age
which he lays bare.
Even when he produces abstract action painting–which isn't
the case with his *Gray Mirror*–Richter is, by contrast, the heir
of the "absorptive" tradition that dominated modernism.
Maximum absorption is achieved with the black monochrome,
the antithesis of the mirror. So we may marvel at the paradox
of the absorbing mirror.

Mark Rothko
Untitled, 1951

Joan Miró
Peinture (Le toréador), 1927

The painter of the past was interested in what he saw *in* the
mirror or *through* the window; the modern painter is more
interested in the mirror or window *per se*. Abstraction made
the picture plane opaque, and attention was shifted toward
the vibration of colors, the form or matter of the medium, the
stroke and the way of applying pigment, the framing and posi-
tioning of the work in space.

197

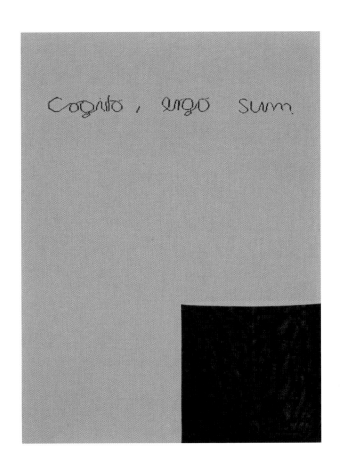
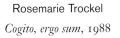

Rosemarie Trockel

Cogito, ergo sum, 1988

Blinky Palermo

Untitled (für Kristin), 1973

When painting turned its back on the representation of the visible, its field both shrank and intensified, focusing on the specifically visual problems which have always been the prime concern of painters. But the field of painting also broadened almost *ad infinitum* when painters felt free to work on the most unexpected surfaces, with novel techniques and in the most varied of forms and formats.

face-to-face

Ellsworth Kelly
Blue Curve, 1996

Art critic Clement Greenberg defined modernism in painting by the ever-growing tendency to assert the flatness of the support—a definition that is certainly not contradicted by the examples shown here, ranging from Russian Suprematism to the most contemporary painting.

But Greenberg didn't follow the ethical thread of his aesthetic thinking very far. He might have done better to speak in terms of facingness rather than flatness, because it is indeed the face-to-face with the other that is involved in the best abstract painting.

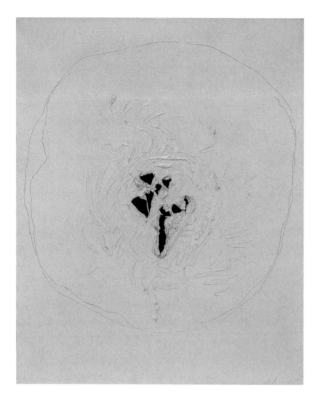

Lucio Fontana
Concetto spaziale, 1962

Robert Ryman
Untitled #1004, 1960–1961

Yves Klein
Monochrome I.K.B., 1957

Robert Ryman
Untitled, 1965

Nikolai Suetin
Composition avec la raie jaune, 1930

Robert Ryman
Untitled, 1961

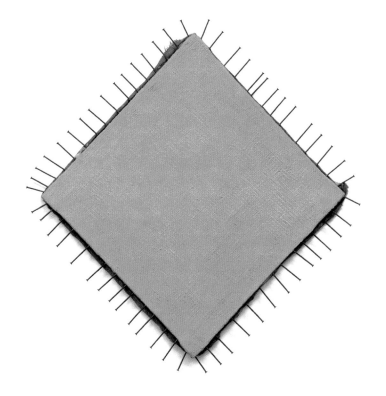

Günther Uecker
Das gelbe Bild, 1957–1958

Eric Cameron
Lettuce, 1979

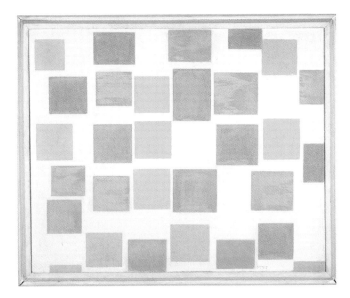

Piet Mondrian

Composition n°3 avec plans colorés, 1917

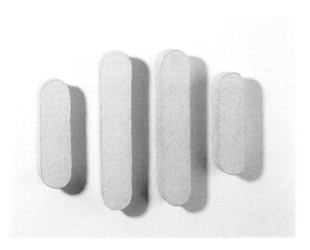

Richard Tuttle

Pink Oval Landscape, 1964

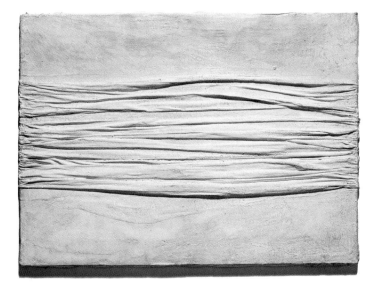

Piero Manzoni

Achrome, 1960

Have you noticed how Tchelitchev's young man stares intensely at you? Well, the other pictures are also looking at you. And have you noticed how he's got one eye bigger than the other?

Robert Mangold

Untitled, 1973

Robert Mangold

Untitled, 1973

Pavel Tchelitchev

Tête de jeune homme, 1925

It's as if the right half of his face were twenty inches closer to you than the left half. Painting is often a matter of finding the right distance. To each his or her own.

Marthe Wéry
Peinture Venise 82, 1982

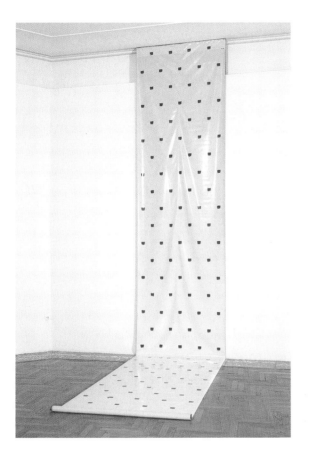

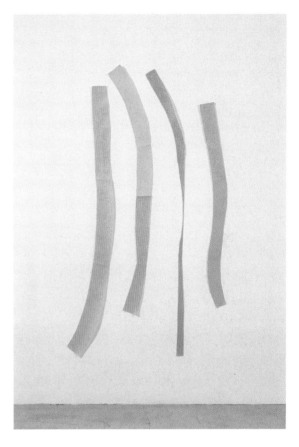

Niele Toroni

Travail / Peinture (Empreintes de pinceau n° 50), 1969

Guy Mees

Verloren ruimte, 1990

Here's the human figure again, which in the case of video
is self-explanatory. Seventeen men, not a single woman.
Dressed like workers, whose features attest today's multi-
ethnic and multi-cultural America.

vis-à-vis

Gary Hill
Viewer, 1996

They are immigrant workers. The foreigner. The other.
Here is a work that confronts you with the otherness of
the other—in the singular, as the title says: *Viewer*. Who
is looking at whom in this work?

portraits

Jean Fautrier
Portrait de ma concierge, 1922

The image of stars belongs to the public, and Warhol doesn't make their portrait. He makes that of the society of the spectacle. To portray an *individual*, it is as if you had to descend the social scale and zero in on the intimate sphere, like Fautrier with his *Portait de ma concierge*.

Andy Warhol

Dolly Parton, 1985

Andy Warhol

Dolly Parton, 1985

Günter Umberg

Untitled, 1999–2000

And what of the photo of Eleanor? The beloved woman.
And what of the nape of Vera's neck? Again the beloved
woman. And the face of this dead man, basked in
diaphanous light? Perhaps it's only in love and death that
the individual and the universal can touch one another.

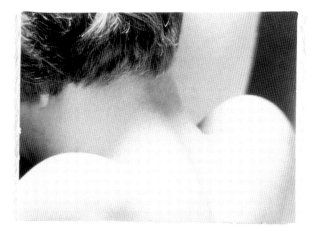

Raoul Hausmann
Untitled (Épaules), 1927–1933

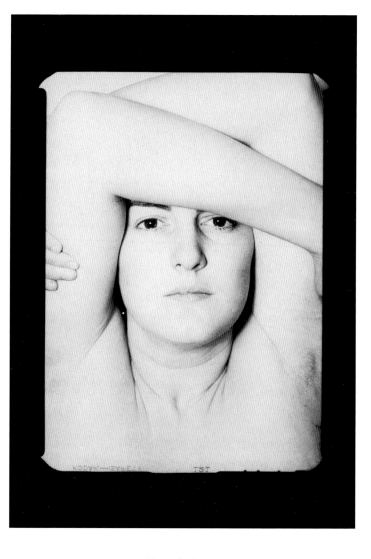

Harry Callahan
Eleanor, Chicago, 1950

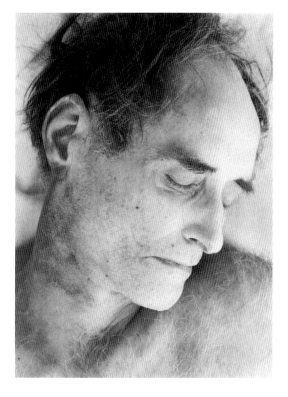

Rudolf Schäfer
Totengesicht, 1986

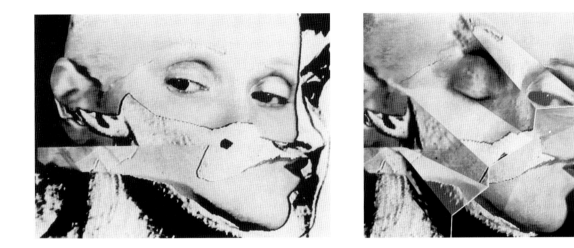

Valie Export
Untitled, 12, 1–2, 1989

 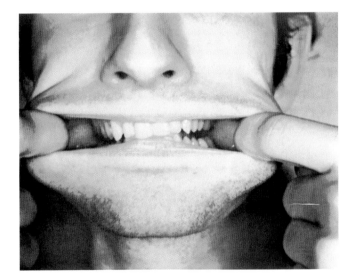

Bruce Naumann
Studies for Holograms (a), (e), 1970

Elsewhere it's all grimaces, irony, and deconstruction. Nowhere more than on the representation of the human face did modern art confront the limits ot its own legitimacy.

Roni Horn
You Are the Weather, 1994–1996

Has the artist produced a hundred-faceted portrait of the personality of this young woman? No. She is simply reacting to the climatic conditions in which she is plunged. Each series shows her bathing in the hot, cold, luke-warm, or icy water from a spring or a pool in Iceland. Who's the "you" in *You Are the Weather*? Could it be that the young woman is reacting to the coldness, warmth, luke-warmth, or iciness of your gaze? Her shivering flesh incarnates *you*, in the second person, while her gaze addresses you and seems to ask, a hundred times over: "What do you want of me?"–the very question with which the "you" opens onto the "us."

you

Here we are

Édouard Manet

Un bar aux Folies-Bergère, 1881–1882

Alas, kings furiously strive after war; we the peoples should strive after love.

Victor Hugo

Murdering the species is the work of the species. The SS is no different from us.

Dionys Mascolo

Pacts

What, we? How, we? Who's this we? Only a being endowed with speech can say "we," and as there are no other speaking beings besides us on this planet, we is we. Just we? We ourselves? We all? You and I. I, now! Who's this I? The reader is irked and the author embarrassed. He'd decided that, save in a few calculated spots, he wouldn't write in the first person singular. He's used the conventional "we" that enables a writer to summon his readers to his cause, and which goes unheeded as long as the writer is uttering general truths—or deemed as such, or imposed as such. Convenience of language, abuse of power, mandate of confidence received from the readers? From the publisher, perhaps? From society? From language? No sooner have you paused to ponder over it, than an abyss opens up in that simplest of little words, the pronoun of the first person plural. The author didn't want to shatter the convention of language behind which he has taken shelter up till now. Perhaps it was already shattered, for those readers irritated by his style, or in disagreement with what he has written. At the moment of tackling the art of the century from the "Here we are" angle, he has simply realized that he could no longer write in the guise of the conventional "we," and this even less so because it is precisely with this particular difficulty that the art of the century has wrestled. This will be our theme—and our thesis. When a convention comes up for discussion, there's every chance that it is already no longer a convention.

In any civilization you care to name, the artist's trade obeys conventions. These conventions are technical and aesthetic rules which lend substance to the professional know-how of their guild, and are negotiated with that part of society which maintains and commissions them. An artistic tradition is stable when artists gracefully submit to the taste of their patrons, and when the latter cultivate respect for the artists—in other words, when artistic conventions are what all conventions should be: a pact, a tacitly or explicitly signed agreement between two parties who are acquainted with each other, and who know who they are and what they want. The avant-garde is born—can be born, is bound to be born—when these conditions no longer exist: when no one knows any longer whom art is addressing, and when no one knows any longer, either, who is legitimately an artist. It was no accident that the pictorial avant-garde was born in France, in the midst of the Salon tiffs, for France alone had invented that odd institution which has no equivalent anywhere else. The "French exception," which France's cultural press is quite touchy about these days, is actually a very old bone. It should come as a surprise to no one to learn that it dates back to Colbert. *Per se*, the Salon wouldn't be quite such a noteworthy institution were it not an offshoot of the *Académie royale de peinture et de sculpture*, founded in 1648 following a petition mounted by the court painters and looking for all the world like a *coup d'état*. In exchange for their unconditional allegiance to the power of the throne, the petitioners set their sights on, *and obtained*, monopolistic control over access to the profession—yet another French exception which still weighs with all its clout on today's art education in France. Less than twenty years later, those happy few, cocooned in exclusive contracts binding them to the royal household and shielding them from outside competition, decided—God knows why—to broadcast their work before the eyes of the whole nation. Beneath this contradiction between the conditions of exercising their trade and the conditions of displaying its product— monopoly on the part of artists, free access on the part of viewers—there smoldered an explosive situation from which the avant-garde would duly emerge, almost two centuries later. But *les anciens*—as the founders of the Academy christened themselves—didn't actually decide anything. They allowed themselves to be swept along in a process whose long-term consequences they failed absolutely to gauge, and all the more so because they weren't in a position to foresee the social changes that would undermine the foundations of the *ancien régime* and lead to its eventual downfall. They saw nothing but the outstanding advantage they had just gained as a result of their petition: that the idea of an art whose intent was to be aristocratic, and which wasn't content just to be an art for the aristocracy, should be *institutionalized*; and that the technical and aesthetic rules of their trade should be given a legitimacy tantamount to a mandate on the part of the only social class they were really addressing. Once granted as if in nobility lied the very essence of art, this legitimacy delegated, disseminated, and diffracted the royal authority in a body of painting professionals invested with the power to lend it visual representation. The opening of the Salon to the people was an aberration from this point of view.

How did it come about? In 1655, a royal warrant confirmed the Academy's monopoly over access to the profession, reinforced in 1664 when Colbert increased its subsidy fourfold. The new statutes specified that "each year there will be a general assembly in the Academy on the first Saturday of July, at which each of the officers and academicians will bring some piece of their work to be used to decorate the premises of the Academy for just a few days, and then remove them if they so see fit." Such is the origin of the earliest Salons. The exhibition was quite clearly not intended to be a public one: the general assembly of the academicians simply provided them with the opportunity to show their works to one another, in a spirit of emulation. But in 1667, again at Colbert's instigation, it was decided to hold a biennial exhibition lasting a fortnight starting at Holy Week, outside under the arcades of the Palais-Royal or in the courtyard of the Palais Richelieu. Until the seventh exhibition in 1683, this custom was upheld, then it was interrupted until 1699, when the eighth exhibition was hung in the Great Gallery of the Louvre. The year 1673 saw the publication of the first *livret*, the equivalent of our modern exhibition catalogs, proving that in that year the exhibition was a public one, albeit relatively unassuming. It was definitely public in 1699, since the *Mercure de France* reserved a few lines for it. An exhibition was also put on in 1704 to celebrate the birth of the Duke of Brittany, followed by another in 1706, opened on 25 August, the feast day of St. Louis. Until the eclipse of the *ancien régime*, this date would mark the opening of the Salon, though this term was not used to describe the exhibition until the following one held in 1725, when, for the first time, it occupied the "*Salon carré*" in the Louvre on the occasion of Louis XV's wedding. All these festive occasions suggest that the Salon was part of the pomp and circumstance of the court, put on display for the populace, yet anything but addressed to it. Nobody could have imagined that before long it would be one of the places where modern citizenship would be constructed. For lack of money, the next Salon wasn't held until 1737, when it assumed a certain independence, turned into a yearly affair, and was duly fleshed out: at the 1737 exhibition, 286 works by 69 artists were shown. Throughout the 18th century and nearly all of the 19th, in spite of countless ups and downs, interruptions, moves to various premises, and changes in the supervisory authority, the Salon would carry on being the great institution that orchestrated French artistic life and subjected it to the control of the state. It was not until the disastrous Salon of 1880, mentioned in Chapter One, that the edifice started to crack, and it was not until the creation of the *Salon des Indépendants*, four years later, that the state lost hold of its monopoly and the *Académie des Beaux-Arts* revealed itself to be the bastion of academicism that it had become. In the meantime, the avant-garde had come into being.

What was planted in France's artistic landscape by the creation of the Salon was nothing less than a time-bomb. We should never stop being amazed by the unheard-of decision—even if it was made unaware of its consequences—to expose, on a regular basis, the work of living artists, approved by the Academy, to the verdict of the crowd, the people, all and sundry. The public flocked to the Salon—and here was the time-bomb—in numbers that swelled exponentially. Diderot spoke of 20,000 visitors to the Salon in 1765. For the year 1783, estimates ranged, depending on the source, between 100,000 and 600,000 visitors. This latter figure would double in 1846. The number of visitors at the Salons of 1827, 1831, and 1841 was estimated at one million, a figure that exceeded the entire population of Paris. And for the World's Fair held in 1855, the official attendance figure was 891,682 visitors, no more, no less. We know this because, for the very first time that year, admissions were all paid and automatically counted by turnstiles. The organizers must have been disappointed because, for the following Salon, in 1857, free admission on Sundays was introduced. This measure attracted almost one and a half times the number of paying visitors clocked in during the week—a sign, if ever there was one, of the success of the Salon among the lower classes. So anyone could visit the Salon, no matter what social class they belonged to, and people didn't refrain from attending. Nor did they refrain from pronouncing verdicts. A public arena for personal aesthetic judgment was accordingly created, glaringly contravening the protective measures taken by the Academy in order to maintain its aesthetic standards and the continuity of its tradition. From the outset, the mixture of social classes at the Salon was staggering. Respectable society was no longer on its own home ground at the Salon, and it sensed as much, unsure whether to rejoice or panic. A multitude of writings attest all this. In 1725, the *Mercure de France* recounted that "during this splendid exhibition, an endless array of Viewers of every condition, gender, and age" was to be seen. The same phrasing recurred fifty-five years later, this time signed by one Pidansat de Mairobert, who referred to "this admixture of every order of the state, every rank, gender, and age." In 1755, the *Mercure de France* published an article with the title: *Doubts about the Existence of a Public*, where it was noted that "every society has claimed to be the true public, like good company. Through this division, good taste has become problematic, real belief dubious, and the authority of a legitimate public has ceased to be unique." As the critic Fréron observed at the same moment, in *L'année littéraire*, "Few people are knowledgeable, and everyone claims to be." To which Sébastien Mercier added, in his *Tableau de Paris*, written in 1767: "What is missing is a rallying point and, as Paris never speaks with one and the same voice, it is an indefinable compound. Does the public exist? What is the public? Where is it? Through what organ does it display its will?" Needless to say, what emerges from these doubts about the existence of a public is not that nobody visited the Salon, but rather that artists no longer knew whom they were addressing when they showed their work at it. Guardians though they may have been of the monopoly of artistic legitimacy, by no longer knowing whom they were addressing, they would end up doubting the authority from which they had received their mandate. The decline of the Academy into academicism during the 19th century has its roots in these very doubts on the existence of a public in the 18th. To increase the pressure that would make the stylistic breaks of the avant-garde necessary, the feeling of the loss of identity of the "natural" art public would have to spill over into a new social arena, made possible only through the advent of the modern, bourgeois public sphere. Before the Revolution, there could be no question of any such thing. Nonetheless, this feeling did gather momentum throughout the 18th century, as the crowds, which would never actually be granted the status of fully legitimate public, flocked to the Salon.

Toward the middle of the 19th century, access to the Salon for one and all, regardless of class, was a *fait accompli*. "I have seen bourgeois folk, workers, and even peasants," said Zola. There wasn't a single painter in France who, aware that his career depended on his success at the Salon, wasn't seized by this alarming question: for whom was he painting? Those most sensitive to their time, still steeped in the aristocratic values of high art, were conscious that they had to consider the aspirations of a heterogeneous throng whose breath they could feel on their necks as they painted. For us, who are sadly so easily reconciled with the fact that contemporary art only speaks to the small circle of people who are acquainted with its codes, the wholesome appetite for painting on the part of the 19th century masses almost defies understanding. We might find it suspect: the populace went to the Salon the same way it went to the theater, to look at the *parterre* audience at least as much as the stage. Yet this is an historical fact. The whole population of Paris, and then some, at the 1831 Salon! Such numbers make it simply impossible to think that just the educated elites went to the Salon. The country squire, the *nouveau riche*, the craftsman from the *faubourgs*, the fishmonger's wife, and the factory worker—the whole Human Comedy jockeyed for position at the Salon, opining, applauding, and guffawing. Everything suggests that the Salons were one of the first forms of mass entertainment, within which the aristocratic tradition of high art strove, willy-nilly, to maintain its integrity and ward off the corruption issuing from the plebeian taste for vulgarity, garishness, facile seduction—that is, to put it with an anachronistic word, kitsch. With hindsight, it isn't too hard to see that, in the guise of tradition, it was academic art that toppled over into kitsch, and the burgeoning avant-garde which kept tradition alive. And not just any old tradition—the aristocratic tradition of high art, no less. The irony of all this is missed only by those reactionaries who still haven't understood a thing about the vaccine strategy, and whose ranks are swelling, thanks to the laziness of some left-wing intellectuals bothered by the avant-garde's "elitism" and who prefer to take at face-value the avant-gardistic discourse with which—granted—the avant-garde saw fit to justify itself. Greenberg is a better guide, he who made such a careful distinction between avant-garde and avant-gardism. He knew that the avant-garde was the only real defence of tradition and, in a famous 1939 article, *Avant-garde and Kitsch*, he named the enemy by name: "Self-evidently, all kitsch is academic; and, conversely, all that's academic is kitsch." But Greenberg's idea of kitsch was too simplistic, and he refused to take into account the innumerable borrowings made by the avant-garde from the most vulgar manifestations of the ambient culture. He failed to adequately delve into the fact that, if the love of kitsch is the unconscious enjoyment of the corruption of one's own taste, in the eye of some observer it may well be the very conscious enjoyment of the corruption of someone else's taste. One of the themes recurring regularly in descriptions of the Salon, from the 18th century on, is that of the artist laying low in the crowd, observing it, recording its reactions, and using all this for his own ends. Never solely with the aim of detecting the crowd's taste, the better to please it. Perhaps more to take sustenance from the crowd's vindicative pleasure at trampling the royal rugs in the Louvre. Artists are workers, ennobled far too recently to have forgotten as much. Before long, they would think of themselves as aristocrats in the etymological sense, but released from their alliance with a class whose decadence they had witnessed, like everybody else. It is perceptible, since Watteau, that the best artists took the pulse of the Salon, having understood that new social pacts were under negotiation there, quite physically, shoulder to shoulder, and that, for a painter, those things were the very stuff of his art. The Salon was an impressive interchange where the emerging social classes undertook an apprenticeship in their respective mores, idioms, and fashions, and rubbed shoulders with each other outside the usual relations governed by status, protocol, and the hierarchies of the working place. Conflicts could be suspended in it, or be playfully enacted in the harmless form of aesthetic argument—class struggle sublimated as taste struggle. The birth of the pictorial avant-garde can't be separated from this social laboratory, even if the latter is not the only thing involved. To be sure, the artistic upheavals of modernity would have appeared even if France hadn't invented this strange institution, since they did indeed appear in other countries, with a slight time lapse. But it is an historical fact that the history of the avant-garde, or modernism, was played out in Paris, on the stage of the Salon (or the Salons) up until the First World War.

When painters exhibit in conditions where they deal with anyone and everyone without distinction, what becomes of the conventions of their trade? To grasp this, the emphasis must be put on the convention as a pact, not as a technical-aesthetic rule. If the partners in the pact are vague, the pact will be uncertain, and the artists are not responsible for this. They are only responsible for being in and of their time and, above all, for understanding that any broken pictorial convention signals a pact broken with one faction of the public, at the same time as a demand for a new pact possibly addressed to another faction. Reducing these factions to the struggle between academicism and avant-garde is too simple. No doubt, there are the Academy, the jury, the Beaux-Arts schools, but none of this fine society holds an opinion that is, by definition, monolithic, conservative, and backward-looking. No doubt there are sensitive and daring critics, a few enlightened art lovers and collectors, and an artistic and literary intelligentsia who will defend the avant-garde, but there is also a conservative bunch of critics, along with a narrow-minded middle class, an uneducated populace, and philistines of every stripe. Last of all, there are, from time to time, in those social classes least educated and least encumbered by academic culture, sensitive individuals, artists by temperament if not by trade, who instinctively gravitate to the works that count. All painters have to cope with the indeterminate Salon public; nobody can hope to please all the people all of the time; they all paint with an anonymous crowd of unpredictable reactions looking over their shoulder. Painters experience the contradictory expectations of this crowd like aesthetic *desiderata*, tastes and prejudices that come to them from others; but they experience them with brush in hand, in front of their canvas. Thus it is aesthetically, with their sensibility, and through the mediation of the technical constraints of their trade, that artists sense the need to conclude a pact with an addressee who is unspecified and divided by social conflicts. For a Salon artist (and *all* artists, whether modern or *pompiers*, were Salon artists in the 19th century), the crowd was always present, even when he'd rather have ignored it and painted only for himself, insofar as he couldn't avoid dealing in his work with that momentary state of aesthetic consensus represented by the conventions of his medium. These conventions were presented to him in very tangible technical forms. They were his supports, his tools, his pigments and their bonding agents; they were the professional gestures he had learned to make and the visual effects he had learned to like; they were the means of achieving a certain surface quality, a certain impasto, glaze, or scumble; they were the studio recipes, the tricks, sleights of hand, and habits of the trade he had assimilated. They were also the chromatic harmonies that pleased him and the dissonances he would venture to make; the respective parts of drawing and of color; the compositional methods he mastered or would seek to master; the styles he knew, having tried his hand at them; his way of looking at the world through the more or less conscious filter of tradition—of a tradition. Thus, the painter experiences both technically and aesthetically the conventions of his medium, which doesn't keep these conventions from being conventions, or in other words, from embodying a great many pacts which haven't been signed solely among painters, but rather between the guild of painters in the course of its history and the public getting a certain idea about painting as a result of its contact with their works. Shrewd, indeed, would be the person who might unravel, within the conventions of the medium, the share of professional customs and the share of the public's expectations; they are as inseperable as the heads and tails of one coin. So, it's under the aesthetic pressure of his technical constraints that an artist worthy of the name either accepts or breaks a convention—that is, the pact. Conversely, it's under the pressure of the authority of the pact in force within a given social segment, possibly countered by the desire pressing for another pact with another fraction of society, that he either accepts or aesthetically transgresses a technical constraint. By breaking the convention (the rule), avant-garde artists provoke the public to take stock of the fact that, by being uncertain, the convention (the pact) is, in practice, already broken and must be renegotiated, on a case-by-case basis. Conversely, by breaking the convention (the pact), avant-garde artists make the conventions (the rules) of their trade the arena of negotiation. With whom?

To sign a convention with someone, you need someone opposite you, and you need to know who that person is. The painter would have to know whom he's painting for, and the middle-class Parisian visiting the Salon would have to know whom he's dealing with. Let's take the 1851 Salon. (It's interesting both for the exorbitant number of works on view—four thousand—and for its political context, because it opened just one month after Louis-Napoléon's *coup d'état*.) With whom should the middle-class Parisian strike an aesthetic deal? With the dignified Edouard Dubufe, showing a *Portrait of Mme. F.* in the manner of Ingres? With the disconcerting Chassériau, whose *Sappho* wavered endlessly between Ingres and Delacroix? With the suave Gérôme and his *Gynaeceum*? With Corot, waxing mythological for once? Or should he bargain with the new school known as the realists: Tassaert, Antigna, Haussat, Lacoste, Pils, who are a bit too common to his taste? Would he go so far as to accept that Millet's *The Sower* and *The Binders*—both so unfinished and so dashed off, but which stir him to emotion not to say repulsion—embody the new conventions in painting? How can we expect this middle-class Parisian to know whether Mr. Courbet, whose name was on everyone's lips and whose *Burial at Ornans* enjoyed pride-of-place at the Salon despite a hostile jury, was a dangerous revolutionary preaching hatred for art, as Chennevières claimed, or whether, as Champfleury maintained, Mr. Courbet had invented the art of the real? The middle-class Parisian was all at sea. He had the feeling—and it wasn't at all a mistaken one—that certain artists had come to an understanding, over his head, with the jury, and that others (to hell with the jury!) had made a deal with the devil. And these artists, too, had better know the identity of that devil to whom they'd sold their souls. Nothing was sure on their side of the pact, either. Shouldn't Mr. Courbet himself have decided whether he was addressing the Paris intellectuals or the countryfolk of Flagey and the gravediggers of Ornans, or even the bourgeois of Besançon, on whom he tried out the painting before dispatching it to the Salon? And what applied to Courbet also applied to the others; Gérôme was in the same boat. He wasn't any too sure whom he was painting for, either: for the jury, for the members of the Institute, for the crowd flocking to the Salon, for his master Gleyre, for Théophile Gautier who, three years earlier, had been so complimentary about his *Cockfight*? Or for the museum— that is, for the public of the future? All painters were asking themselves the same question, brush in hand: with whom must the social pact be negotiated, and how? In so far as the rules of the trade were only of concern to those in the trade, the negotiation was undertaken, for the artist, with his specific tradition. In so far as they implied a pact with this anonymous public, which the very existence of the Salon invited to have a say in matters of art, the negotiation must be undertaken with everyone and anyone. And given that artists had started to depend more and more on public recognition for their professional status, the negotiation must be undertaken with a specific tradition, of which those in the trade were no longer the only guardians, but which proceeded via the verdict of the crowd. Try and unravel that.

It is hard to imagine, today, to what extent 19th-century French artists were reliant upon the Salon when it came to official acknowledgement and the means of acquiring a private clientele. How to convince or win over the jury so as to be admitted to the Salon, and, once admitted, how to reach the public that mattered (government officials, potential purchasers, influential critics), became issues of strategic importance for all painters. But seducing the jury and the public that mattered was not enough. You also had to arouse the crowd's interest; draw in the throng in front of your picture and keep it there, enthralled; stop it from being distracted by your rivals' works; instantly move it, and get the picture to stick in its memory. You had to be sure you were talked about in the press, for success at one Salon was the best passport to the next one. All those things that young film-makers in our own day and age cannot afford to ignore. If they want to find a producer for their second movie, they must not only have received subsidies for the first film, preferably been selected at Cannes, and had one hell of a write-up not only in *Les Cahiers du Cinéma* but in the popular press as well, but must also, if possible, have sent box office figures booming. There is no better parallel than the one with the film industry, to get a tangible idea of what Salon painting was: an art that had turned into mass entertainment. Same thing from the public's vantage point. It might help to imagine the Salon of the Manet years like a large multiplex moviehouse where each hung painting screens a different film. The Saturday night crowd, arriving in couples and gaggles, knows as it enters that it'll give in to the pop-corn and can-of-Coke ritual, but it doesn't yet know what film it will opt to see. They are no film buffs, really, but they can talk about fifteen hit movies, and they know all the stars. They have a vague idea about what they've come in search of: a fiction that will transport them beyond the humdrum daily round, a well put together story that keeps them riveted to their seat, two hours of fun, making them laugh or cry, from which they emerge moved but not changed. These expectations are quite similar to those of the average Salon-goers. Portraits and still-lifes were the short accompanying films shown before the main program, history painting, or what had become of it. David had long since passed away, and it was almost as long since Paul Delaroche had invented the "historical genre," which had been such an unrelenting success since his *Enfants d'Édouard* shown at the 1831 Salon and his *Jane Grey* shown in 1834. English history was an inexhaustible mine of dire and sinister intrigues, bristling with suspense, which a Frenchman couldn't fail but find thrilling. Those who had other tastes had the choice between various historical epics and orientalist hammam scenes, Napoleonic battles where not a single gaiter button was missing from the uniforms, and—latest fashion, latest thrill—the "peasant genre," made popular by Jules Breton, an especially spectacular example of which had pride of place at the 1882 Salon, not far from *A Bar at the Folies-Bergère*: Léon Lhermitte's *The Harvesters' Pay*. Not forgetting, needless to add, sex all over the place, under the most varied of pretexts and the most transparent of alibis. Indeed, there were conventions by the dozen at the Salon, and they were virtually identical to those that we can reel off when we look at a Saturday night multiplex program. Firstly, painting is a spectacle, rendered by means of a technique that culture has had time to assimilate, to the point where it comes across as identical with natural vision. The invention of monocular perspective during the Renaissance has provided this technique. Photography recently mechanized it. Film would add movement to it. Secondly, painting tells stories, like film, even if in this respect it is at a disadvantage. As we have seen, Manet came up against this handicap as early as his *Surprised Nymph*, as if he had been jealous of film without even knowing it. Most of his contemporaries didn't even raise the issue. Either they chose subjects so well-known that people had no trouble recreating the narrative, on either side of the moment picked out by the picture, or they so reduced the narrative to anecdote that it was contained in one single image. 19th-century painting saw the disappearance of all that highly sophisticated culture of the significant gesture that had informed discussion about the pictorial representation of action, from Poussin to David. Gestures became *outré*, unambiguous and conventional. Same disappearance of the culture of expression and physiognomy formerly exalted by Lebrun, the principal founder and first director of the Academy. Conventions were hardened and simplified to become accessible to as many people as possible. Thirdly, the story told by the picture takes place within four walls, but the fourth wall is missing. It gets replaced, unbeknownst to the characters, by a window. The action takes place in the picture as if on a theater stage—or as if on a cinema screen. Here, too, the fourth wall is missing unbeknownst to the characters, who live out their story as if they were all alone in the world. Let's keep Diderot's Susannah in mind, chaste as she was because she was unaware of the beholder's presence. If a painting convention does exist, whose pact-like nature stares you in the face at the slightest transgression, it is indeed this one. Conventions are fragile when they admit their conventional character. All it takes is for a movie actor to look the camera "in the eye" for us to be instantly wrenched out of the fiction and become self-conscious about sitting in the movie theater. Jean-Luc Godard used this procedure more than once, and its modernist and self-referential character, as "film about film," is patently evident. But Godard is the Manet of film, unless Manet is the Godard of painting. At the time when the existence of the Salon started to have serious effects on the practice of painters—in other words, in Diderot's day and age—nobody was ready yet to break this pact, and still less to want to draw up a new pact around a broken one. On the contrary, painters of that period took extraordinary measures to let the viewer know that the characters in the painting were unaware of being beheld. We appreciate what Manet grappled with in aiming at the precise opposite. Which brings us to the fourth of the conventions shared by Salon painting and multiplex movies, the pact around which all the others take shape—suspension of disbelief, what else?

What is it, under these conditions, that sets Godard apart from Luc Besson, i.e., *mutatis mutandis*, the avant-garde painter from the academic painter? This latter is aware of his immediate social interest and subjects his technical and aesthetic wherewithal to it; he targets, or thinks he's targeting, a clientele, or—less cynical but less intelligent, too—he thinks he's serving perennial and universal values, whereas he's unwittingly adjusting to the taste of those who bring him honors and material advantages. He deals with his medium as if it were transparent, and this medium thus becomes the means—which is precisely what the word medium entails—in the service of a purpose which is to reach the public with which the pact is signed and sealed in advance. His strategy of address is selective, even and above all when he wraps it in a universalizing discourse. The other is a receiver at the end of a chain of communication. The avant-garde painter, more sensitive to the fragility of aesthetic pacts but infinitely more ambitious when it comes to their scope, more alert, more alarmed, and possibly more panicked by the indeterminacy of his addressee, addresses his medium as if it actually embodied this addressee. For him, the other is not at the end of a chain of communication, and the medium is not a channel or a means (which doesn't mean that it is an end in itself). The medium is the other in the second person. It incarnates and materializes the addressee's otherness. Indeed, because the medium of painting is made up of the technical and aesthetic conventions of the trade, its matter and materials may well be oil on canvas, plus the way to use them; its real substance is the pact. And where there is a pact, there is an "us." And where there is an "us," there is an "I" and an other. How are you to unravel the conventions of the trade that are valid for this "us" from those that aren't—or aren't any longer, or aren't yet—when you don't know who is the other in the "us," except by questioning the conventions themselves? And how are you to question them, except by addressing them? But how then are you to make visible the fact that you have addressed a convention? When you're a visual artist, you ought to visualize things. How, except by making the convention opaque, so as to make visible the pact hiding in the technical-aesthetic rule, and show that the pact depends on us? That it's contingent, like all pacts? How are you to bring this contengency into play, except by subjecting the technical rule to an aesthetic test on the part of the viewer? And how are you to test this rule, except by mishandling it, breaking it, or abandoning it? The modernist or avant-garde painter subjects the other to whom he addresses his work to the challenge of renegotiating the technical and aesthetic conventions of the medium by acquiescing to the broken or abandoned convention; in other words, by drawing up a new pact around a broken one. Rather than asking his public to ratify the quality of his painting within the existing conventions which, at any given moment in history, define what a painting should be, the modernist painter asks it to bring its aesthetic judgment to bear on these very conventions. To sign and seal a pact about a pact. Orthodox modernism, in the wake of Greenberg, translated this with the formula: painting-about-painting. Abstract painting where form is concerned, self-reference where content is concerned. And the latest theories, in the wake of Duchamp, translate this with the formula: art-about-art. Meta-art testing the social conventions of the artworld. Both discourses are obsolete. There is more in modernism than the "meta-pact"; the one invented by Manet is not this kind of pact. The time has come to revisit the period when the artworld was known as the Salon and when the premises of abstract painting were laid down by the man who invented painting in the second person. His testament hasn't yet had the last word.

Manet, our legacy

So, we're in January 1882 and Manet, afflicted by locomotive ataxia—a degenerative disease related to multiple sclerosis and possibly resulting from syphilis—feels that his condition will not give him time to round off his *œuvre* as he wished. He is just fifty years old and surmises that the long life accorded Titian or Rembrandt is not going to be for him. Just as he embarks on the large painting he is planning for the next Salon, he is still possibly hoping for public recognition, and he has no idea that this painting will truly become his testament in the days to come. He quite simply savors the idea of transporting the Salon visitor to the Folies-Bergère, which have been recently restored and become the must destination of night birds and tourists. A superb set for the new scene of modern life he has in mind, this fashionable *café-concert*—where the social classes intermingle and sample the new forms of mass entertainment dazzling Paris—is, moreover, a place not that different from the Salon. There, as in the Salon, the different social classes rub shoulders with each other, buy and sell one another forbidden pleasures, and play the game of appearances and pretenses. The banker has come there to slum it, the demimondaine to play at being the worldly woman, and the bourgeois to pose as a Bohemian; barmaids supplement their meagre pay with occasional prostitution; and everyone is involved in temporary intercourse, usually of an erotic and venal variety, which infringes upon class barriers and boundaries. The way social conventions are transgressed in places such as the Folies-Bergère suggests more than one analogy with the way artistic conventions are renegotiated at the Salon. Manet is well aware of all this. The difference is that, in the cabaret, people deal with other people through the mediation of various exchanges of money, consumer goods, and services, and that, at the Salon, people deal with artists through the mediation of their work. Let's stay with this for a moment—the word "mediation" doesn't quite ring true. We have already seen as much with regard to Ryman, and we are beginning to glean the historical reasons for it: rather than addressing his public *through the mediation* of his medium, the modernist or avant-garde painter—the painter who paints in the second person—addresses his medium while he is at work, and then addresses his finished painting to the beholder. The address takes place in two stages. Manet didn't address us through the mediation of the *Bar at the Folies-Bergère*. Not knowing who makes up this us, he addressed himself, *while painting*, to the painting conventions of his day, in all their uncertainty and contradictoriness. This was the address that motivated him throughout the execution of the painting, until the end result called *A Bar at the Folies-Bergère*. Then, by signing the painting and assuming responsibility for it, he addressed it to us. Like Ryman refraining from adding to his canvas the one touch too many that would make his art topple into *peinture soignée*, Manet abandoned the *Bar* to its "definitively unfinished" state (Duchamp's expression), and abandoned to the *Bar* the responsibility of presenting itself on its own and adressing us. It is on this two-tier address that the new pact hinges. The first stage takes place in the studio, the second in the Salon. Hence the importance of the final touch, which not only crystallizes the moment when the painter, as the first beholder of his picture, gives way to the second, but also symbolizes the picture's transportation from the studio to the Salon. Hence, likewise, the importance of the model. Unlike Ryman, Manet is figurative. He has a model in the studio, and it is to this model addressing the beholder that he hands over the responsibility for addressing the picture to us. The whole question is now one of knowing if the model does the mediation, and if so, in what sense.

So let's venture into the studio and watch Manet at work on *A Bar at the Folies-Bergère*; it is by watching him paint that we shall have some slight chance of understanding what it meant, for him, to address the conventions of his medium. With a bit of luck, we shall even be eye-witnesses to the invention of painting in the second person, in all its complexity. The gaze of the *Surprised Nymph*, the bristling cat in *Olympia*, Victorine's blush in *The Railroad* and Suzon's in the *Bar* all involve the second phase of the address, the moment of the "here you are" when the pact is signed and sealed. It was during the first phase that the pact was hammered out, while the painter was at work. Admittedly, the scenario that follows is speculative, but it is

Édouard Manet

Study for *Un bar aux Folies-Bergère*, 1881

based very closely on the painting's x-ray and what it helps to recreate in terms of the painter's successive pentimenti. Manet has not in any way embarked on his painting with the aim of turning it into his last will and testament. Before his eyes is the sketch he's just made on the basis of a few preliminary jottings done on the spot, and he is in the process of transcribing it onto a large canvas. The sketch shows a sidelong view of one of the balcony bars, the barmaid, and her reflection in the mirror behind her. The mirror also reflects the image of the audience for the show on the balcony opposite, as well as that of a little fellow wearing a hat and clutching a cane, who is off-screen, and who was modeled, as we have seen, by the painter of military subjects, Henri Dupray. The point of view, which is lower than in the final version, is also considerably more to the right, and also off-screen, as indicated by the right-hand edge of the bar. The scene is plausible despite the absence of any frame around the mirror. We can see that there is a mirror thanks to the barmaid's reflection. We can also see, thanks to the reflection of the little fellow with the cane, that a transaction is under way between the barmaid behind her bar and someone who is on our side of the bar—or picture. We may already wonder whether Manet indeed has the intention of transporting the Salon visitor to the Folies-Bergère, or whether he's not trying to transport a Folies-Bergère customer to the Salon as well.

Any kind of transport calls for a vehicle. Manet set great store by the fact that his model should be a real Folies-Bergère barmaid, something quite new. In the Victorine days, he had never shied away from getting his favorite model to play the part of a person observed in real life, like the street singer spied coming out of a café scoffing cherries, who wouldn't pose for him. For the *Bar*, he is keen on having model and character really overlap: the barmaid is to be the vehicle that will transport to the Salon what the painter has really seen at the Folies-Bergère. This decision was already made at the moment of the sketch, which shows us a barmaid with frizzy hair, hands clasped at her waist, turning her head toward the little fellow with the cane. But on the brink of transposing the sketch onto the definitive canvas, Manet opts for

Édouard Manet

X-ray of *Un bar aux Folies-Bergère*

a change in casting. He must have found the barmaid in the sketch either too vulgar or not moving enough for the final painting. He's had another model come to his studio, a fair-haired young woman with a ruddy complexion, called Suzon. Suzon duly poses, her hands clasped just like her colleague, but her eyes staring straight ahead—a direction of the gaze that is essential to her function as vehicle. It's because we see her seeing us that Suzon is in the Salon. The x-ray shows that, at this stage, the whole picture is just a blueprint transcription of the sketch, except that Manet has straightened the barmaid's face, and thus caused her to lose her eye-contact with the customer at the bar and transfer it to the viewer. He must have realized, at this juncture, that the viewpoint of this latter had to be central. No longer any question of putting it to the right, off-screen. Suzon is seen head-on, while her reflection refers to an oblique viewpoint. Something is no longer quite right here. The perspective is incoherent and, what's more, the picture is out of balance. Should he give up on the frontal viewpoint and risk destroying Suzon's expression, virtually perfect from the first try? Manet can't bring himself to do that. Or should he just get rid of the reflection or put it in its proper place, almost invisible behind Suzon's back? That would be a pity. The viewer might no longer understand that there is a mirror in the painting, a *mise-en-abyme* that's crucial to the status of the fellow with the cane who—and this now starts to become clear—doesn't depict merely a Folies-Bergère customer; he, too, is a vehicle, transporting the Salon viewer into the painting. How to solve this dilemma? If only Suzon could keep her eye-contact with the Folies-Bergère customer *and* with the real Salon visitor, she would act as a go-between, and do the mediation. Her gaze would address her partner in the story being told by the picture and, unbeknownst to her, address the picture to the viewer by the same token. Manet, in short, wants to have his cake and eat it too: a picture that doesn't "know" it is being looked at, and a beholder who does know that the picture "knows" it is being looked at. Is this compatible with the minimum of verisimilitude required by the laws of optics? As a pragmatist, the painter has a mirror set up in his studio. To shift the reflection of Suzon to where it already is, as in the sketch (the x-ray shows Suzon's head reflected in the place of the globe on the pillar in the background), he simply has to turn on its axis the mirror rising behind the barmaid's back, bringing the right side closer to him. No sooner said than done. Manet glances over the scene, which confirms the verdict of the sketch's transcription: the picture would be too laden on the right, with those two adjoining blue-black masses represented by the barmaid's jacket and its reflection. He pivots the mirror further to bring the reflection a bit more to the right, so as to detach it from Suzon and form a distinct mass that no longer throws the painting off balance. Manet plays with his mirror, and swiftly brushes in the reflection more or less halfway between the place where it was in the sketch and the place where it will be in the finished picture. In the process, he unclasps Suzon's arms and has her hands resting on the edge of the bar, thus lending her not only the symmetry and monumentality required by the head-on composition, but also a physical prop to relieve her tiredness. She has been on her feet for hours, obliged to smilingly serve all those men ordering drinks, bantering with her, sizing her up, and, in some cases, making dubious propositions. From the very first brush strokes, Suzon has shed her smile and wears her ineffable melancholy pout and her lost look. Indeed, her face is painted without any pentimento, unlike Victorine's in *The Railroad*. Little by little her figure gets fleshed out; her character acquires density, social meaning, and humanity. And the picture begins to take shape. But at this moment, the reflected figure of Henri Dupray, transposed directly from the sketch, is no longer suitable. The little fellow with the cane is a bit pathetic, and decidedly Lilliputian beside the statuesque Suzon. So Manet decides to redo him, and there occurs a second change in casting, with a more impressive gentleman, sporting a proud moustache and wearing a top hat, to replace the little fellow. It is another painter, Gaston La Touche, who stands in for Dupray in this role.

Here is La Touche, with his incredible name, back once again. He would only become worthy of his name when, in making Suzon blush, he would incarnate, in the second person, the final touch to the painting. We haven't quite gotten there yet. La Touche probably replaces Dupray quite simply because his physique is better suited to the job. The important thing, at this stage, is that a painter should be playing the role of the customer. A real painter, a colleague and a contemporary, someone active at the same time as Manet, and the male counterpart to the real barmaid physically transported from the Folies-Bergère into the studio on rue d'Amsterdam. Manet has put himself in the painting by proxy. There is nothing new about that. The idea of delegating to a figure in the painting the task of representing the painter dates right back to Alberti who, in his *Della Pittura*, recommended putting in a corner of the painting, in the foreground, a figure called the *festaiulo* or admonisher who, with his forefinger pointing at the depicted scene and his face turned toward the viewers, would present the *istoria* being narrated by the painting. This character is looking at the viewer, but not so as to tell him or her: "look at me," but rather: "look at what's going on in the painting." The *festaiulo* is both the presenter of the scene represented, and the painter's delegate addressing the beholder in his name. What he presents to the viewer is the finished picture. Unlike the *festaiulo*, La Touche is not—or not yet—the representative of the painter who has finished his painting. He represents Manet *at work*, inasmuch as he is presented addressing the barmaid, the way Manet himself is addressing the painting conventions of his time. The clue, if it is one, is well-hidden. We may well wonder if it's not earmarked exclusively for future art historians, who will have done their detective work and discovered that the man in the top hat was posed for by a painter, and then by another painter—something that Salon spectators and present-day museum visitors alike are not supposed to know in order to appreciate the work. We may indeed wonder about this, not because it's flattering for us, as art historians, but because tossing out clues, like you'd toss a bottle into the sea, in the hope that someone might one day stumble upon them, could well be a way of addressing the painting conventions of the period, while signifying, to whoever might discover therein the secret of the new pact, that this pact is by no means a convention. One of those bottles thrown into the sea recently reached its destination, when an art historian, Juliet Wilson-Bareau, discovered that the door and the window visible just to the left of Victorine's hat in *The Railroad* were the door and window of Manet's studio, located at that time at N° 4, rue de Saint-

Petersbourg. So the *Bar* isn't the first time that Manet has himself represented at work by an element in the painting for which he has offered no clue, but which itself is one. In the *Bar*, through a colleague, and in *The Railroad* by his working place. It is probably not irrelevant that he had felt this need in the very painting where, for the first time, he had the beholder incarnated, in the second person, in the flushed complexion of its female character.

Like the decision to get a Folies-Bergère barmaid to play her own part, the decision to have himself represented in the painting by a colleague was made at the moment of the sketch. In the painting? More precisely, in the mirror that is in the painting, in other words, in front of the scene depicted by the painting. Dupray's role, taken over by La Touche, becomes more complex. The dear colleague represents Manet at work while also depicting the Folies-Bergère customer who, himself, should in the end incarnate the Salon visitor, who, in turn—as we have seen in the previous chapter—still needs my own presence in order to become "really" alive. And to top it all, one imagines that it is also as the first viewer of his painting that Manet has himself represented by his representative in it. Heavens, what an imbroglio. Forgive me for waxing technical, but the words here are of paramount importance. Representing, depicting, and incarnating are not interchangeable. Neither Dupray nor La Touche depicts Manet, for neither man has his features. Neither man incarnates him, either. This isn't their role, and never will be. Dupray and La Touche represent Manet. When you have yourself represented by someone else, you don't have yourself incarnated by that someone. The Congresswoman you've voted for doesn't incarnate you in the House of Representatives. Manet chose the two men, one after the other, to be his delegates, because they were, like him, representatives of the corporate body of painters. Lastly, they don't remotely represent—in the sense that the Congresswoman represents—the fellow with the cane or the man in the top hat to whom they lend their features, and they only incarnate them in the most conventional sense, namely, by acting as models, in the studio. Which means they don't incarnate them at all, unless you're content with basing incarnation in painting, conventionally, on suspension of disbelief—whereas this is, obviously, the broken pact. Let's leave Dupray now, since he's just been replaced by La Touche, whose role is to represent the painter without depicting him, and to depict the beholder of the scene without representing him. And without incarnating either of them. But at the moment of the final touch, when La Touche would at last deserve his name, he would end up incarnating, in the second person, the painter as the first viewer of the painting at the very moment when he yields his place to the second viewer. The pact would then be signed and sealed.

Hold on, the final touch hasn't yet been put down—far from it. Let's get back to the studio in rue d'Amsterdam, where Manet is hard at work on the *Bar*, anxious about placing Suzon's reflection where her face-to-face with the man in the top hat would come across unambiguously, without, however, causing her to lose eye-contact with the viewer. He can now try out various mirror angles with his models—Suzon not budging, and La Touche whom Manet asks to stand facing Suzon so that their eyes would meet. By pivoting the mirror, he further shifts the reflection of the

Jean-Louis Forain
Le Bar aux Folies-Bergère, 1878

young woman toward the right, once, twice, and brushes it into the picture. (The x-ray proves that the reflection underwent three successive rightward shifts, the last one kept.) The barmaid's encounter with the man in the top hat is now very close, even intimate. Manet will hang on to it, even if the reflected image of the couple no longer has any verisimilitude in the mirror, whose gilded frame, along with the frontal point of view, obliges us to imagine it as being parallel to the picture plane. (You actually have to imagine Manet—like someone in computer graphics working with Photoshop—pasting into the parallel mirror an image seen in the oblique mirror, and thereby robbing the viewers of the clues that might help them understand the mirror's rotation.) It must be during this trial-and-error process that he realizes that La Touche's reflection in the oblique mirror falls (or could be made to fall) in the same spot as Dupray's in the parallel mirror of the sketch. Dupray had stood a bit in front of the righthand edge of the bar, a place perfectly accessible for a customer in the real Folies-Bergère, as is shown by a gouache by Jean-Louis Forain, a painter-reporter decidedly less imaginative than Manet, and whom we can therefore trust when it comes to the realism of the setting. If, in the sketch, Dupray appeared to be talking to the barmaid, this is because she turned her head his way. La Touche, for his part, is facing Suzon across the marble countertop installed in the studio, and Manet is looking at the couple in the oblique mirror. As he starts to outline La Touche's silhouette over Dupray's, he realizes that he is no longer looking at anything like the same spectacle as the one he had before his eyes when he was painting the sketch. On the one hand, La Touche's back blocks him from seeing Suzon; on the other, the oblique mirror offers him a view of La Touche head-on and Suzon from behind. Something clicks in his mind. Manet asks La Touche to move to where Dupray was, and straightens the mirror (fig. 1). His reflection is identical to what it was in the oblique mirror a minute ago, when La Touche stood facing Suzon (fig. 2).

Manet has just realized that if two positions of one and the same character can yield a single reflection, then he will not only have managed to make Suzon keep her eye-contact with the Folies-Bergère customer *and* with the Salon viewer, but he will also have managed to *prove* that such is the case. The decisive fact that one and the same reflection of the man in the top hat, in a mirror that has meantime been pivoted, should serve for his two successive locations "in reality," establishes an equation, clinched by the even more decisive fact that Suzon's reflection is compatible only with the oblique mirror, whereas the reflection of the man in the top hat is compatible with the parallel mirror as well.

How do artists come by their consciousness? And consciousness of what? The click in Manet's mind is purely intuitive, and accompanied by intense intellectual excitement, as if the painting knew something that remained unconscious in the artist. Manet has clearly not proceeded by way of the bird's-eye view to which the commentator is reduced. He has discovered by chance, and in retrospect, that the painting was conceived as it is constructed, and he doesn't seek either to explain or to explain to himself the incredible condensation of meaning whose potential wealth he glimpses in the intensity of his excitement. But he reacts instantly and plants a clue in the picture which proves that *A Bar at the Folies-Bergère* was consciously conceived as it is constructed, even if its conception had germinated in his mind during its execution and was not in any way a calculated plan. The clue is the small vase of flowers on the bar countertop. Off to the right, on the edge of the frame, just above Suzon's lace cuff in the mirror, we can see the reflection of a rose hastily brushed in, its green stalk turned toward us. There's only one way to explain its presence there: the mirror is oblique and has been pivoted at the same angle, precisely, as the angle required to place the reflection of Suzon and her interlocutor right where they are. Everything fits. Speculative as it may be, the scenario of the painter's successive pentimenti suggested earlier makes the conception of the painting described here compatible with the way Manet worked—about which we have some information thanks to the x-ray. The painter has stumbled upon his discovery quite by chance, and achieves full awareness of what he has done only in retrospect. But at the moment

Édouard Manet

Un bar aux Folies-Bergère,
1881–1882

when he realizes that, in disguising the rotation of the mirror, he has obliterated the irreducible lapse of time separating the man in the top hat from himself in his two successive positions, he also understands that he might get it to say something that is troubling him. He has a foreboding that before long his illness would kill him, and that the *Légion d'honneur*, which he has recently been awarded through the good offices of his friend Antonin Proust, would not, for all that, make his painting any more comprehensible to his contemporaries. He feels that he is going to die without the new pact sought out in *Surprised Nymph*, *Olympia*, and *The Railroad*, being signed by the Salon visitors to whom his paintings were addressed in his lifetime. In short, he knows that his real public is his posterity, and he senses the possibility of bequeathing it a picture-testament which, in extraordinarily condensed form, sums up his lifetime of effort.

Once again, slow down the big dipper making its loop-the-loops in the head! View the film frame by frame, cut the soundtrack, hush the pom-pom music, freeze the trapeze artist in mid-flight, and set up a meditative silence around the painting. Don't think that anyone's going to utter the ultimate truth about this painting, but indulge in a bit of theoretical daydreaming. Like a scribe copying out what he sees without understanding it, commit to paper scenarios which are engulfed in the breach between the two moments presupposed by the conception of the painting. It's the same man who's addressing the barmaid, askance and head-on, but it's not the same man at the same moment. Let's go with him from the first of these two moments to the next, and to make our task that much easier, let's turn the *Bar* into a film. Let's pretend it has been filmed in a sequence shot, of which the film-maker has kept just the first and the last frames, overlaying them one on top of the other. The storyboard, drawn up in plan, would be like a cartoon going from figure 1 to figure 2: the mirror pivots on its axis while the gentleman moves on his arc of a circle, the two movements being synchronized in such a way that the reflection of the gentleman in the mirror doesn't budge. Figure 3 represents this double movement halfway. Suzon, posing, holds her position throughout the sequence. The camera, static, is at the apex of the visual pyramid, where Manet's and the beholder's eyes are. The set has been

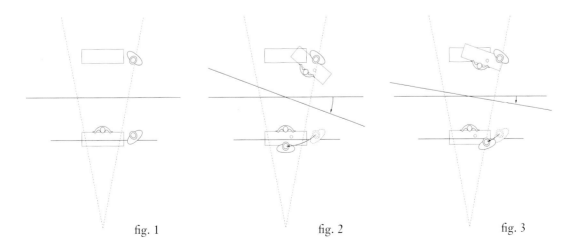

fig. 1   fig. 2   fig. 3

recreated in Manet's studio. We, for our part, are in a multiplex moviehouse—sorry, we're at the Courtauld Institute, in London; but no, we're in Paris, at the 1882 Salon; who are we? For the time being, consenting victims of illusion, quite prepared to suspend our disbelief. So we are in the Folies-Bergère, and the man in the top hat is walking up to the bar, from the right. He is off-screen and hasn't yet managed to catch the barmaid's eye, unlike his counterpart in the sketch, but his reflection is already in the frame. The film is in period costume, and we have no problem recognizing an ordinary bourgeois, somewhat stiff in his clothes, who's come in search of fun and adventure at the *café-concert*. In the credits, we've been told that a certain Gaston La Touche, a painter by trade, lent his features to the character. But the last thing on our minds, engrossed in the film as we are, is that this La Touche is not at the Folies-Bergère but actually in Manet's studio, and assigned by the artist to a dual role: that of representing him in his capacity as a painter, and that of depicting the customer on the screen. In his first role as a representative, he has a triangular relationship with, on the one hand, the female model and, on the other, the mirror, which is a picture within a picture, or a screen within a screen. He is the understudy for Manet at work, busily transferring Suzon onto the canvas (here, there is no further analogy possible with film). In his second—depicting—role, he is in front or, at most, on the threshold of the scene, and still off-screen. If he does depict the man in the top hat on the screen, this is solely through his reflection. The mirror bounces him back to the place occupied both by the customer in front of the scene and by a cinema-goer who's arrived late and hasn't yet taken his seat in front of the screen— sorry, a Salon viewer approaching the painting from the side and from the right, the way the customer approaches the bar. Here La Touche takes on a third role, that of the vehicle transporting the Folies-Bergère customer into the Salon. All this without having budged yet from his eccentric position. But now he is budging. And the mirror pivots, perfectly synchronized. The effect is fantastic. The barmaid remains totally motionless, as does the gentleman's image in the mirror. But the barmaid's reflection shifts to the right and moves toward his, while he himself enters the screen, and his back eclipses the view of his reflection for a short while, then the

Stop

« Une marchande de consolation aux Folies–Bergère », *Le journal amusant,* 1882 reflection of Suzon and, lastly, Suzon herself. In the last image, he has come to stand between her and us. How irritating: the latecomer to the film disturbs the whole row without waiting for the end of this thrilling meeting scene, and passes brashly in front of us. And how fascinating, too, for this filmgoer is our man in the top hat! In *The Purple Rose of Cairo*, Woody Allen fared no better. The effect is all the more fantastic, irritating, and fascinating because the film has come from the George Lucas studios, where computerized special effects work their wonders, and because the reflection of the balcony where we are sitting hasn't pivoted with the mirror, as it should have. Nor has the mirror's frame. It's stayed doggedly parallel to the screen while the man in the top hat has walked over to the barmaid. This is the storyboard of the film that Manet didn't make but which, to all appearances, the caricaturist Stop has seen.

That's enough of cinematographic analogies. Stop saw things right when he deemed it okay to correct Manet by interposing Suzon's interlocutor between her and us. He understood that the Folies-Bergère customer had indeed been transported to the Salon, but as one viewer too many. Undesirable, irksome, and obstructing the other visitors' view. Has Stop also understood that it wasn't this particular viewer to whom Manet was addressing his finished painting, but to him, Stop? Or to every other ideal or posthumous viewer who would understand, like Stop, that the customer, depicted by his reflection in the mirror, is also and very paradoxically presented to us negatively? That is, through his absence from the space in front of the bar—or the *Bar*? One thing is sure: Stop has understood that in order to see the man in the top hat from behind, he himself had to be behind the man. That he himself was not that man, *alias* the undesirable Salon viewer. The place of the posthumous or ideal viewer is that of the painter, at the apex of the visual pyramid. As we shall see in a moment, Manet has managed to *prove* that the painter's place is behind that of the man, and that, if you have a good look, there is no other place for him—or us—to occupy. Yet the feeling we have about our position in front of the *Bar* is not spontaneously this one, so irresistible is the temptation to identify either psychologically or erotically with the customer, and so powerful the impression that this identification is desirable in order to get the gist of the picture. We're right. We must take a place very close to the bar so as to address Suzon, make her blush, incarnate ourselves in the second person in her very complexion, and thus sign the new pact that will give life to the painting without resorting to suspension of disbelief. But then, in the very moment when we sign the pact, who are we? The Folies-Bergère customer? Yes, it's our presence in front of the painting that finishes incarnating the customer. The Salon visitor? Yes, Manet made no distinction between painting for the Museum and for the Salon. Whether we are at the Courtauld in the year 2000 or in Paris in 1882, we run the risk of being that one obtuse viewer too many who, throughout Manet's entire life, didn't want to understand anything about the new pact, and whom Manet did not address. To address him would have been to flatter his expectations, give him hammam scenes filled with hysterical nudes, or Napoleonic battles with not a gaiter button missing. Rather than give in to this, Manet preferred to address the medium of painting, by challenging and capsizing its conventions. But there's a nuance here: that particular Manet, who didn't address the Salon-going public, was Manet at work, Manet painting, Manet in his studio, Manet who had himself represented in his picture by La Touche. At the moment when he put the final touch to the canvas—the touch that would redden Suzon's cheeks—it was La Touche again whom he delegated to make Suzon blush by addressing her with some seductive compliment or dubious proposition. We are also this La Touche who represents Manet but depicts the customer. We are him without incarnating him, without having him represent us, and without him depicting us. Nobody does the mediation in this sequence of transfers that excludes nobody from the address. For at the moment when, with the final touch added, Manet signs the *Bar* and becomes the first viewer of his own finished painting, he rejoins the Salon crowd at the same time as he carries the picture there, and abandons it to the expectations of the second viewer who, by his or her touched presence, will activate the fantastic see-saw of the blushing barmaid.

It is the same man who addresses the barmaid from the side and face-to-face, but it isn't the same man at the same time. It is the same painter who addresses the conventions of the painting of his day and age, and who addresses his finished painting to an indeterminate public, but it isn't the same painter at the same time. It is the same "we" standing in front of the finished painting, but it isn't the same "we" in the same time, depending on whether we're among the obtuse viewers of Manet's day or among those future viewers to whom he bequeathed his testament. The lapse of time that separates the man in the top hat from himself between his two theoretically successive positions has at least three meanings: the time of work, from the first touch to the last; the time of the last touch and the painter's withdrawal; the time of the stage entry of the second viewer. And the cycle—the rotation of the triangle, rather—can be repeated with the third viewer, then the fourth, and so on, ad infinitum. At each turn of the triangle, the posthumous or ideal viewer, who Manet asked to understand him by literally stepping into his shoes, comes, by definition, to place herself there where the painter was. There is no other place for her to occupy but the apex of the visual pyramid, as in good old perspective. Perspective is a weird thing. It mathematically establishes the sensation intuitively felt by all beholders of a picture that they're standing precisely where the painter was, no matter where they are in front of the picture, even if their point of view is extremely oblique. This sensation results from the fact that pictures are flat; and so, too, the sensation that makes us feel that the eyes in a portrait follow us when we move, or the sensation that spontaneously makes us correct the distortion of the screen when we are sitting at the end of a row in a moviehouse. Manet—and this is the least we can say—was as a rule not the painter who showed the greatest respect for the laws of perspective, he who was so offhand, so untheoretical, so apparently nonchalant, and so indifferent to verisimilitude. At first sight, *A Bar at the Folies-Bergère* stacks up perspectival anomalies with quasi-perverse pleasure. This is our Manet driven by the desire to be understood but viscerally incapable of giving in to the expectations of the public to achieve as much. He probably found that by putting, for once, the Salon viewer into the picture, albeit in a mirror, he had already been too didactic. As a result he intentionally cranked up the number of perspectival anomalies, such as the bottles on the left of the bar, whose reflection is no more in its right place than that of the couple. But from the moment he became aware of the theoretical advantage he could derive from his altogether empirical game with the rotation of the mirror, perspective became a matter of paramount importance to him. He didn't use it to construct his painting; rather, he relied on it to provide those viewers puzzled by the inconsistencies of the mirror, yet curious enough to seek immanent visual explanation in the painting, with just enough clues to allow them to deduce from the vanishing point the spot where they are placed in front of the painting.

But where is the vanishing point? The only clearly indicated orthogonal, or vanishing line, is the lateral edge of the marble bar reflected in the mirror. Two intersecting orthogonals (or one intersecting with the horizon) are required to determine the vanishing point, but Manet doesn't offer us any other that has the degree of certainty of the first, nor does he offer us any horizon. It is intuition, not theory, that comes up with the vanishing point. We are facing the barmaid, and she has been placed directly in the center of the painting. Manet underscored the median line—the bridge of the nose, the medallion hanging from Suzon's neck, the spray of flowers tucked into her bodice, the row of pearl buttons, and the crease that ironing has left in her skirt, bisecting the flare of her jacket—the artifice couldn't have been more obvious. The vanishing point can only be found, intuitively, at the intersection of the extension of the edge of the reflected bar and the *visual* median line of the painting. The x-ray reveals that Manet made a couple of stabs here. A first vanishing line representing the edge of the bar departs from a point between the apéritif bottle on the extreme left of the counter and the bottle of Bass to its right. Its prolongation intersects the median line of the painting between the barmaid's eyes. The definitive vanishing line runs parallel to this one, shifted just a tad to the right, starting from a point between the bottle of Bass and the first bottle of champagne, and intersecting the median line at Suzon's mouth. The spatial shift is very small indeed, but the symbolic shift is considerable, as if Manet had been insisting that what was at stake in the face-to-face encounter between Suzon and her customer was not the specularity of gazes, but the reciprocity of addressed speech.

Don't be in any doubt that, in a moment, Suzon will respond to the man who's made her blush with his address to her. But that moment is not in the picture; it's in what the picture has bequeathed us. Would Manet have wanted to give Suzon back the use of words? It's very possible. The symbolic shift of the vanishing line suggests, in any event, that he's understood that he had first robbed her of it. And with Suzon, women. As with Olympia's suitor and the *flâneur* in *The Railroad*, even women must have seen themselves incarnate in the man with the top hat at the moment when he addresses Suzon and when she answers in her flesh, by blushing, involuntarily, and not by addressing him in words. This is a role women are thoroughly entitled to find unpleasant: insofar as they're endowed with speech, they are turned into "guys," and insofar as they're women, like Suzon, they only have their body to reply with. They may very well reach the conclusion that *A Bar at the Folies-Bergère* is a picture that isn't addressed to them. Some have. They might also reach another conclusion, something more subtle but no less problematic, which weighs with a considerable historical weight on incarnation in painting in the western tradition. Men monopolizing speech while women are granted the power to incarnate, in their bodies, the word received—doesn't this remind you of something? "And the Word was made flesh." God the Father inseminating the Virgin Mary through her ear and being incarnate in her in the second Person of the Trinity—this is the founding moment of the Christian narrative, whose three steps we've travelled, in this book, in reverse order: Annunciation, Incarnation, Resurrection. It is also the founding theorem of a theology of the image invented in Byzantium in the 8th and 9th centuries by the iconodules—or those who venerate icons—in their struggle against the iconoclasts. Since these latter had accused them of worshipping idols—in other words, of lending divine substance to a mere *thing*—they riposted with a analogical theory, whose argument goes roughly like this: just as the Son of God, who is the image of his Father, was born from the virgin womb of a woman impregnated by the divine word, so the icon, which is the image of the image, is born from the virgin surface of a wooden panel inseminated by the painter's work. So don't accuse us of adoring bits of wood! We know how to tell a God incarnate in his image apart from this image in turn incarnate in an image's image. In this theory, the painter doesn't take himself for God; at the most he has a role akin to that of the archangel messenger bringing God's word to Mary. Once the painter has prepared the wooden panel by applying to it coat after coat of white gesso and sanding them, he draws the outline of the figure without ever closing it, for, like Mary's womb, the panel is a finite space designed to accommodate the Infinite. He then applies color to it in successive coats which bring

Robert Rauschenberg
Mother of God, ca. 1950

the image to light, and he ends up by inscribing the icon's name on it, to signify that the word is incarnate therein. The Eastern church kept this iconic tradition virtually unaltered, but it was the Western church that made the most of all its artistic and ideological potentialities. The theory developed around the second Council of Nicaea, in 787, was the remote foundation for the injunction received by the Baroque painters at the Council of Trent, between 1545 and 1563, to put all the power of images at the service of the church's propaganda.

Manet had certainly no knowledge of the theological bedrock of his practice, but, like all his colleagues, he was dependent on a long tradition which had assimilated its tenets, secularized them, and forgotten their origins, but in which they remained subterraneanly active. They would stay active throughout the history of modernist painting. That particular pact wasn't broken by modernism. The lack of finish of modernist painting, its deliberate "Cistercian" poverty, the emptying-out that drove it to the monochrome, indeed to the threshold of the blank canvas, all can be interpreted as modern versions of *kenosis*, where the Byzantine icon inscribed the grace of an Absent. There is an early Rauschenberg painting titled *Mother of God* which is almost literally the incarnation—the apposite word, if ever—of the Byzantine theory. Rauschenberg wouldn't have known all its analogical subtleties, which shows to what extent it continues to do its underground work in the history of western painting— and not just painting but the entire history of images—unbeknownst to artists. Nobody has gone quite so far as to interpret *A Bar at the Folies-Bergère* as an Annunciation in disguise, but some have seen in the posture of the barmaid, arms spread and palms up, an iconographic borrowing from the imagery of the Immaculate Conception that invaded Catholic France from 1854 on in the form of medals and pious images, before long parodied again and again by anti-clerical literature. It was in that year that Pope Pius ix proclaimed the dogma of the Virgin being born free of original sin, and rebooted the Marian cult, with the obvious aim of reasserting the church's authority over its "eldest daughter," and with the hardly more disguised aim of putting the brakes on the emancipation of women. In the *Bar*, there's no more than the slight shift of the vanishing point from Suzon's eyes to her mouth which attests a desire in Manet to break with a thousand-year-old pictorial and religious tradition which assigns gender to profoundly inegalitarian statuses before paintings—and before creation. This is not much, and nothing proves it was intentional. But Manet was sensitive to the social tremors of his day, and especially to those which affected gender relationships. Despite the egalitarian one-to-one exchange of looks that is so perceptible in *Olympia* and *The Railroad*, these paintings still postulated a male viewer, and Manet could not be unaware of this when, in the *Bar*, he explicitly put him into the picture. The fact is that the Salon was governed by a relative equality of the sexes that was rare everywhere else and absolutely unthinkable in the Folies-Bergère. Dated as far back as the 18th century, etchings depicting the crowd at the Salon show us almost as many women as men. By 1882, a visit to the Salon had become one of the favorite leisure activities of women of the bourgeoisie, who went there unchaperoned, often with other women friends or accompanied by their children. By contrast, the only women you were likely to come across at the Folies-

Bergère were the dancers on stage, the demimondaines in the stalls and in the circle, the prostitutes in the aisles, and the barmaids behind their bar. No self-respecting woman would have ventured into that shady world—and definitely never alone. Thus, sexual difference introduces a serious asymmetry in the crossed transfers of Folies-Bergère customer to the Salon and Salon viewer to the Folies-Bergère. It may be that female visitors at that time found nothing to find fault with. For someone sensitive to present-day feminist issues, there is in Manet's testament something intolerable or, at the very least, unfulfilled, which puts a strain on his legacy. For a woman artist of today, the legacy is even heavier to bear: what is the point in having invented incarnation in the second person, if it remains modeled, no matter how sub-terraneanly, on the Incarnation in the second Person that underpins the Christian narrative? What is the point, if speech and creative inspiration remain the privilege of men and if the place of women is still that of the receptacle, the wooden panel, the virgin canvas, the medium? Women are barred from creation by a theory which casts the masculine and the feminine in this way. There is strong need for a new theory of the image incarnate which will enable women artists to occupy, in relation to their creative work, a position other than that of "virgin and mother," imposed upon them by the Christian doctrine of incarnation. When an artist, male or female, receives the legacy of a predecessor, it is, if all goes well, in order to make something new with it.

Remake

Vancouver, 1979. Jeff Wall's *Picture for Women* is quite obviously a remake of *A Bar at the Folies-Bergère*. Why this title, *Picture for Women*? An image—or a painting, the English is ambiguous—addressed to women? Apparently because *A Bar at the Folies-Bergère* seemed to Jeff Wall to be a picture addressed to men, and also because the question of address mattered to him, an indication of his early awareness of mod-ernism's true content. Wall was still a young artist in 1979, and he had only recently found the medium that suited him. Like everyone else, he had done monochrome painting as a student before briefly venturing into conceptual art—like everyone else, too. It was in a context overdetermined by the reception of Duchamp's work that he produced his first piece, *Landscape Manual*, in 1969, in a spirit akin to Dan Graham's *Homes for America*, Robert Smithson's *A Journey to Passaic County*, and Ed Ruscha's little photographic books. Shortly thereafter, he bowed out of this scene and went to study art history at the Courtauld Institute, where he became acquainted with the work of Velázquez, Géricault, Goya, Manet, Degas, Seurat, and Munch, and wrote two dissertations examining the political prehistory of conceptual art in Dada-Berlin, John Heartfield, agit-prop, and Duchamp. When he resumed his artistic activities, in 1977, it was with his first transparency, *Faking Death* (a work he has since rejected), and after immersing himself in film, to the point of flirting with the idea of a career as a film maker.

There is cause to think that Jeff Wall's essential contribution to contemporary art lies in his invention of a novel medium. He is indeed known for being the first artist—prior to Alfredo Jaar and Dennis Adams—to use large cibachromes (color photos on transparent film) set in light-boxes similar to those advertising panels lit from within that you see in airports and on bus stops. But once the surprise effect has worn off and the impact of the images has been assimilated, the medium appears secondary. Wall merely "turned up the volume" to keep in pace with the level of intensity of a cultural environment where neither painting nor small-format photography could hope to compete with the seductive power of film and advertising. The real surprise caused by his work in the late 1970s lay rather in restoring pride of place to a 19th-century *pictorialist* genre of photography, of which Rejlander had been a much appreciated representative in his day, and has been a much decried one since: photography in the "directorial mode," staged and composed like a *tableau vivant*, and emulating painting. A rather academic genre, at that, whose theatricality brings it dangerously close to Salon painting. It was risqué. For an eye trained on abstract, minimal, and conceptual art, it even bordered on sacrilege. However, it is just that kind of training you would have needed in order to see that Wall was not working from within one of the traditions that had stood up to abstraction and had laid claim to realism—all ideological tendencies lumped together, traditions such as *Neue Sachlichkeit* in Germany, *Retour à l'ordre* in France, *Valori Plastici* and *Novecento* in Italy, Socialist Realism in the Soviet Union, or Precisionism and the *American Scene* in the United States. No, Wall belonged squarely to the modernist tradition ushered in by Manet, and seemed to want to go back to Manet's time as if toward a point where history forked in two directions, only one of which it explored. This is what makes his art unique. Manet is undoubtedly the first modernist painter in Greenberg's sense, but he is also the first *and the last* painter of modern life in Baudelaire's sense. Maybe not the only one: Daumier, Degas, Caillebotte, and a couple of others might well vie with him for this title. But none of these painters, including Manet himself, had any real progeny in this particular direction. They didn't give rise to a genealogy of artists capable of

Jeff Wall
Picture for Women,
1979

talking about the world in painting with the documentary wealth that Baudelaire lent the painter of modern life, but rather a genealogy of painters who sacrificed the world in order to save painting. This was abstraction. A hundred years later, it took a young artist who had experienced first-hand the risk of sterility in this genealogy, now that it had come up against the "last" monochrome, to decide to turn back to the point of bifurcation called Manet, in order to explore the path not taken by the history of modernist painting. Needless to say, he had to sacrifice painting on the way.

The medium that replaces painting in Wall's work is photography. In 1977, his light-boxes were something quite new, as was the scale of his enlargements; novel, too, was the advent of a curious category of artists who make photographs but don't call themselves photographers; in this context, what was most surprising was the activity of an artist who, precisely like the young Manet, felt the need to fill his works with learned iconographic allusions to the pictorial tradition. But photography, for its part, had not been a new medium for a long time already. Wall doesn't use photography the way a photographer does, like a medium focused on reality and sampling fragments of it. He uses it to make *tableaux*. He is, we might say, a "painter who makes photographs." A modernist painter? We've seen that rather than treating the conventions of his medium as transparent, the modernist artist addresses his medium. How do you make visible the fact that you've addressed a convention? By making it opaque, so as to reveal the pact hiding in the technical-aesthetic rule, something modernist painters did by literally making the transparency of the picture plane opaque. Whence the famous flatness dear to Greenberg. Well, photography is technically incapable of making the picture plane opaque. Whereas in a painted picture, even an illusionistic Old Master painting, the impasto of the pigment, the painter's touch, the grain and texture of the canvas, and so on, all attest the physical presence of the picture plane, the latter is invisible in a photograph. This is what caused Greenberg to say, in the opening sentence of a 1946 article about Edward Weston and Walker Evans: "Photography is the most transparent of the art mediums devised or discovered by man," adding a little further on, as if he had foreseen Jeff Wall: "… it would seem that photography today could take over the field that used to belong to genre and historical painting, and that it does not have to follow painting into the areas into which the latter has been driven by the force of historical development." In short: photography doesn't have to be modernist and, what's more, it doesn't have the means to be modernist, either.

Picture for Women gives it those means. Defining modernism, as Greenberg does, by the opaqueness of the convention and the flatness of the support, puts the emphasis on the pact drawn up around a broken pact. Wall seems to have realized that this discourse has worn out, and acknowledged receipt of Manet's testament by putting the emphasis on the address, which is the gist of the new pact. Let's bear in mind that the modernist painter addresses his medium while he is at work, and, once the painting is finished, addresses it to his public. Yes, but what about the photographer? In photography, the time of the making is reduced to the split-second of the shutter's click. The photographer doesn't have the painter's leisure of addressing his medium stroke by stroke, nor can he treat the image as a living interlocutor whose

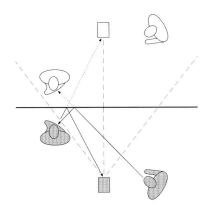

"responses" he experiences in himself. Almost everything that a painter experiences, brush in hand, during the execution of his work, is condensed, for him, in the snapshot. For the modernist painter, the address is two-tiered; for Wall the painter-photographer, the two tiers, or phases, merge into one. Question: did he address his medium at the same time as he addressed his picture to women? The image is life-size, like the *Bar*. The picture plane intersects a long wooden shelf, as it does the marble counter in the *Bar*. A young woman looks at us from behind the shelf, her hands resting on it, like the barmaid, but clasped. Instead of being in the center, she is off to the left of the image and her eyes are looking askance. To the right, almost in the spot where the Folies-Bergère customer was standing, there is a man—posed for by the artist—holding the remote shutter release of a camera that proudly stands right in the middle of the composition, at the vanishing point of the perspective. We swiftly realize that the camera has snapped itself in a mirror, and has captured the very instant of its own shutter action. And this is where things get complicated. Where's the mirror in *Picture for Women*? The allusion to Manet's painting has us spontaneously placing it behind the young woman, despite the absence of her reflection at her back. But we are mistaken. We are not mistaken, on the other hand, in putting Jeff Wall in the mirror he photographs, and thus in front of it, like the man in the top hat. The exchange of looks, and the disturbing sensation that this exchange is not an exchange, is the fascinating thing. Without it, there'd be nothing to stop us thinking that the whole scene has been arranged without a mirror in front of another camera, worked by another operator. The young woman is looking at us, but where's Jeff Wall looking? At her, yes, in her direction, but his gaze somehow lacks precision. If the photo had been taken by a second camera, clearly Wall would be seeing the woman from behind, which doesn't tally with our impression. It's only by proceeding by way of a bird's-eye view of the whole scene and its reflection, that we end up understanding that he's looking at her head-on, in the mirror; that the mirror isn't behind her, but actually *is* the picture plane; and that the young woman is thus on the same side of the mirror as the photographer—and as the beholder. The female beholder? *Picture for Women*, the title reads. The young woman who posed for the photo is among them. Has she freed them from the unpleasant obligation of identifying with a male beholder in order to bring the image to life, as was the case in front of *A Bar at the Folies-Bergère*? Sure. Conversely, does she oblige the male beholder to identify with a female one, as the title suggests? Not necessarily. Jeff Wall addresses his slightly anxious and dubitative eye to the young woman, who doesn't return his gaze. She addresses hers—a firm and intelligent and almost severe one, devoid of seductiveness or entreaty—to the camera that she sees in the mirror. The latter represents us (in the Congressman's sense), without either incarnating or depicting us. The camera is, in the image, the neutral stand-in for the male or female spectators which we are, before the image. It's up to us to incarnate it by taking its place. Its gender depends on us.

Picture for Women—the title—makes promises that the work doesn't keep, while the work keeps promises that the title has never made. Splendidly. So it goes with works of art; they're never where you expect them to be. Address to the medium and address to women cannot be told apart in Jeff Wall's work, and not just in *Picture for Women*. You must be thoroughly acquainted with his art to realize both that he is a romantic artist who does his utmost to hide it, and that, like any romantic artist, he combines political utopia and address to femininity. This is where he's at his most vulnerable. Doesn't the plural, in *Picture for Women*, shroud a singular? There's every reason to wager that the personal reasons why Wall called this work *Picture for Women* don't have a whole lot to do with what should make the choice of such a title more than disconcerting for us, at the stage we're at in our reading of *A Bar at the Folies-Bergère* and its remote theological underpinnings. But when an intelligent and rigorous artist sticks with a title, when he decides that it is appropriate because it has imposed itself on him, it's not necessary to presuppose that he's fully aware of its implications. There they are, regardless of him. A theoretician—and even a practitioner—of the Byzantine icon would, in any event, unsurprisedly draw the equation: "addressing the medium = addressing women." Or rather, *woman*, singular. Mary, the

Jeff Wall
The Destroyed Room,
1978

new Eve, mother of us all. That the panel acting as the support for the icon should be to the Virgin what painting is to Woman, namely the medium of incarnation, is the daily bread not only of the iconodule theologian, but of the least talented painter of icons as well. Despite the plural, *Picture for Women* doesn't break the equation. Let's say, rather, that it extracts it from a lengthy repression and that it sheds light on its banality and violence, taking shelter behind the theological sophistication. Banality and violence are even all that remains of theological sophistication when the equation is relieved of its analogical structure and becomes "painting = woman." "I paint with my prick," Pollock allegedly said. This produced some very beautiful pictures. De Kooning's *Women* are also very beautiful. But all this beauty nevertheless leaves us with the feeling that a pact hasn't been broken by modernism, which ought to have been, a pact among men at the expense of women, a male bonding in which the fathers of abstract painting and more than a few of their descendants have found one another. It is worth quoting in full this edifying excerpt from Kandinsky's *Reminiscences*, written a year or two after his shift to abstraction: "This is how I've learned to fight with the canvas, get to know it like a being resisting my desire, and subjecting it to this desire by violence. At first, it stands there like a pure, chaste maiden, with clear gaze and heavenly joy—this pure canvas that is itself as beautiful as a picture. And then comes the imperious brush, conquering it gradually, first here, then there, employing all its native energy, like a European colonist who with axe, spade, hammer, saw, penetrates the virgin jungle where no human foot has trod, bending it to conform to his will." All is said, even the rape of the dark continent by colonization. Let's take a look at *The Destroyed Room*, the first cibachrome Jeff Wall produced after *Faking Death*, shortly before *Picture for Women*. It's Kandinsky's text after the *acting out*. Or even before and after. A woman's bedroom has been destroyed, her wardrobe scattered all over the place, all the shimmering finery of her seductiveness flung onto the floor, her sex raped. The disembowelled mattress is her, afterwards. The little statuette dancing the dance of the seven veils, like Salomé in front of Herod, is her, too, before (her skirt is the same color as the sheet). And the upturned table, with its immaculate formica top tipped toward the picture plane just as the bed is tipped backwards, is her once again, before. We are left in no doubt as to the consciousness the artist has of the history he has inherited: the gaze moves from the virgin canvas to a slashed Fontana. Jeff Wall has made an image that condenses in one snapshot what Kandinsky, de Kooning, and Fontana all experienced brush in hand and fantasies in their heads, and addresses the ensuing disaster to us. Who's this us? All of us, men and women alike: *The Destroyed Room* was first shown in a display window giving onto the street, addressed to anyone and everyone.

We two, we all

Anyone and everyone, all of us, or in everyday language: you and me. The pronoun "we" has interesting properties. To begin with, it's the first person plural, which doesn't seem like very much at all, but already means two things: that "we," like "I," designates the speaker, and that it's a plural. "We" can range from "the two of us" to "all of us," but clearly you don't make up a *we* if you're on your own. Secondly, like all deictics, the word "we" is mobile and available to any speaking being, but it is an empty word. It doesn't express either who it's constituted by, or how many members it includes, or anything about what they have in common. Last of all, it can be broken down in two ways, but it doesn't say which: either into "they and I" or into "you and I." In the first instance, it excludes from the "we" those persons whom the speaker is addressing; in the second it includes them in it.

   Scarcely have we noted these three purely formal properties of this very simple little word, which we use casually a hundred times a day as if it were transparent, than it assumes a formidable opaqueness, and raises a thousand and one questions having to do with—how shall we put it?—its *flesh*. To do with the plural, first. "We" refers to a collective, a group, or a community, even in the royal "we" used by the high and mighty of this world, or in the conventional "we" used by authors to associate their readers with what they are writing. Save in exceptional and always somewhat disquieting cases, where a group speaks with a single voice, the speaker sets him- or herself up as the group's spokesperson, simply because s/he says "we" rather than "I." By what right? Has s/he been appointed to speak for the others, and in their name? Is s/he a legitimate representative of the group? Does s/he speak with authority? Already, the whole political question—the issue of power and its legitimacy—is swallowed up in the first person plural status of the pronoun "we." Next, as far as its nature as an empty, available, and mobile form is concerned. The word "we" doesn't express who this "we" is, a member of whom takes the floor in the name of the others, nor does it say of how many members the group is made up. Shouldn't another deictic, a finger pointing one by one at each member of the group, for example, inform the listener who hears someone say "we" about their identity? Or shouldn't the listener be informed in some other way about the identity category that gives to the empty form of the pronoun its substance? We francophones, we women, we contemporary art-lovers, we grocers, we old people—the categories can be very heterogeneous. Or, to the contrary, very structured, in binary contrasts: we Serbs, we Kosovars; we Israelis, we Palestinians; we Tutsis, we Hutus; we Chechens, we Russians. By these latter examples it can be surmised that "we human beings," in other words, "we all," is not that easy a thing to say. It is understandable that, if we add this particular example: we Nazis, we Jews, this might seem impossible to some. Lastly, the third and most noteworthy of the properties of the pronoun "we" is also the most formal, because it doesn't display the content, substance, or identity of the we, but solely its relationship to the address. Take for example a "we two" whom we shall call Adam and Eve, so as not to make anyone jealous. Eve says to Adam: "We love each other," and Adam, enthralled, runs off to proclaim their love from the rooftops. Both of them spoke of the couple they make, but for Eve it was "you and I" and for Adam "she and I," simply because Eve was addressing Adam and Adam was addressing the rest of the world.

   The example is a silly one, but appropriate for getting across the fact that all the issues revolving around the pronoun "we" touch it in its *flesh*. Sexual flesh, mortal flesh. For starters, who says that Adam and Eve love each other? They were created to have offspring and then die, and endowed by their Creator—sorry, by natural selection—with the organs and hormonal metabolism necessary to this end. They desire each other and engage in intercourse at times—but who knows whether they love one another?—and the rest of the time they're on their own, seeing to who hunts and who gathers, each happy-go-lucky about themselves and the other. Their awareness of their difference and their separateness, and of what love might well mean, will come to them with the Fall, poor things, when they will dream, in hindsight and with the nostalgia which embellishes the past, that everything was hunky-dory in paradise, that they were united night and day, for better not for worse, merged together, and that there was no need for Eve to appoint Adam or for Adam to delegate Eve to speak in their name. Oh yes. In its earthly paradise, humankind basked in the amniotic fluid of Mother Nature blessed by God the Father. Some people have not renounced the dream. Before the Fall, Adam and Eve deserved no credit for loving one another, and even less for spreading their love to the rest of humanity. They *were* humanity. We two, we all, same thing. And same struggle, which didn't fall on deaf ears in the next generation. As soon as humankind numbered four, it counted one man too many, and started waging the fratricidal wars that have been the fodder—canon fodder—of its history ever since. But let's not go too fast. Let's still suppose that they are in paradise, our friends Adam and Eve. They are in love. Eve says as much to Adam: "We love each other, you and I," and Adam says: "We love each other, she and I"—to whom? They are the only human beings in the world. To the little birds, perhaps, like St. Francis of Assisi? Yes, to God. From the third property of the "we" there issues an admirable consequence that everyday language spontaneously recognizes when it uses the words "you and I" to mean "we all." Unless it is addressing a being—or a Being—outside humanity, the expression "we all" *must* be translated by "you and I." Actually, a "we" that is broken down into "they and I" cannot refer to us all, because it is leaving at least one individual out of the we: the addressee. All it takes is one outcast—just one—for humanism not to be universal.

Ah! big words. Too many crimes have been committed and too many treasons perpetrated in the name of humanism and universality for anyone to hear these words once again without wincing. Yet humans are hopefully still here for a long time to come, and on a planet that is now globalized. How are we to do without big words? Possibly by using little ones. Very simple little words like "we" and "*voici,*" light, moveable deictics, available to one and all, free, content-less words, but words which make us reflect on their formal properties. The advantage of the formal properties of words over the content of words is their abstraction. The advantage of pronouns over nouns, and substance-less deictics over substantives, is that they are exclusively formal. And the advantage of works of art over other products of human desire is that they deal with their contents formally—in short, treat big words as little ones. Artists have nothing original to say about what is pompously called the great humanist themes—life, death, love, war, happiness, grief, etc.—nothing, at least, at this level of generality. It's into forms, into their work on form, into formal invention, that they put what they have to say. In art, form is content. The modernist discourse has to be well-worn for "formalism" to have become a dirty word and "abstraction" the dated reference to a school of painting that is a mere century old, as if Khmer statuary, Olmec pottery, and Fang sculpture were less abstract than a Kandinsky or a Fontana, on the pretext that they embrace the human figure. To understand why abstraction was an *explicit* necessity in the 20th century, we would be best advised to proceed by way of a formal analysis of little words like "we" than by way of the great humanist themes. The abstract or modernist artist addresses the conventions of his or her medium. Conventions are social pacts. The content, material, substance, or subject matter of a pact is what links the partners of the pact together. Examples: belief in one and the same god—and the pact is a religious one; obedience to one and the same law—and the pact is a legal one; interest—and the pact is an economic one; the city's welfare—and the pact is a political one; carnal desire—and the pact is a sexual one; love or friendship—and the pact is an affective one, and so on. These categories are seldom pure, and the links rarely detached from their opposite. Just think of military alliances struck up out of interest, despite mutual hatred, or of the camaraderie that unites sportsmen, despite the competitiveness, or of political solidarity, or economic rivalry, or—because this is what we're dealing with here—the love of art. The substance of these pacts is complex, variable, enigmatic, and mixed, but the substance of their substance—their flesh—is the pact itself. An *us*. By addressing his or her medium, the modernist painter addresses the us. Yet it is not possible, formally—in this case, grammatically—to address an us. You address a *you*, for the addressee is perforce in the second person. Addressing the pact as such would be dealing with an us as if it were a you, while dissolving a pact would be dismembering the us. By breaking the convention, the modernist artist apparently dissolves the us in its substance. She actually grasps hold of a property of the us that is not substantial but formal, in order to dismember it—hence the association almost invariably made between modernism and formalism. This property is precisely the one that the pronoun "we" has: its ability to be formally broken down in two ways, either into a "they and I" or into a "you and I," without affecting the substantial identity of the partners of the we—the same people are involved. A we or an us broken down into a "you and I" contains a pronoun in the second person. It is because the pact to which the modernist artist addresses her request for a new pact is a we which has the form of a "you and I," that she can, without betraying, address herself to it. Dealing with this "we" as if it were a "you" is thus to remove the "I" from the "you and I." The artist withdraws from the pact she addresses, hence the "kenosis" of modern art. She withdraws from her work as both author and authority. She sets her materials free, she listens to them, she lets them act as they see fit, she grants them an autonomy which they have not been prepared for by their nature as simple technical means. She deals with them with the respect due the other, that other being addressed.

As we have seen, the avant-garde begins when people no longer know whom art is addressing. And when you no longer know whom you should be addressing, there's every chance, too, that you will no longer know, either, in whose name you are speaking. And vice versa: when you are no longer certain that you're a legitimate representative of the "we," the identity of the "you" wavers. The Greek poet, the bard, used to be the spokesman of the city. He had a place in society because he was appointed by the community to address it. Greece is the paradise lost of modernity, sung about with nostalgia by the early Romantics, when they imbued it with an ideal of universalism inherited from Christianity and secularized by the Enlightenment. All the artistic utopias of modernity bear the mark of the political dream of this paradise lost projected into the future. Its tenor is the same everywhere: the artist *must* address all, and s/he *can* if s/he is mandated by all. The dream embraces the whole human race, guided toward progress, freedom, and happiness by a particular avant-garde, depending on the author, but in which artists are usually the avant-garde of the avant-garde. "In this great undertaking, artists, men of imagination, will open up the way," observed Saint-Simon. Here we are back with the big words. The invention of art in the second person is the inversion of the romantic utopia: the artist can say s/he is mandated by all if s/he addresses all. S/he can speak in the name of a we which is a *we all*, if s/he considers it as a "you and I." This is likewise a utopia. Its advantage is that it is concrete and aesthetic rather than ideological. It eschews big words and gets incarnated in the works. If it came into being in France, this was probably because the very specific conditions of the Salon offered those artists who were most sensitive to their time—with Manet foremost among them—a concrete and incarnate perception of humanism and universality which, today, proves to be a formidable antidote to big words. Humanity—that lofty notion—flocked to the doors of the Salon in the form of a throng with heterogeneous tastes, talking loudly and smelling bad. Anyone and everyone, the *hoi polloi*, people like you and I. But the price hitherto paid by art in the second person has been exorbitant. It's abstraction: people have been removed from artworks. They have stopped being represented in them, because artists could no longer legitimately call themselves the representatives of the community. The social conditions which would have enabled them to regain the place of the Greek bard within the community weren't there, and utopia does not replace reality. The aesthetic pacts which modernist artists sought to sign with their public are singular, joining individual work to individual beholder, or, even more singular: *this* touch in *this* touching picture striking *this* sensitive chord in *this* individual. By addressing you, and you, and you too, without presupposing in these "you"s anything shared, modernist art alienated itself from the *you all* to whom it was addressed. So modernism is still absorbing the utopian debt of Romanticism. It doesn't *want* to know whom artists represent or whom they're addressing, and this is why the fantasy of the merger of artists in the *we all*, where the difference between mandate and address is erased, periodically recurs. Joseph Beuys, who never ceased to proclaim that everyone is an artist and that creativity defines man, was the last great romantic artist, in whom all the threads of the modern utopia converge: the Greek thread, the Christian thread, the revolutionary political thread, and even the Marxist or Marxian thread—the thread of an anthropology which defines man's humanity through labor power. But Beuys sacrificed himself on the altar of modernity, and these days everyone is brooding on the bereavement of utopias. Those disappointed artists and intellectuals who started talking about postmodernity in tones of bitter irony some twenty years ago were, if you will, the avant-garde of actuality. The fall of the Berlin Wall caught up with them. There are no longer many people left to

Sylvie Blocher
Three of Us, 2000

lament the paradise lost that lay on the other side of it. The big words have been buried, but who is still raising the issue of the legitimacy of the artist in speaking for all of us? The world is attending to its affairs and art is business as usual. Abstraction, figuration, who cares? There is a market for every taste, and contemporary art addresses the artworld, period. What gets forgotten is that art—which is probably as old as humankind and its fratricidal wars, as old as politics and its power struggles, and certainly as old as religion—is one of the major modes, separate from the religious, the political, and the economic, in which human beings have fabricated an "us" to attest the *us*. Take "us" to mean here: forms of co-existence, and *us*: the flesh of the social bond. The alliance of flesh with a form is what has been defining works of art ever since Adam and Eve.

There is always food for thought in the titles that Sylvie Blocher gives her works, and *Adam et Ève* (1993) is one such title. Others, like *Elle et Lui* (1995), *Entre tú y yo estamos nosotros* [*Between You and Me There's Us*] (1995), *them(selves)* (1998) and *Three of Us* (2000) all involve those little words called pronouns. *Three of Us* took eight years to gestate and was billed from the outset as a piece about flesh, which it actually is, now that it's done: a triptych of circular video images projected like tondos and showing extreme close-ups on the human body, patches of skin, genitalia, body parts mutually touched and touching. It is the third part of a trio of works which the artist has gradually thought of as a triptych itself, with the title first given to the first part, *Déçue la Mariée se rhabilla* [*Disappointed, the Bride Put her Clothes Back on*] (1991). The second, *Le partage du secret* [*Sharing the Secret*] (1992) was an installation work comprising nine plywood volumes of various forms and, already then, a tondo-shaped video projection. It showed the artist's lips silently mouthing a text by Maurice Blanchot, precisely titled "Le partage du secret." In spite of the tondo that links this piece to *Three of Us*, a full eight years separate the two works, during which the artist has been intensely active both on a theoretical and on a practical level—an activity that turns out, in retrospect, to have been a prerequisite for the execution of her project on flesh. A work taking incarnation as its subject matter called for a new theory at the same time as a new practice regarding the image incarnate. We shouldn't be surprised that this theory has come into being through the work of a woman: it is primarily for women artists that Manet's testament dragged in its wake an inequality with respect to creation that's as old as Christianity.

The video image incorporated in *Le partage du secret* showed the artist's own mute mouth. In the aftermath of this piece, Sylvie Blocher became gradually convinced that if she was to go on using video, she would have to film other people rather than herself, address them first, and let them talk: "I couldn't give substance to flesh if I didn't give the figure a face. First of all, I had to deal with addressed bodies." Out of that conviction arose the concept of *Living Pictures*, which she elaborated in 1994. She embarked that year on a series of video works bearing that generic title, and for which she gave herself the following motto: *rendre la parole aux images*—to give images back their speech. The first, *L'Annonce amoureuse* (1995), was shot on the occasion of the Saint-Denis film festival, *Actors on Screen*, and featured the thirteen young French actors and actresses who had been nominated for the Michel Simon prize for exceptional performances in films made that year. This piece marks a turning-point in her work, and the springboard for a series which, to date, consists of ten or so *Living Pictures*. So, in *L'Annonce amoureuse*, it is actors and actresses who do the talking, as chosen by circumstance. The artist asked them to address the camera and make an "amourous announcement." She said "*annonce amoureuse*," allowing various related *annonces* to suggest themselves, such as "*annonce publicitaire*" (advertisement) or *L'Annonce faite à Marie* (the Annunciation in Paul Claudel's eponymous play). Of course, "declaration of love" was the primary meaning she attached to the expression, "*annonce amoureuse*," and she made that clear. In the camera's stead, the actors and actresses were at liberty to imagine whomever they wanted. Since they were addressing the camera framing their faces in close-up, and looking straight at it, they could hardly ignore it, the way movie actors are usually taught to do, so as to create the illusion that the spectators are privy to a scene that is only intended for them by tacit agreement. The thirteen "announcements" were spliced together end-to-end in the editing, the artist having allowed herself the choice of a sequence within each take but not the possibility of cutting and choosing within that sequence. The

Sylvie Blocher
Living Pictures /
L'Annonce amoureuse,
1995

piece—an installation with projection on a large screen—was shown for the first time at Saint-Denis in March 1995, during the festival, set up in an old chapel bathed in half-light. The screen, thin and translucent, unframed and apparently unsupported, was hung from thin steel cables, and set slightly a-slant in space. On the floor stood seventeen sheets of plywood, cut out in the shape of stylized pieces of furniture, looking like standard furnishings for a model apartment. Their dimensions had been taken from an Ikea catalog. The video tape of *L'Annonce amoureuse* defies description, so disarmingly simple is its aesthetic form. The end-to-end editing lets each of the young actors and actresses speak in turn. The frame is tight, the editing too. Silences are long and inhabited. The visages are unshielded and naked, and yet very physical. The eyes are naughty, or sexy, or downright sexual. Or shy, or cocky, or desperate, or packed with seduction, but always, always full of demands. There are raucous shouts and tinkling giggles on the soundtrack, and a fair number of slips of the tongue. None of the actors control their expression. When viewing the tape, the sensation of being addressed is incredibly strong, yet that of being addressed as the beloved one is totally absent. The content of *L'Annonce amoureuse* makes it a very moving work for anyone who hasn't silenced within themselves the call for love, but its form prohibits any romantic identification with the beloved ones. The outcome is that the projection splits the public in two: those who are touched and those who are not, or rather, who won't allow themselves to be touched. Those who accept and those who reject the new pact.

At issue in *L'Annonce amoureuse* is indeed the new pact, one notch further than Manet and the abstract art that stemmed from him: acknowledging receipt of the vanishing point's symbolic shift from Suzon's eyes to her mouth, and, in so doing, giving images back their speech; basing incarnation on the address to the medium and on the sessaw effected, as the artist says, by the fact of "dealing first of all with addressed bodies"; undoing any possible confusion between address to the medium and address to *woman*, which is after all still the case in modernism and abstraction. A whole program, tantamount to nothing less than trying to once again take up the issue of incarnation from where the second Council of Nicaea had left it, and blazing a novel trail for its solution, a trail which no longer assimilates the medium to a virginal womb fertilized by the word of God—or raped by Kandinsky's brush. Well, if the painter's medium is oil on canvas plus the way to use it, the filmmaker's or video artist's medium is the actor's performance and the camera to capture it. In *L'Annonce amoureuse* the address to the medium begins with the address to the actor, or actress. Isn't this the point of departure of the Annunciation? "Hail, Mary. Blessed art thou among women." Yes, but there are three essential differences between *L'Annonce amoureuse* and the Annunciation. The first is that the artist's word is neither the word of a God the Father nor the word of a messenger angel, but the word of a woman. The second is that the actors and actresses nominated for the Michel Simon prize belong to both genders. And the third is that in the Annunciation, God was in charge of the casting. Mary was the chosen woman, and it was her acquiescence to her election among all women which prompted her to answer: "I am the servant of the Lord," and then duly conceive. Mary's acquiescence, it should be noted in passing,

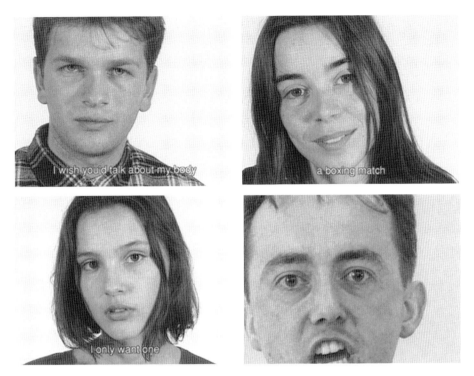

Sylvie Blocher
*Living Pictures /
L'Annonce amoureuse,*
1995

caused Sylvie Blocher to conceive a piece titled *La Vierge Marie est une mère porteuse non payée et soumise* [*The Virgin Mary is an Unpaid and Submissive Surrogate Mother*]— which is enough to hint at the twist she imparts to the iconodule doctrine. When the artist pounced on the Michel Simon award ceremony to make *L'Annonce amoureuse*, she didn't handle the casting herself. She accepted as a given the thirteen young actors nominated on the basis of their acting talent, all competing for the same prize. They had acted in different films and would not be acting together in *L'Annonce amoureuse.* They formed what Sylvie Blocher first called a "fictitious community," and a bit later a "pseudo-group"—people brought together quite by chance on the basis of a certain shared characteristic. Unless they feature a single individual, all the *Living Pictures* call upon "pseudo-groups"—this is a rule: artists from the same gallery, citizens from the same city, residents of the same apartment block, players in the same sports team, or members of the same profession, like the Toronto cab-drivers in *them(selves)*, who also have in commom that they are all immigrants. Here, the common characteristic was that they were young performers with only one or two films, at most, under their belts. A good actor is a piece of clay in a director's hand, and, to be a good actor, you need this particular psychology, not really comprised of submissiveness, but involving all the same a mix of malleability, a desire to please, and a measure of "femininity" and "hysteria," which a good director will know how to exploit for the public's benefit. This psychology forms the basis for the pact which unites the director, the actor, and the audience—a pact which Blocher radically breaks. She addressed the performers with a request that forced them to confront their own freedom. When she approached them, individually—explaining to them that what they would have to do, if they agreed to the rules of the game, would be neither fiction cinema nor reality-show nor any kind of psychoanalytical outpouring—she was keenly conscious of the fragility of their young careers. Some would be forgotten, like so many actors who never get a second chance; others would possibly be bidden to become stars, or, alternatively, find their calling on the other side of the camera. (Both have happened: Gaël Morel has become a film maker, while Elodie Bouchez, Mathilde Seigner, and Virginie Ledoyen have all been propelled to stardom.) She knew, then, that in accepting her invitation, these young men and women would be exposing their budding self-image as professional actors. The game was not without its stakes for them; doubly so in that, far from having to bring to life a character and say its lines, they were being asked to be themselves and make up their own text. One may imagine their helplessness facing an artist equally helpless inasmuch as she had given up all the postures of authority usually ruling a film shoot and reassuring those involved: the postures of author, scriptwriter, and director. The only solid pact binding the artist and the performer was the loss of part of their authority on either side. Otherwise a sort of floating contract with several unknown factors, for both parties completely open-ended as to results, must have been the basis for their consent. Chief among the unknowns was the question of whether the actors were going to act their declaration of love. Can you stop an actor from acting? When you're an actor, can you refrain from acting?

Some of the young actors and actresses thought their *métier* would carry them through the assignment easily. Isn't a good actor supposed to cheat persuasively? It was for these actors that the shooting experience proved to be the most difficult—though it was hard for all of them—for they hadn't realized that all the conventions of their *métier* had been turned upside down and inside out. They had been trained to be aware of the camera's presence but to ignore it; now they were asked to look the camera "in the eye" while being oblivious of its presence. Trained to address their partners on the movie set and no one outside; now their addressee would be their partner in life. Trained never to stare at the camera unless it personified a protagonist in the story; now the camera would personify a protagonist in their story who was never part of the script. It was not just the conventions of their *métier* as actors that had been turned upside down and inside out, but the whole social pact which makes people in multiplex cinemas on a Saturday night laugh and cry. By accepting the rules of the game set forth by the artist, the actors and actresses in *L'Annonce amoureuse* drew up a new pact around a broken one. What did it consist of? When an actor is instructed by the film director to momentarily break the convention which has it that the whole action should take place on a stage where the fourth wall is missing, and to address the camera directly by looking it "in the eye," it is the audience that he imagines in the camera's stead and addresses. Not so in *L'Annonce amoureuse*. In the camera's stead is the beloved one. Or perhaps we should say behind the camera, through the camera, on the other side, in that mysterious space where all actors in full-flight project the audience of the finished film. It is an item of Hollywood folklore that the place behind the camera should be marked and occupied by a chair with the director's name on its back. When shooting a *Living Picture*,

Sylvie Blocher leaves the director's place conspicuously empty. No chair in that spot, nor anywhere else. She monitors the image on a screen from a position alongside and slightly in front of the model, so as to make her presence felt while being out of the frame and to open a void at the back of the camera. And she never sits down, she stays on her feet, never offering herself any more comfort than she offers the model. It is this physical void, this withdrawal of the author, and this renunciation of authority which enable the camera to presentify the beloved one for the actor.

The originality of *L'Annonce amoureuse* is that the film is made up of thirteen love stories of couples, only one of whose partners appears on the screen. The other is outside, on the same side of the screen as the audience. Not in the film, with the actors, but in life, and in more than one sense, because the actors address their declaration of love to their significant other. Each one of the thirteen couples is by definition a "we two," but what is noteworthy in this work is the composition of the "we two" as far as the address is concerned. Between the two heterogeneous forms of the "we two," referring either to "he and I" (or "she and I"), or to "you and I," the choice is unhesitatingly: "you and I." We'll never know who is the "you" in these "you and I"s, and even less so if the message has come through. In some instances, we don't know the gender of the beloved one who is absent from the screen. Nothing proves that the love affairs of these young men and women are all heterosexual. But we do know with certainty that the couple is face-to-face, and that the "you" is not on the screen. This is the originality of *L'Annonce amoureuse* as compared with multiplex movies. But as compared with Manet? Ever since *Surprised Nymph*, the film—sorry, the painting—has been made up of a story about a couple only one of whose partners appears in the picture. How does Sylvie Blocher take the problem of incarnation a notch further than Manet? In *A Bar at the Folies-Bergère*, Manet delegated to La Touche the function of… the touch, in every sense of the term: he put the final touch to the picture by making Suzon blush; he possibly imagined that he'd scored a hit (*faire une touche*); he has touched the poor girl, he has seduced her, or hurt her, or angered her, who knows? His role was to activate the seesaw of "touching-being touched," which would ensure that the viewer would in turn be touched by the involuntary blushing of the young woman. Suzon's feelings didn't count; they were just a way of winning over the viewer's emotions. Apparently, it hadn't crossed Manet's mind that a female viewer might identify with Suzon rather than with the man in the top hat, and that she might take offence at the fact that the viewer was supposed to be touched by the humiliation of a woman. Bringing a woman to blush is such a cliché of male vanity—and of violence, too, innocuous as it may be—that one feels embarrassed for Manet for having resorted to such a stale stratagem in order to activate incarnation in the second person. If it were merely a matter of feminist sensibility, he could be forgiven on the ground that this issue was less developed in his day than in ours, but there is more to the matter than this. Also involved is what incarnation in the second person owes to Incarnation in the second Person, and the mortgage this debt puts on the future of art, today. *A Bar at the Folies-Bergère* is indeed an Annunciation, in its own totally secularized way. And so is *L'Annonce amoureuse*. It is even more explicitly an Annunciation, if only by dint of its title. In both instances we are dealing with addressed speech incarnated in the addressee's body and returned to the sender as a manifestation of its flesh. For this is what is meant by the flesh of the image, or the image as flesh: it is a body that has been addressed and which manifests it; it is what a body incarnates of the word received. With Manet, the body is female. With Blocher, both genders are concerned. The emotion of the actors and actresses is palpable in the image. Even with those you feel are trying to act their declaration of love, control of their facial expression eludes them: between the slips, the wavering voice, the tears and the nervous giggles, the endless silences, broken—as in the case of this boy who blushes red like a peony and finally lets out a coy: "*T'es belle*"— by a sentence which isn't the one they'd planned to say, what is given us to see and hear are the touching manifestations of their flesh touched. The French word best suited to these manifestations is *maladresse*, clumsiness, inasmuch as it is often the clumsy, inadvertent, involuntary, *poorly addressed* part of what a person intentionally communicates to us that makes us find him or her touching. Are these manifestations an equivalent to Suzon's blushing? Like it, do they achieve the reversal of a message addressed as a message returned to sender, without it being addressed at all? Yes, but with one additional transferral, which shifts the seesawing of the message and changes everything. Sylvie Blocher herself assumes the function of La Touche, Manet's stand-in. But rather than seeking to stir up trouble among her models by way of some dubious proposition (the way we can easily imagine the man in the top hat issuing such a one), she asked them to talk. Not just to talk but, quite explicitly, to utter an addressed word; not just addressed, but addressed to the person of their choosing; not just of their choosing, but of their amorous choosing. It's as if, rather than announcing to Mary that she is the chosen woman through whom the Messiah shall be incarnated, the archangel Gabriel had asked her to choose her god or her man, and then asked her to anounce to him that she wants to be made pregnant by his works—or that she already is! Begging her models to make a declaration of love is not as banal and innocent as asking them to say: "Pass the salt." In a way, Sylvie Blocher was begging love from them herself. But not for herself. For X. In answer to her request, the actors and actresses then addressed to their beloved one a declaration of love which in most cases conveyed, and not surprisingly, an intense demand for love. You have to be a saint to say: "I love you" without implying: "Tell me that you love me." With Manet, it was the blushing that effected the seesaw of the address; with Blocher it's the fact that any declaration of love carries a quasi-automatic built-in reversibility of address—a desired one, needless to say, hoped for, begged for, often surreptitiously imposed on the addressee, all things that the declaration of love of the actors and actresses in *L'Annonce amoureuse* amply confirm—but which, here, doesn't depend on our willingness to respond in order to be activited. When the tape is projected, we viewers take the place of the absent beloved one. However, nothing is stronger in *L'Annonce amoureuse* than the sensation that these declarations of love are not addressed to us. If we are touched, then we are touched, as in Manet, by the inner turmoil unintentionally betrayed by the flesh of the models—which doesn't prevent us from being likewise touched by their demand for love, but inasmuch as it is palpably not being addressed to us. This is possibly what the artist sought to say when, in the wake of the *Living Pictures*, she formulated the concept of *double touché*, associated in her mind with the concept of *double sexué*. The medium is no longer in an exclusively female position. The void behind the camera, which presentified the beloved one *for the actor*, also presentifies *for the artist* the X which, *for the public*, will state the enigma of incarnation in the finished film. Sylvie Blocher could well have chosen another theme or content for her piece, something less intimate, less problematic, and less romantic than a declaration of love. The piece would not have been so successful. She has had to "crank up the volume" to an extreme level of sentimental intensity in order to make visible, as if it were her subject, that the work is successful to the degree that the viewers respond to a demand for love with their love for art.

Isn't this the demand that every work of art addresses to us? Of course, but this is so rarely said, even among those people who answer to the beautiful name of "art lovers," especially if it is modern, modernist, or avant-garde art which is their preference. Love is not numbered among the bellicose virtues associated with the word avant-garde. "Strategy" is on everybody's lips but "love" gives rise to embarrassed smiles. It's not serious, not intellectual enough, quaint, not to say queer. It smacks of schmaltzy romanticism, in a nutshell, of femininity, or, worse still, effeminacy. Even those feminists who are eager to denounce the fuddy-duddiness—phallic, in this particular case—of Kandinsky when he intones: "This is how I've learned to fight with the canvas, get to know it like a being resisting my desire, and subjecting it to this desire by violence," are wary of giving in to what they take—or are afraid might be taken—for cheap sentimentalism. It's odd. As if love were reserved for human beings of the female sex; as if it were steeped in charitable feelings and nothing else; as if it didn't imply an ethical relationship to the other and to otherness; and as if it didn't concern all of us, both genders. The lid of censorship weighs on love in treatises on aesthetics, in art criticism, and in the way art history, especially that of the avant-gardes, is written, and this must certainly indicate some significant measure of historical repression. You don't need to be a cynical psychiatrist to recognize that love is transference neurosis. Better to be a historian and wonder why hysteria—that *female* prototype of transference neurosis—surges up, or up again, in the midst of that huge cultural crisis of paternity which shook the 19th century, with the death of God as backdrop. Or better to be an artist, and a woman, and look for a way of bringing images into being other than issuing from the nervous pregnancy of a Virgin fertilized by the Paternal word. This is what Sylvie Blocher strives toward—and she is certainly not alone—in her *Living Pictures* and in the theoretical work accompanying them, convinced—let's quote her—that: "If modernity has created potentials, one of its great failures has been its relationship to authority and the feminine. The fathers of modernity have either covered up or killed their feminine side. Not 'women' but the feminine which they carried within them." It is not the Kandinsky quote which will prove her wrong. Under the lid of the modernist repression of the feminine seethes romanticism, that major disease of love contracted in the aftermath of the disenchantment of the world and the death of the Father. We haven't finished absorbing its utopian debt, witness Beuys. And beneath the lid of romanticism seethes Christianity or, rather, Christianity without God. Its theory remains to be written, its practice perhaps to be invented. It's a huge construction site many people are working on right now, which is a good sign. Artists can contribute their stone, alongside philosophers, political thinkers, and even—why not?—theologians, if they are brave enough to confront the void. The anthropological definition of the religious is "that which links," involving the *we* where its flesh is concerned and the "you and I" where its form is concerned. Christianity is the first universal religion and the first one founded on this unique principle: "love thy neighbor as thyself"—an ethical value which cannot be reduced to transference neurosis. You'd have to be either crazy or depraved to dare say that this value is not a value, and you'd have to be blind to history not to see that, for the past two centuries at least, it has no longer essentially been a religious value, but that it has changed into a political one. Isn't *Solidarnosc*, to take a fairly recent example, a political name for love, and one which means "we all"? *We* ranges from *we two* to *we all*. The death of God altered the deal to the point of having apparently made humanism impossible and universalism suspect. Art could well have foundered, been crushed beneath the weight of big words too cumbersome to bear. But no, it reacted by working on little words such as deictics and pronouns. The expression "we all" *must* be translated by "you and I" rather than "they and I," because it could no longer be addressed to a Being outside humanity. It is not for nothing that the question of the address to one and all has been at the core of the new pact which the avant-garde tried to draw up around art. Because modernity had stopped triangulating the relationships among humans by the common reference to a Father, up there, it became a necessity for art to work at other triangulations, opening onto an X. Some people think that it is possible to cope without triangulation, by deploying all human relationships in the flatness of immanence. History teaches us, until further notice, that this is not possible, and that it is dangerous to repress the third tip of the triangle: there are too many Stalin-wanabees and too many televangelists keen to set themselves up there. As far as art history is concerned, it also teaches us something: that artists—the great ones—have always been aware of the misunderstandings on which those social pacts were based, which gave them an apparent place within the community. Even the Greek bard. They have all obscurely felt—how should I put this?—that art was older, or closer to the common anthropological plinth, than religion. The priests have not had the last word.

The Salon

On the history of the Academy and the Salon, in addition to the essays mentioned in Chapter One, see in particular:

Nathalie Heinich, *Du peintre à l'artiste, Artisans et académiciens à l'âge classique* (Paris: Minuit, 1993).

Andrée Sfeir-Semler, *Die Maler am Pariser Salon 1791–1880* (Frankfurt-am-Main / New York: Campus Verlag; Paris: Ed. de la Maison des Sciences de l'Homme, 1992).

Théodore Gosselin, *Histoire anecdotique des Salons de Peinture depuis 1673* (Paris: E. Dentu, 1881).

Francis Haskell, ed., *Saloni, gallerie, musei e loro influenza sullo sviluppo del'arte dei secoli XIX e XX.* (Bologna: Proceedings of the xxivth International Congress of Art History, 1979).

Harrison C. and Cynthia A. White, *Canvases and Careers, Institutional Change in the French Painting World* (Chicago: University of Chicago Press, 1965–1993).

Thomas Crow, *Painters and Public Life in Eighteenth-Century Paris* (New Haven, CT: Yale University Press, 1985).

Richard Wrigley, *The origins of French Art Criticism. From the Ancien Régime to the Restauration* (Oxford: Clarendon Press, 1993).

On attendance figures for the Salon:

For 1765: 20,000 according to Diderot in his *Salon de 1765.*

For 1783: 100,000 according to the *Journal de littérature, des sciences et des arts;* between 500–600,000 according to the *Observations générales.* These figures seem far-fetched. Carmontelle estimated the daily number of visitors at the 1785 Salon at between 700 and 800, yielding a total attendance of between 21,000 and 28,000. See Wrigley, p. 80, who gives the figure of 20,000 booklets sold for 1783. The exact figure is 18,387, given by Udolpho Van de Sandt, 'La fréquentation des Salons sous l'Ancien Régime, la Révolution et l'Empire,' *Revue de l'Art,* 73, 1986. Van de Sandt multiplies the number of booklets sold by a factor of three and offers a sensible, ableit non-demonstrative, explanation of this coefficient.

For 1846: 1,200,000 according to the *Journal des artistes.* According to *L'Artiste,* there had already been 1,000,000 Salon visitors in 1841. In 1836, the *Moniteur universel* estimated that 30,000 people had flocked to the Salon on opening day, and *Tam-Tam* that, a fortnight later, half the population of Paris had been to the show. See Wrigley, p. 80.

For 1857, when admission-free Sundays were introduced, see Sfeir-Semler, pp. 50–51: 181,586 paying visitors, as compared with 265,180 visitors taking advantage of the free-on-Sunday offer, yielding a total of 447,766. The population of Paris at that time was 1,174,000.

The various quotations from the *Mercure de France,* Fréron and Mercier are taken from Wrigley, pp. 85, 103, 105.

Manet

There is plenty of literature on *Un bar aux Folies-Bergère.* See in particular:

Timothy J. Clark, 'A Bar at the Folies-Bergère,' chapter 4 of *The Painting of Modern Life: Paris in the Art of Manet and his Followers* (London: Thames & Hudson, 1985).

Bradford R. Collins, ed., *Twelve Views of Manet's 'Bar'* (Princeton, NJ: Princetown University Press, 1996). With contributions by Carol Armstrong, Albert Boime, David Carrier, Kermit S. Champa, Bradford Collins, Michael Paul Driskel, Jack Flam, Tag Gronberg, James D. Herbert, John House, Steven Z. Levine, and Griselda Pollock, and an introduction by Richard Shiff.

Ruth E. Iskin, 'Selling, Seduction, and Soliciting the Eye: Manet's *Bar at the Folies-Bergère,*' *Art Bulletin,* March 1995.

Novolene Ross, *Manet's* Bar at the Folies-Bergère *and the Myths of Popular Illustration* (Ann Arbor, Mich.: UMI Research Press, 1982).

Juliet Wilson-Bareau, 'Cafés-concerts and the Folies-Bergère,' *The Burlington Magazine,* April 1986.

Robert Bruce-Gardiner, Gerry Hedley, Caroline Villers, 'Impressions of Change,' in *Impressionist and Post-Impressionist Masterpieces: The Courtauld Collection* (London and New Haven: 1987). (On the x-ray of the *Bar.*)

Thierry de Duve, 'How Manet's *A Bar at the Folies-Bergère* is constructed,' *Critical Inquiry*, 25, Autumn 1998. With a critical response by James Elkins, and a response to the response.

On the allusion to the iconography of the Immaculate Conception in *Un bar aux Folies-Bergère*, see:
Michael Paul Driskel, 'On Manet's Binarism: Virgin and/or Whore at the Folies-Bergère,' in *Twelve Views of Manet's 'Bar.'*
Michael Paul Driskel, *Representing Belief: Religion, Art, and Society in Nineteenth Century France* (University Park, PA: Pennsylvania State University Press, 1991).

On the discovery of Manet' studio in *Le chemin de fer*, see:
Juliet Wilson-Bareau, *Manet, Monet, and the Gare Saint-Lazare* (New Haven, CT: Yale University Press, 1998).

On the issues of Annunciation, Incarnation and Resurrection, their importance for pictorial aesthetics, and the relationships between western art and Christianity, see:
Marie-José Mondzain, *Image, icône, économie* (Paris: Seuil, 1996).
Alain Badiou, *Saint Paul, La fondation de l'universalisme* (Paris: PUF, 1997).
Thierry de Duve, 'Come On Humans, One More Stab at Becoming Post-Christians!,' in *Heaven*, exhib. cat. (Liverpool Tate Gallery, 1999).
Slavoj Žižek, *The Fragile Absolute: or, Why the Christian Legacy is Worth Fighting For* (Verso: New York, 2000).
Alexandre Leupin, *Fiction et incarnation* (Paris: Flammarion, 1993).
Alexandre Leupin, *Phallophanies* (Paris: Éditions du regard, 2000).

Wall

On the link with Manet, see:
Jeff Wall, 'Unity and Fragmentation in Manet,' *Parachute*, 35, Summer 1984 ; repr. in Arielle Pelenc, Thierry de Duve and Boris Groys, *Jeff Wall* (London: Phaidon Press, 1996).
Thierry de Duve, 'The Mainstream and the Crooked Path,' *ibid.*

On Jeff Wall's art and its relationship to photography and painting, see:
Els Barents, 'Typology, Luminescence, Freedom, Selections from a conversation with Jeff Wall,' in *Jeff Wall, Transparencies* (Munich: Schirmer/Mosel, 1986).
Thomas Crow, 'Profane Illuminations, Social History and the Art of Jeff Wall', *Artforum*, February 1993.
Frédéric Migayrou, *Jeff Wall, Simple indication* (Brussels: La lettre volée, 1995).

Greenberg's comment on photography can be found in:
Clement Greenberg, 'The Camera's Glass Eye: Review of an Exhibition of Edward Weston,' *The Collected Essays II.*

On the possible invention of a new medium, see:
Rosalind Krauss, '"… And Then Turn Away?" An Essay on James Coleman,' *October*, 81, Summer 1997.
Rosalind Krauss, 'Reinventing the Medium,' *Critical Inquiry*, 25, Winter 1999.
Rosalind Krauss, '*A Voyage on the North Sea,*' *Art in the Age of the Post-Medium Condition* (London: Thames & Hudson, 1999).

Kandinsky's citation from his 1913 *Reminiscences* is to be found in:
Wassily Kandinsky, *Complete Writings on Art*, Vol. 1 (Boston: G. K. Hall & Co., 1982), pp. 372–373.

Blocher

On the link with Manet, see:
Thierry de Duve, 'On Incarnation: Sylvie Blocher's *L'annonce amoureuse* and Édouard Manet's *A Bar at the Folies-Bergère*,' in Carolyn Bailey Gill, ed., *Time and the Image* (Manchester & New York: Manchester University Press, 2000).

On Joseph Beuys, the romantic background of his utopia, and Blocher's own situation vis-à-vis Beuys, see:
Max Reithmann, *Joseph Beuys: La mort me tient en éveil* (Toulouse: ARPAP, 1994).
Thierry de Duve, 'Joseph Beuys, or the Last of the Proletarians,' *October*, 45, summer 1988.

Thierry de Duve, 'Kant after Duchamp' and 'Archaeology of Practical Modernism,' chapters 5 and 8 of *Kant after Duchamp*.

Thierry de Duve, *La déposition* (Paris: Dis Voir, 1995).

On the *Living Pictures*:

Sylvie Blocher,' *Le double touché*, or, Gendering the Address', in *Time and the Image*.

Sylvie Blocher, '*Living Pictures* en général,' *Trafic* 23, 1997.

Thierry de Duve, 'People in the Image / People before the Image: Address and the Issue of Community in Sylvie Blocher's *L'annonce amoureuse*,' *October*, 85, Summer 1998.

Sylvie Blocher, Interview with Marc Donnadieu, *Ninety*, 23, 1997.

Sylvie Blocher, 'An em@il Interview, March 1998,' in *them(selves)*, exhib. cat. (Toronto: Art Gallery of York University, 1998).

Paul Ardenne, *Contemporary Practices* (Paris: Dis Voir, 1999).

Sylvie Blocher, 'A Talkative Silence', interview with Hou Hanru, in *Insisting Memories: Marina Abramovic, Sylvie Blocher, Stan Douglas, William Kentridge, Bill Viola*, exhib. cat. (Gainesville: Harn Museum for Art, University of Florida, 2000).

Here we are

Philippe Bazin
NÉS, 1998–1999

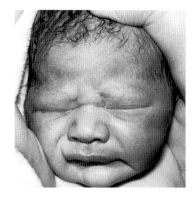

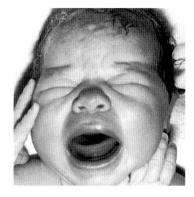

overture

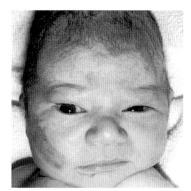

Thirty-seven newborn babies photographed in the first
five minutes after their birth all say together "Here we
are." We, humans? We, works of art? We, the humans
in images? We are the content, subject, substance,
and *flesh* of works of art.

Max Dean

As yet Untitled, 1992–1995

Or is the first "we" to be formed that of the couple made up of the work and its beholder? What does it share that is human? Nothing less than the life and death of the images, here. If you put your hands against the robot's hands, the image is saved, otherwise it's destroyed.

Henri Matisse
La Perruche et la sirène, 1952

Ann Veronica Janssens
Untitled, 2000

in-common

Jean-Michel Basquiat
Riding with Death, 1988

So, life and death. Is there any artist who has sung the joy of living with more exuberance and sensuality than Matisse? He was 83 when he made this collage! No life without death, however. The partner of Matisse's little blue mermaid is this horseman of the apocalypse astride a human skeleton, painted by Basquiat six months before he died. What secret correspondence makes the shape of the horseman echo that of the mermaid?

Christian Boltanski
L'Album de la famille D., 1971

It's a pity for Baudelaire that when he wrote his famous
essay, *The Painter of Modern Life*, he had Constantin
Guys in mind rather than Manet. One of the subjects of
modern life which Manet painted often was gender relations. The extraordinary thing here is the uncertainty in
this couple's relationship. At times the man looks like he's
trying to pick up the woman, and "coming on strong," and
she looks like a respectable married woman. At other
times the man looks as if he's head over heels in love
with her, and she looks like a demimondaine giving him
the once over and thinking: "Keep talking, honey." But the
most extraordinary feature is the café waiter keeping an
eye on them from the rear of the picture. Or is he looking
at us? Who knows...

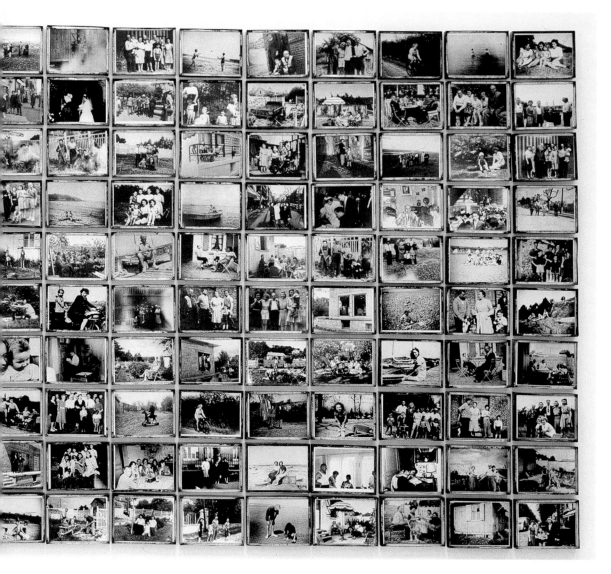

Édouard Manet

Chez le Père Lathuille,
en plein air, 1879

Jeff Wall

A Ventriloquist at a Birthday Party in October 1947, 1990

James Ensor

Squelettes se disputant un hareng-saur, 1891

Like Manet, Jeff Wall is a painter of modern life, but one who paints with photography. He stages his photos the way a classical painter would stage his paintings. Their subject? Us. His work explores the thousand and one facets of social life. Here, childhood. A birthday party that supposedly took place in 1947, to which the unseen parents invited a young woman ventriloquist, who makes her puppet talk, to amuse the kids. The artist explains that in 1947 few households had TV. But maybe the image also tells us what it means, for art, to make images talk.

277

Constantin Brancusi
Le Baiser, 1923–1925

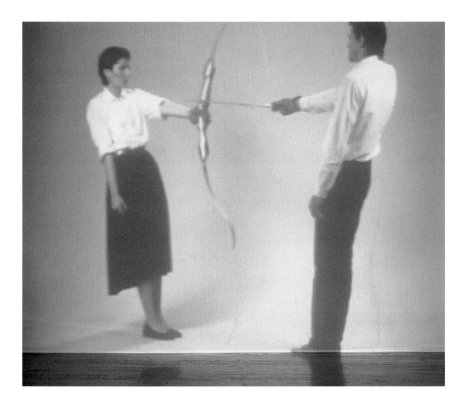

the two of us

Marina Abramovic & Ulay
Rest Energy, 1980

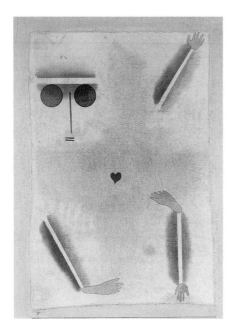

Paul Klee
Hat Kopf, Hand, Fuss und Herz, 1930

Sylvie Eyberg
1998, 28,5 x 38 cm, 1998

"We" can range from "we two" to "we all." Here we're in
an intimate drawing cabinet, at times erotic, always sen-
sual, where various aspects of "the two of us" are
explored—tender or violent, not always happy, not always
within the norms, and not always together in the picture,
either.

Marc Chagall
Clair de lune, 1926

Andy Warhol
Male Couple, 1950's

Joseph Beuys
Drei Mädchen, 1958

Joseph Beuys
Bewegungsstudien, 1955–1956

Joseph Beuys
Der Tod und das Mädchen, 1957

Joseph Beuys
Untitled (Akt), 1958

The time has come, since we're talking about *us*, i.e.
about the *pact*, to emphasize that the avant-gardes broke
the bonds with the past much less than we imagined, at a
time when, to win their right to exist in the face of

Joseph Beuys
Mädchen mit Ball, 1948

Auguste Rodin
*Femme nue de profil, dans
la posture du port d'armes*, UNDATED.

Joseph Beuys
Untitled, 1958

Auguste Rodin
Le Génie, UNDATED

a hostile tradition, they carried on a discourse of rupture
and clean slates. It is hardly fifteen years since Beuys
died, and already the extreme delicacy of his watercolors
likens them to Rodin's.

Joseph Beuys
Untitled (Torso), 1958

Joseph Beuys
Aufsteigende, 1952

Auguste Rodin
Trépied,
UNDATED

Auguste Rodin

Danseuse nue de dos, jambe droite haut levée,
UNDATED

Blinky Palermo
Fernsehen I, 1970

Auguste Rodin

Femme nue debout, tenant à mi-cuisse un vêtement,
between 1898 and 1903

Blinky Palermo
Fernsehen II, 1970

Blinky Palermo
Fernsehen V, 1970

Blinky Palermo
Fernsehen IV, 1970

Blinky Palermo
Fernsehen III, 1970

"We two" divides "we all." The philosophical name of "we all" is the universal, which the French Revolution translated by "Liberty, Equality, Fraternity." Where did sorority go?

Valerie Mannaerts
Untitled, 1996

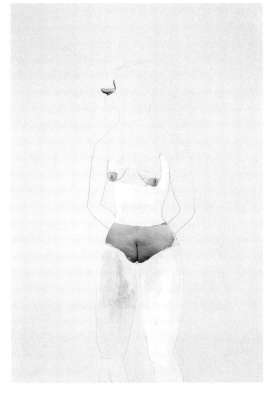

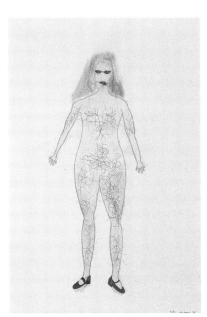

Valerie Mannaerts
Untitled, 1998

Valerie Mannaerts
Untitled, 1996

Even if, in a future near or far, we were to reproduce by cloning or God knows how, humankind will always be divided into two by sexual difference. It's time to gender the universal.

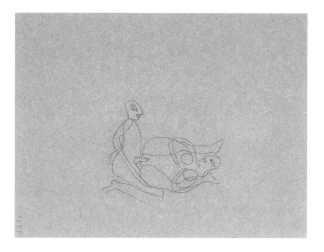

Sylvie Blocher
La violence c'est le lisse, 1995

Sylvie Blocher
La violence c'est le lisse, 1995

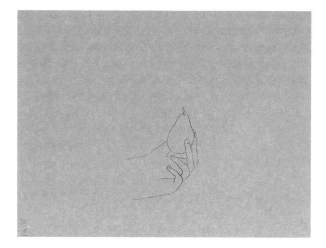

Sylvie Blocher
La violence c'est le lisse, 1995

Thomas Huber
En sainte, 1994

Andy Warhol
Two Heads and Clasped Hands, 1950's

Sue Williams
Woman with Kitten, 1991

Pablo Picasso
Deux figures et un chat, 1902–1903

Tamsir Dia
Untitled, 1993

Nancy Spero
Acrobat Totem, 1988

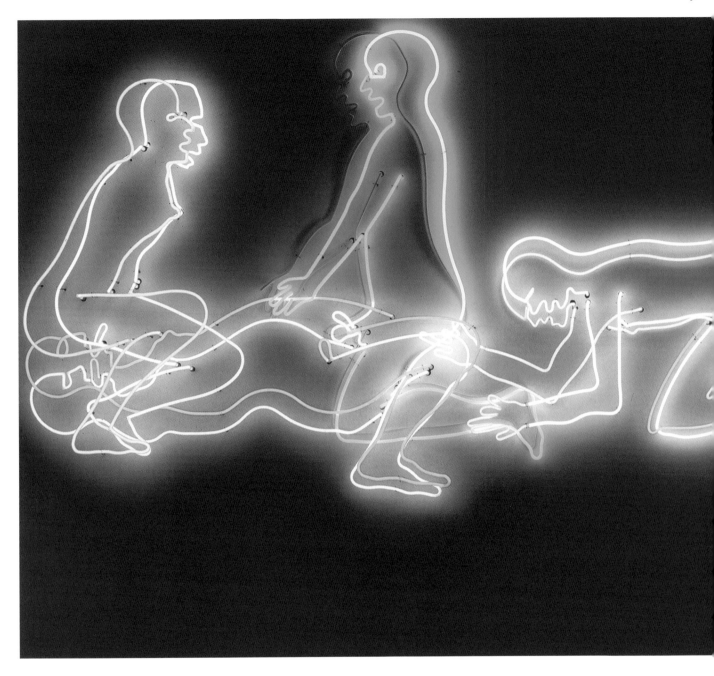

Nobody better than Nauman is able to lend almost abstract,
and yet explicit, form to the violence of human relationships.
Does *Seven Figures* propose some merry erotic utopia to
go from "we two" to "we all" via group sex?

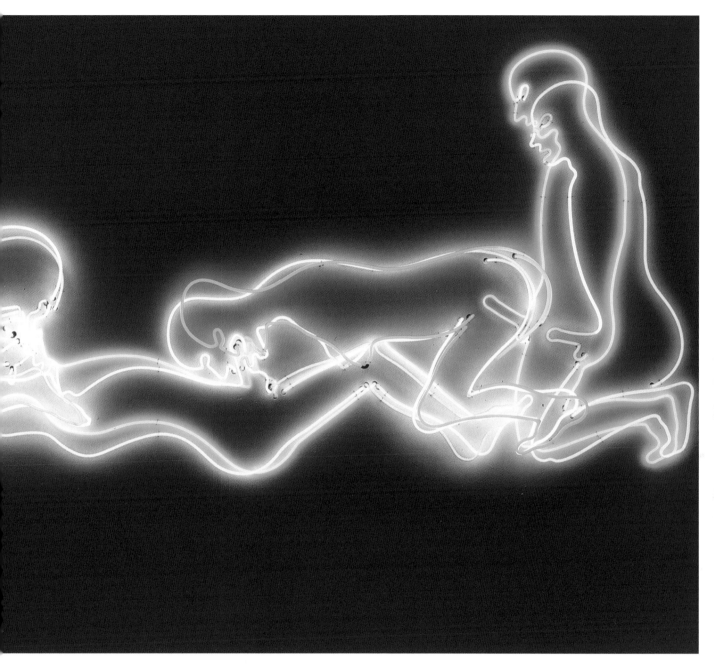

Bruce Nauman
Seven Figures, 1985

Sex, here, is an engine, a mechanism, and an allegory of
desire when it is chained by domination. Humor is the
sublime form of despair.

Sylvie Blocher
For ever, 2000

Giving images back their speech doesn't have much sense unless it means this: giving the people in images back their speech. The people here are inhabitants of Brussels from both linguistic communities recruited by small ads. You and I. A "pseudo-group," says the artist, people brought together at random in the same work of art, people who haven't chosen one another and whom the artist hasn't chosen either.

They came before the camera as families—rarely complete, by the way. The artist added a somewhat specific clause: the children should be about forty, the age when parent-child relations tend to be sorted out—if they ever get sorted out at all. The family is the microcosm where all social relations are elaborated, and where emotional bonds are at their strongest. And it's a "pseudo-group."

Alain Géronnez
*Rue de Bruxelles, Rude Brussels Road,
Ruhe Brüsselerstraße, Ruwe Brusselstraat*, 1994–2000

Where are we? In London there's a *Brussels Road*, and
in Cologne there's a *Brüsselerstraße*, evidence of the
abruxellation of Europe. They are conflated here by Alain
Géronnez, who has drawn his own *Rue de Bruxelles* in
the Palais des Beaux-Arts.

abruxellation

all of us

Angel Vergara

Straatman, 2000

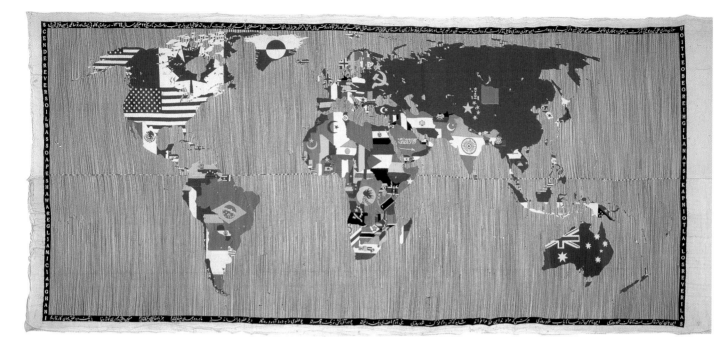

Alighiero e Boetti
Mappa, 1989–1992

Marijke Van Warmerdam
Voetbal, 1995

History and geography. We all. Boetti's great planisphere,
woven by Afghan women who took refuge in Pakistan,
dates from just before the fall of the Wall, and thus represents a world which is already no longer ours.

André Cadere
B 142 0000 3 = 35 = = 12x13 =, 1974

Michel François
L'Arpenteur, 1993

Immigrant kids all dream of being Ronaldo, and if the dream remains a dream for most of them, at least for the boy filmed by Marijke Van Warmerdam there is the miniature miracle of the ball balanced on his head for the fourteen minutes the video lasts. And what if the ball were the earth?

Clifford Possum Tjapaltjarri
Warlugulong, 1992

Michel François
Les Casseurs de cailloux, 1994

We all. History and geography. The Australian aborigines are extraordinary painters, and Tjapaltjarri is one of the most acclaimed. This painting is the topographical reading of a part of Papunya territory and recounts a Dreaming, a dream dreamt by ancestors and interpreted by the artist. Lungkata, the blue-tongued lizard-man, lit a huge bush fire in which his two sons perished for having killed a sacred kangaroo. The explosion in the middle of the canvas is the fire, the wavy marks are those of the snake Yarapiri... Some meanings remain secret.

Rodney Graham

L'Arbre de la Révolution, 1993

Why is *The Tree of the Revolution*–planted at the time of the French Revolution at Bourlémont, in Belgium–upside down? Because in a camera, like in our retina, the world appears upside down? Or because in revolutions the world is all topsy-turvy?

mensch tot... mensch tot

Sylvie Blocher & Gérard Haller
Nuremberg 87, 1987

Over images of the Nuremberg *Parteigelände*, the voice of German actress Angela Winkler recites three hundred first names of men and women which could well be yours or mine. Sylvie Blocher has said this about *Nuremberg 87*: "We wanted that unspeakable thing to be borne by a 'We all' and not just by the Jewish community."

Jef Geys

De gevallen verwittiging, 1985

The bronze letters of the Hebrew alphabet have fallen off the wall in *The Fallen Warning*, but their mark is still there, the mark of the words *Mene, Mene, Tekel, Upharsin*, written by a mysterious hand on the wall of the palace of Balthazar, tyrant of Babylon, announcing the downfall of his kingdom. The episode occurs in the Bible, in the Book of Daniel.

Marianne Berenhaut
Vie privée, 1993

Michel François
Pas tomber, 1996

Michel François

Le Drapeau, 1997

Frédéric Bruly Bouabré
La Haute Diplomatie, 1982–1994

Michel François
Jeu de mains, 1991

Felix Gonzalez-Torres
Untitled (Portrait of Dad), 1991

Felix Gonzalez-Torres died of AIDS in 1996, and his whole oeuvre is an act of transmission. You can take a candy, it is a communion with the departed. It's for children not yet born that we must remember the dead, for humankind doesn't stop with the living.

Panamarenko
Donderwolk, 1970–1971

taking flight

LIST OF THE WORKS

* Works not in the exhibition
** Works not reproduced

Marina ABRAMOVIC & ULAY, *Rest Energy*, 1980 [We]
Video installation
Musée d'art contemporain de Lyon

ABSALON, *Proposition d'objets quotidiens*, 1990 [I]
Wood, cardboard, and plaster under plexiglas; 30 x 140 x 60 cm
Collection Claude Berri, Paris

Giovanni ANSELMO, *Verso l'Infinito*, 1969 [I]
Incised iron, transparent varnish, grease; 36 x 19.5 x 16.2 cm
Courtesy Galerie Micheline Szwajcer, Antwerp
Photo: Moortgat

ARMAN, *Diabelli*, 1971 [I]
Resin, plexiglas, wood, metal; 80 x 43 cm
Private collection

Hans ARP, *La Trousse du naufragé*, 1921 [I]
Assemblage of six pieces of wood on wooden plank; 19 x 32 cm
Musée d'art moderne et contemporain, Strasbourg

ART & LANGUAGE, *Untitled Painting*, 1965 [You]
Mirrors, canvas; 2 parts, 119.3 x 58.3 x 10.9 cm each
Collection of the FRAC Nord-Pas de Calais, Dunkirk
Photo: S. White

Richard ARTSCHWAGER, *Mirror and Wood Construction*, 1962 [You]
Mirror on wood; 59.7 x 45.7 cm
Collection of the Artist, Hudson, New York

Richard ARTSCHWAGER, *Blp*, 1969 [I]
Painted steel; 105 x 35 x 35 cm
Fundação de Serralves Collection, Porto

Richard ARTSCHWAGER, *Hair Sculpture-Shallow Recess Box*, 1969 [I]
Rubberized horsehair; 30.5 x 24.1 x 29.2 cm
The Dorothy and Herbert Vogel Collection, Ailsa Mellon Bruce Fund, Patrons' Permanent Fund and Gift of Dorothy and Herbert Vogel, © 2000 Board of Trustees, National Gallery of Art, Washington
Photo: Philip A. Charles

Jean-Michel BASQUIAT, *Riding with Death*, 1988 [We]
Acrylic and soft pencil on canvas; 248.9 x 289.6 cm
Private collection; courtesy of The Menil Collection, Houston
Photo: Hester & Hardaway

Philippe BAZIN, *NÉS*, 1998–1999 [We]
37 black-and-white photos, 45 x 45 cm each
Collection of the Artist

Linda BENGLIS, *Pour Daum # 2*, 1979 [I]
Plaster on wire mesh, gold leaf, and oil paint; 48.2 x 27.9 x 16.5 cm
The Dorothy and Herbert Vogel Collection, Ailsa Mellon Bruce Fund, Patrons' Permanent Fund and Gift of Dorothy and Herbert Vogel, © 2000 Board of Trustees, National Gallery of Art, Washington
Photo: Lyle Peterzell

Linda BENGLIS, *Untitled*, 1979 [I]
Gold leaf and red and blue paint on metal wire frame; 48.2 x 19 x 7.6 cm
The Dorothy and Herbert Vogel Collection, Ailsa Mellon Bruce Fund, Patrons' Permanent Fund and Gift of Dorothy and Herbert Vogel, © 2000 Board of Trustees, National Gallery of Art, Washington
Photo: Lyle Peterzell

Marianne BERENHAUT, *Vie Privée*, 1993 [We]
Mixed media, table desk, card-trays; 140 x 120 x 85 cm
Collection of the Artist

Joseph BEUYS, *Mädchen mit Ball*, 1948 [We]
Pencil and pink watercolor on sallow background; 25 x 16.6 cm
Stiftung Museum Schloss Moyland, Sammlung van der Grinten, Bedburg-Hau

Joseph BEUYS, *Aufsteigende*, 1952 [We]
Pencil and walnut stain on light-yellow notepaper, lightly corrugated edge at top and bottom; 20.9 x 29.7 cm
Stiftung Museum Schloss Moyland, Sammlung van der Grinten, Bedburg-Hau

Joseph BEUYS, *Bewegungsstudien*, 1955–1956 [We]
Pencil and watercolor on light-yellow notepaper; 15.9 x 13.2 cm
Stiftung Museum Schloss Moyland, Sammlung van der Grinten, Bedburg-Hau
Photo: Walter Klein

Joseph BEUYS, *Der Tod und das Mädchen*, 1957 [We]
Pencil and walnut stain on light-yellow notepaper; 21 x 29.7 cm
Stiftung Museum Schloss Moyland, Sammlung van der Grinten, Bedburg-Hau
Photo: Maurice Dorren

Joseph BEUYS, *Drei Mädchen*, 1958 [We]
Pencil and watercolor on light-yellow notepaper; 20.8 x 14.6 cm
Stiftung Museum Schloss Moyland, Sammlung van der Grinten, Bedburg-Hau
Photo: Walter Klein

Joseph BEUYS, *Untitled (Akt)*, 1958 [We]
Pencil and pink watercolor on fine white notepaper; 20.8 x 29.3 cm
Stiftung Museum Schloss Moyland, Sammlung van der Grinten, Bedburg-Hau
Photo: Walter Klein

Joseph BEUYS, *Untitled (Torso)*, 1958 [We]
Pencil and walnut stain on light-yellow notepaper; 30 x 40.2 cm
Stiftung Museum Schloss Moyland, Sammlung van der Grinten, Bedburg-Hau
Photo: Walter Klein

Joseph BEUYS, *Untitled*, 1958 [We]
Pencil and green watercolor on light-yellow notepaper; 29.5 x 21 cm
Stiftung Museum Schloss Moyland, Sammlung van der Grinten, Bedburg-Hau
Photo: Walter Klein

Joseph BEUYS, *Wirtschaftswerte*, 1980 [I]
Various utensils and foodstuffs from the GDR, metal shelves and massive plaster beam with butter, several paintings (oil on canvas, dating from the time of Karl Marx, 1818–1883); 290 x 400 x 265 cm
SMAK, Gent
Photo: Dirk Pauwels

Sylvie BLOCHER & Gérard HALLER, *Nuremberg 87*, 1987 [We]
16-mm film transposed on video, 9'; with the voice of Angela Winkler
Collection of the Artist
Photo: Sylvie Blocher

Sylvie BLOCHER, *La violence c'est le lisse*, 1995 [We]
Drawing transferred to recycled paper; 19.2 x 25.8 cm
Private collection

Sylvie BLOCHER, *La violence c'est le lisse*, 1995 [We]
Drawing transferred to recycled paper; 19.2 x 25.8 cm
Private collection

Sylvie BLOCHER, *La violence c'est le lisse*, 1995 [We]
Drawing transferred to recycled paper; 19.2 x 25.8 cm
Private collection

Sylvie BLOCHER, *Living Pictures/For ever*, 2000 [We]
Video installation, 17', shot with inhabitants of Brussels
Collection of the Artist

Alighiero e BOETTI, *Mappa*, 1989–1992 [We]
Embroidery on canvas; 255 x 580 cm
Collezione Giordano Boetti, Rome

Christian BOLTANSKI, *L'Album de la famille D.*, 1971 [We]
150 photographs; 22 x 30 cm each
Collection of the FRAC Rhône-Alpes / Institut d'Art contemporain, Villeurbanne
Photo: Yves Bresson

Louise BOURGEOIS, *Single I*, 1996 [I]
Fabric doll; 213.4 x 132.1 x 40.6 cm
Courtesy Cheim & Read, New York
Photo: Nic Tenwiggenhorn

Constantin BRANCUSI, *Sculpture pour aveugles; "Le Commencement du Monde"*, 1914 [I]
Marble; 17 x 29 x 18.1 cm
Philadelphia Museum of Art: The Louise and Walter Arensberg Collection, Philadelphia
Photo: Graydon Wood

Constantin BRANCUSI, *Le Baiser*, 1923–1925 [We]
Brown limestone; 36.5 x 25.5 x 24 cm
Collections of the Centre Georges Pompidou / Musée national d'art moderne, Paris
Photo: Photographic archive of the collections of the Centre Georges Pompidou / Musée national d'art moderne, Paris

Constantin BRANCUSI, *Socle*, after 1928 [I]
Two elements: poplar and limestone; 92 x 58 x 59.05 cm
Collections of the Centre Georges Pompidou / Musée national d'art moderne, Paris
Photo: Photographic archive of the collections of the Centre Georges Pompidou / Musée national d'art moderne, Paris

George BRECHT, *Untitled*, 1962–1986 [I]
Reconstruction from 1986 with artist's agreement
Wood, paint, paper, fresh oranges; 82 x 45 x 42 cm
Collection of the Musée d'art contemporain de Lyon

Marcel BROODTHAERS, *Section des figures (Der Adler vom Oligozän bis heute)*, 1972 [I]
Detail 41: anonymous, Eagle's head, recent post-classic 1350–1521
Toltec-Aztec, Tehuacan
Volcanic stone; 120 x 100 x 130 cm
Royal Museums for Art and History, Brussels

* Marcel BROODTHAERS, *Section des figures (Der Adler vom Oligozän bis heute)*, 1972 [I]
Detail 7: anonymous, Eagle with spread wings, Roman
Bronze; 5.6 x 5.3 cm
Staatlichen Museen Stiftung Preußischer Kulturbesitz, Berlin
Photo: Maria Gilissen-Broodthaers

* Marcel BROODTHAERS, *Section des figures (Der Adler vom Oligozän bis heute)*, 1972 [I]
Detail 67: beer bottles, corks, miscellaneous
Photo: Maria Gilissen-Broodthaers

* Marcel BROODTHAERS, *Section des figures (Der Adler vom Oligozän bis heute)*, 1972 (double page in the catalog) [I]
Städtliche Kunsthalle Düsseldorf
Photo: Maria Gilissen-Broodthaers

Frédéric BRULY BOUABRÉ, *La Haute diplomatie*, 1982–1994 [We]
Colored pencils and ballpoint pen on cardboard paper; 82 drawings of 16 x 11 cm each
The Pigozzi Collection, Geneva
© Frédéric Bruly Bouabré, Courtesy: C.A.A.C.

André CADERE, *B 142 0000 3 = 35 = = 12x13 =*, 1974 [We]
Wood and vinyl; 179 x 3.5 cm Ø
Collection Jean-Marcel Gayraud, Paris

Harry CALLAHAN, *Eleanor, Chicago*, 1950 [You]
Silver-salt proof; 20.3 x 12.5 cm
Collections of the Centre Georges Pompidou / Musée national d'art moderne, Paris
Photo: Photographic archive of the collections of the Centre Georges Pompidou / Musée national d'art moderne, Paris

Eric CAMERON, *Lettuce*, 1979 [You]
Gesso on lettuce; 38.1 x 38.1 x 38.1 cm
Collection of the Artist

Eric CAMERON, *Chloé's Brown Sugar*, 1992– [I]
Gesso on a box of sugar; 7.6 x 26.6 x 25 cm
Collection of the Artist
Photo: University of Calgary Com/Media (David Brown and Jim Burton)

Eric CAMERON, *Sonnets from the Portuguese (1656) – for Margaret*, 1992– [I]
Acrylic gesso and acrylic on a small book; 11.3 x 24.7 x 22 cm
Collection of the Artist
Photo: University of Calgary Com/Media (David Brown and Jim Burton)

Eric CAMERON, *Exposed-Concealed: Salima Halladj*, 1993– [I]
Acrylic gesso and acrylic on undeveloped film reel; 13.9 x 25.4 x 8.8 cm
Collection of the Artist
Photo: University of Calgary Com/Media (David Brown and Jim Burton)

Eric CAMERON, *Exposed-Concealed: Laura Baird II, III, V, VI*, 1994/4/6/6 [I]
Gesso on film reels; 10.1 x 7.6 x 5 cm
Collection of the Artist
Photo: University of Calgary Com/Media (David Brown and Jim Burton)

Anthony CARO, *Table Piece VIII*, 1966 [I]
Polished steel; 68.5 x 33 x 50.8 cm
Private collection, London; Courtesy Annely Juda Fine Art, London

Anthony CARO, *Table Piece XXII*, 1967 [I]
Jewel-green sprayed steel; 25.4 x 80 x 68.6 cm
Private collection, London; Courtesy Annely Juda Fine Art, London
Photo: S. Anzai

Denis CASTELLAS, *Untitled*, 1986 [I]
Diverse media; 7 x 10 x 6 cm
Collection of the Artist

* Denis CASTELLAS, *Untitled*, 1986 [I]
Diverse media; 7 x 10 x 6 cm
Collection of the Artist

Denis CASTELLAS, *Untitled*, 1987 [I]
Diverse media; 22 x 33 x 2 cm
Collection of the Artist

Denis CASTELLAS, *Untitled*, 1991 [I]
Cardboard, paper, wire; 80 x 15 x 15 cm
Collection H. Duprat, Claret

* Denis CASTELLAS, *Untitled*, 1991 [I]
Diverse media; 85 x 8 cm
Collection of the Artist

Marc CHAGALL, *Clair de lune*, 1926 [We]
Watercolor and gouache on brown paper; 66.5 x 51.2 cm
Royal Museums of Fine Arts of Belgium, Brussels,
Bequest Madame Alla Goldschmidt-Safieva
Photo: Speltdoorn

Max DEAN, *As yet Untitled*, 1992–1995 [We]
Robot; 175 x 266 x 230 cm
Collection of the Artist
Photos: Isaac Applebaum

Tamsir DIA, *Untitled*, 1993 [We]
Canvas on wood; 31.5 x 71.7 cm
Private collection
Photo: Philippe De Gobert

Marcel DUCHAMP, *Roue de Bicyclette*, 1913; 6th version
1964 [I]
Bicycle fork and wheel on wooden stool; 126 x 64 x 31.5 cm
National Gallery of Canada, Ottawa

Marcel DUCHAMP, *Sculpture morte*, 1959 [I]
Fruit and vegetables in marzipan, insects, paper mounted on wood in
glass box; 33.8 x 22.5 x 9.9 cm
Collections of the Centre Georges Pompidou / Musée national d'art
moderne, Paris
Photo: Photographic archive of the collections of the Centre Georges
Pompidou / Musée national d'art moderne, Paris, Jacques Faujour

James ENSOR, *Squelettes se disputant un hareng-saur*,
1891 [We]
Oil on wood; 16 x 21.5 cm
Royal Museums of Fine Arts of Belgium, Brussels,
Bequest Madame Alla Goldschmidt-Safieva
Photo: Speltdoorn

Walker EVANS, *Trash # 3*, 1962 [I]
Black-and-white photograph, silver contact print; 20.1 x 25.2 cm
Fonds national d'art contemporain du Ministère de la Culture, Paris
Photo: Sylvain Lizon

Walker EVANS, *Trash # 4*, 1962 [I]
Black-and-white photograph, silver contact print; 19.2 x 30.7 cm
Fonds national d'art contemporain du Ministère de la Culture, Paris
Photo: Sylvain Lizon

Sylvie EYBERG, *1998, 28.5 x 38 cm*, 1998 [We]
Black-and-white baryte print, metal; 28.5 x 38 cm
Collection Greta Meert, Brussels

Sylvie EYBERG, *1999, 29 x 21.5 cm*, 1999 [You]
Black-and-white baryte print, metal; 29 x 21.5 cm
Collection of the Artist, Galerie Meert Rihoux, Brussels

Sylvie EYBERG, *1999, 29 x 22.5 cm*, 1999 [You]
Black-and-white baryte print, metal; 29 x 22.5 cm
Private collection

Luciano FABRO, *I Prigioni*, 1994 [You]
Marble; 190 x 170 cm
Courtesy Galerie Micheline Szwajcer, Antwerp

Jean FAUTRIER, *Portrait de ma concierge*, 1922 [You]
Oil on canvas; 81 x 60 cm
Musée des Beaux-Arts, Tourcoing

Jean FAUTRIER, *Le Bouquet de violettes*, 1924 [I]
Oil on canvas; 35.3 x 27.4 cm
Musée de Grenoble

Robert FILLIOU, *Le Siège des idées*, 1976 [I]
Metal folding chair frame (painted), string, index card 16 x 24 cm with
chalk inscription; 74 x 40 x 40 cm
Collection Irmeline Lebeer, Brussels
Photo: Philippe De Gobert

Peter FISCHLI & David WEISS, *Untitled (Equilibrium
Series)*, 1985 [I]
Color photograph; 35 x 24 cm
Collection of the FRAC Aquitaine, Bordeaux

Peter FISCHLI & David WEISS, *Uomo Intimo*, 1987 [I]
Rubber; 16 x 33 x 15 cm
Courtesy Sonnabend Collection, New York

Barry FLANAGAN, *Untitled*, 1985–1986 [I]
Terracotta, Raku technique; 34 x 16 x 12 cm
Collection of the FRAC des Pays de la Loire, Carquefou
Photo: Bernard Renoux

Barry FLANAGAN, *Untitled*, 1985–1986 [I]
Terracotta, Raku technique; 28 x 15 x 15 cm
Collection of the FRAC des Pays de la Loire, Carquefou
Photo: Bernard Renoux

Barry FLANAGAN, *Untitled*, 1986 [I]
Terracotta, Raku technique; 30.5 x 13 x 11.5 cm
Collection of the FRAC des Pays de la Loire, Carquefou
Photo: Bernard Renoux

Lucio FONTANA, *Concetto spaziale*, 1962 [You]
Oil on canvas; 100 x 80 cm
Courtesy Galerie Xavier Hufkens, Brussels

Michel FRANÇOIS, *Jeu de mains*, 1991 [We]
Black-and-white photograph; 30 x 40 cm
Collection of the Artist

Michel FRANÇOIS, *L'Arpenteur*, 1993 [We]
VHS video
Collection of the Artist

Michel FRANÇOIS, *Les Casseurs de cailloux*, 1994 [We]
VHS video
Collection of the Artist

Michel FRANÇOIS, *Pas tomber*, 1996 [We]
VHS video
Collection of the Artist

Michel FRANÇOIS, *Le Drapeau*, 1997 [We]
Giant photocopy; 300 x 400 cm
Collection of the Artist

Lee FRIEDLANDER, *Colorado (Self Portrait)*, 1967 [You]
Black-and-white photograph; 27.8 x 35.3 cm
Collection of the FRAC Aquitaine, Bordeaux

Alain GÉRONNEZ, *Rue de Bruxelles, Rude Brussels Road,
Ruhe Brüsselerstraße, Ruwe Brusselstraat*, 1994–2000 [We]
Photo installation in aluminum; 20 pieces of approx. 30 x 75 cm
Collection of the Artist

Jef GEYS, *De gevallen verwittiging*, 1985 [We]
Powdered pigment and steel; 400 x 700 x 200 cm
MuHKA, Antwerp

* Alberto GIACOMETTI, *La Cage*, 1950 [I]
Bronze; 170 x 34 x 32 cm
Musée de Grenoble

Felix GONZALES-TORRES, *Untitled (Portrait of Dad)*, 1991
[We]
Mints wrapped in cellophane; variable dimensions
On loan from Carlos and Rosa de la Cruz
Photo: Philippe De Gobert

Dan GRAHAM, *Two Staggered Two-Way-Mirror
Half-Cylinders*, 2000 [You]
Glass and metal; 220 x 600 x 700 cm
Collection Banque Bruxelles Lambert, Brussels

Rodney GRAHAM, *L'Arbre de la Révolution*, 1993 [We]
Cibachrome; 225 x 180 cm
Private collection

Raymond HAINS, *Untitled*, 1976 [I]
Torn poster on metal plate; 50 x 43.3 cm
Courtesy Galerie de France, Paris

Raoul HAUSMANN, *Untitled* (attributed title: *Épaules*),
1927–1933 [You]
Silver gelatine on baryte paper, black-and-white photograph; 5.5 x 7.7 cm
Musée d'art moderne, Saint-Etienne
Photo: Yves Bresson

Raoul HAUSMANN, *Regard dans le miroir*, 1930 [You]
Photograph; 19 x 13.5 cm
Collection of the Musée départemental d'art contemporain de
Rochechouart (Haute-Vienne)
Photo: Freddy Le Seaux

Florence HENRI, *Untitled*, 1928 [You]
Silver-salt print; 10 x 7.1 cm

Collections of the Centre Georges Pompidou / Musée national d'art
moderne, Paris
Photo: Photographic archive of the Centre Georges Pompidou / Musée
national d'art moderne, Paris
Photo: Adam Rzepka

Gary HILL, *Viewer*, 1996 [You]
Five-channel video installation / Five video projectors, five laser-disk
players and five disks, five-channel synch box
Photo: Lynn Thompson, Courtesy Donald Young Gallery, Chicago

Roni HORN, *Pair Objects VI c: For Two Locations in One
Place*, 1988 [I]
Forged and machined copper; 2 cones 22.9 x 33 x 33 cm each
Courtesy Galerie Xavier Hufkens, Brussels

Roni HORN, *You are the Weather*, 1994–1996 [You]
Installation with 100 photographs (36 gelatine silver prints and
64 C-type prints; 25.6 x 21.4 cm each)
Courtesy Matthew Marks Gallery, New York
Sammlung Goetz, Munich

Thomas HUBER, *En sainte*, 1994 [We]
Watercolor and pencil on paper; 42 x 29.7 cm
Private collection

Ann Veronica JANSSENS, *Untitled*, 2000 [We]
Heat-sensitive bench with four seats, brushed aluminum
Courtesy Galerie Micheline Szwajcer, Antwerp
Photo: Moortgat

Donald JUDD, *Untitled*, 1965 [I]
Galvanized iron with acrylic plexiglas sheet; 15.2 x 68.6 x 61 cm
The Dorothy and Herbert Vogel Collection, Ailsa Mellon Bruce Fund,
Patrons' Permanent Fund and Gift of Dorothy and Herbert Vogel,
© 2000 Board of Trustees, National Gallery of Art, Washington
Photo: Philip A. Charles

Donald JUDD, *Untitled*, 1967 [I]
Galvanised iron; 12 x 64 x 23 cm
Private collection

Ellsworth KELLY, *Blue Curve*, 1996 [You]
Oil on canvas; 276 x 249 cm
Ellsworth Kelly and Matthew Marks Gallery, New York

Paul KLEE, *Hat Kopf, Hand, Fuss und Herz*, 1930 [We]
Watercolor and feathers on cotton, marouflaged on cardboard and glued
on hardboard; 41.5 x 29 cm
Kunstsammlung Nordrhein-Westfalen, Düsseldorf
Photo: Walter Klein

Yves KLEIN, *Monochrome I.K.B.*, 1957 [You]
Pure pigments and synthetic resin on marouflaged canvas on plywood;
50 x 50 x 5.5 cm
Musée d'art moderne, Saint-Etienne
Photo: Yves Bresson

François KOLLAR, *Lunettes*, ca. 1920 [I]
Silver-salt print glued on cardboard; 22.4 x 16.5 cm
Collections of the Centre Georges Pompidou / Musée national d'art
moderne, Paris
Photo: Photographic archive of the collections of the Centre Georges
Pompidou / Musée national d'art moderne, Paris

Jeff KOONS, *One Ball Total Equilibrium Tank*, 1985 [I]
Glass, metal, distilled water, basketball; 164.5 x 78.1 x 33.7 cm
Collection of B.Z. & Michael Schwartz, New York

Jeff KOONS, *Christ and the Lamb*, 1986 [You]
Gilt frame with mirrors; 197.5 x 142.5 x 17.5 cm
Groninger Museum, Groningen. Acquired with the support of the
Vereniging Rembrandt
Photo: John Stoel

Roy LICHTENSTEIN, *Mirror*, 1970 [You]
Circular wooden frame, oil and magna on canvas; Ø 55 cm
Collection Constance R. Caplan, Baltimore
Photo: Zindman

Bernd LOHAUS, *Münster*, 1991 [I]
Wood; 28 x 1250 x 360 cm
Collection of the Artist

René MAGRITTE, *L'Image parfaite*, 1928 [You]
Oil on canvas, signed bottom left; 54 x 73 cm
Private collection

Édouard MANET, *Chez le Père Lathuille, en plein air*, 1879 [We]
Oil on canvas; 93.5 x 112.5 cm
Musée des Beaux-Arts, Tournai. Bequest H. Van Cutsem (1904)
Photo: Paul M.R. Maeyaert

Robert MANGOLD, *Untitled*, 1973 [You]
Acrylic and colored pencil on hardboard panel; 33 x 33 cm
The Dorothy and Herbert Vogel Collection, Ailsa Mellon Bruce Fund,
Patrons' Permanent Fund and Gift of Dorothy and Herbert Vogel,
© 2000 Board of Trustees, National Gallery of Art, Washington
Photo: Lyle Peterzell

Robert MANGOLD, *Untitled*, 1973 [You]
Acrylic and colored pencil on hardboard panel; 35.6 x 35.6 cm
The Dorothy and Herbert Vogel Collection, Ailsa Mellon Bruce Fund,
Patrons' Permanent Fund and Gift of Dorothy and Herbert Vogel,
© 2000 Board of Trustees, National Gallery of Art, Washington
Photo: Lyle Peterzell

Valérie MANNAERTS, *Untitled*, 1996 [We]
Collage, pencil on paper; 27.5 x 36.5 cm
Collection Eric Decelle

Valérie MANNAERTS, *Untitled*, 1996 [We]
Pencil on paper; 40 x 30 cm
Courtesy of the artist / Galerie Drantmann

Valérie MANNAERTS, *Untitled*, 1998 [We]
Collage, pencil on paper; 50 x 30 cm
Courtesy of the artist / Galerie Drantmann

Piero MANZONI, *Corpo d'Aria*, 1959–1960 [I]
Iron, plastic, wood; 12.7 x 42.5 x 7.4 cm
Collecciò MACBA. Fundació Museu d'Art Contemporani de Barcelona

Piero MANZONI, *Achrome*, 1960 [You]
Material painting with horizontal folds, kaolin on folded canvas; 51 x 70 cm
Collection Dorna Metzger, Turin
Photo: Enzo Ricci

Piero MANZONI, *Base Magica*, 1961 [I]
Wood; 60 x 80 x 80 cm
Archivio Opera Piero Manzoni, Milan
Photo: Orazio Bacci

Henri MATISSE, *La Perruche et la sirène*, 1952 [We]
Paper, canvas, gouache, collage; 337 x 768.5 cm
Stedelijk Museum, Amsterdam

Guy MEES, *Verloren ruimte*, 1990 [You]
Paper, 4 parts; 150 x 190 cm
Courtesy Galerie Micheline Szwajcer, Antwerp

Fausto MELOTTI, *Costante uomo*, 1936 [I]
Plaster; 225 x 55 x 31cm
Collection Marta Melotti, Milan, Archivio Fausto Melotti
Photo: Jean-Pierre Maurer

Mario MERZ, *Salamino*, 1966 [I]
Blanket and neon tube; 90 x 254 cm
Fundação de Serralves Collection, Porto

Joan MIRÓ, *Peinture (Le Toréador)*, 1927 [You]
Oil on canvas; 129 x 97 cm
Former gift of Geneviève and Jean Masurel, acquired through donation in
1994, collection of the Musée national d'art moderne Centre Georges
Pompidou, Paris, in deposit at the Musée d'art moderne de Lille-
Métropole, Villeneuve-d'Ascq

Piet MONDRIAN, *Composition n° 3 avec plans colorés*,
1917 [You]
Oil on canvas; 48 x 61.5 cm
Museum Boijmans Van Beuningen, Rotterdam

Giorgio MORANDI, *Natura morta*, 1951 [I]
Oil on canvas; 30 x 50 cm
Private collection

Giorgio MORANDI, *Natura morta*, 1960 [I]
Oil on canvas; 35.5 x 30.7 cm
Collection Dorna Metzger, Turin
Photo: Enzo Ricci

Bruce NAUMAN, *Studies for Holograms (a)*, 1970 [You]
Silkscreen print; 65.5 x 65.5 cm
Collection Groupe Lhoist, Ottignies – Louvain-la-Neuve

Bruce NAUMAN, *Studies for Holograms (e)*, 1970 [You]
Silkscreen print; 65.5 x 65.5 cm
Collection Groupe Lhoist, Ottignies – Louvain-la-Neuve

Bruce NAUMAN, *Seven Figures*, 1985 [We]
Neon-tube montage; 220 x 465 x 8 cm
Stedelijk Museum, Amsterdam

Luis NORONHA da COSTA, *Objecto*, 1967 [You]
Glass and wood; 60 x 60 x 20 cm
Fundação de Serralves Collection, Porto (Rui Mário Gonçalves deposit)

Blinky PALERMO, *Fernsehen I*, 1970 [We]
Watercolor on pencil on squared paper; 5 x 14.8 x 20.8 cm
Galerie-Verein, Munich
Photo: Engelbert Seehuber

Blinky PALERMO, *Fernsehen II*, 1970 [We]
Watercolor on pencil on squared paper; 5 x 14.8 x 20.8 cm
Galerie-Verein, Munich
Photo: Engelbert Seehuber

Blinky PALERMO, *Fernsehen III*, 1970 [We]
Watercolor on pencil on squared paper; 5 x 14.8 x 20.8 cm
Staatliche Graphische Sammlung, Munich
Photo: Engelbert Seehuber

Blinky PALERMO, *Fernsehen IV*, 1970 [We]
Watercolor on pencil on squared paper; 5 x 14.8 x 20.8 cm
Staatliche Graphische Sammlung, Munich
Photo: Engelbert Seehuber

Blinky PALERMO, *Fernsehen V*, 1970 [We]
Watercolor on pencil on squared paper; 5 x 14.8 x 20.8 cm
Staatliche Graphische Sammlung, Munich
Photo: Engelbert Seehuber

Blinky PALERMO, *Untitled (für Kristin)*, 1973 [You]
Two parts: oil and casein on wood; polyester and casein on plywood;
184 x 115 x 4.9 cm
Kunstmuseum Düsseldorf im Ehrendorf

PANAMARENKO, *Donderwolk*, 1970–1971 [We]
Stainless steel, aluminum, rubberized canvas, felt, leather and perspex;
300 x 500 x 500 cm
Courtesy Deweer Art Gallery, Otegem
Photo: Gerald Van Rafelghem

* Pablo PICASSO, *Deux Figures et un chat*, 1902–1903
[We]
Pencil, watercolor and coloured pencil; 18 x 26.5 cm
Museu Picasso, Barcelona
© Photo Arxiu Fotogràfic de Museus

Pablo PICASSO, *Nature morte: bouteille, cartes et verre
de vin*, 1914 [I]
Oil on panel; 31.5 x 43 cm
Philadelphia Museum of Art, A.E. Gallatin Collection, Philadelphia

Pablo PICASSO, *Nature morte au crâne et au pichet*, 1943
[I]
Oil on canvas; 45.9 x 55 cm
Collection Musée d'art moderne, Céret
Photo: Gibernau

Michelangelo PISTOLETTO, *L'uomo che pensa*, 1962–1993
[You]
Silkscreen print on polished stainless steel; 230 x 125 cm
Collection Banque Bruxelles Lambert, Brussels

Gerhard RICHTER, *Vier Glasscheiben*, 1967 [You]
Diverse materials; 416 x 342 x 198 cm
Collection Herbert, Ghent

Gerhard RICHTER, *Schädel*, 1983 [I]
Oil on canvas; 95 x 90.5 cm
Musée d'art moderne, Saint-Etienne
Photo: Yves Bresson

Gerhard RICHTER, *Kugel (A008623)*, 1989 [I]
Polished stainless steel; Ø 8 cm
Anthony d'Offay Gallery, London

Gerhard RICHTER, *Spiegel, grau (739-3)*, 1991 [You]
Pigment on glass; 100 x 110 cm
Anthony d'Offay Gallery, London

** Gerhard RICHTER, *Kugel (A011121)*, 1992 [I]
Stainless steel; Ø 16 cm
Anthony d'Offay Gallery, London

Gerhard RICHTER, *Blumen*, 1994 [I]
Oil on canvas; 71 x 51 cm
Collection Carré d'Art, Musée d'art contemporain de Nîmes

Auguste RODIN, *L'Âge d'airain*, 1875–1876 [I]
Plaster; 180 x 80 x 60 cm
Commune de Saint-Gilles, Brussels

Auguste RODIN, *Femme nue debout, tenant à mi-cuisse
un vêtement*, between 1898 and 1903 [We]
Graphite and watercolor on cream-colored paper; 32.2 x 25.5 cm
Musée Rodin, Paris
Photo: Bruno Jarret

Auguste RODIN, *Danseuse nue de dos, jambe droite haut
levée*, undated [We]
Graphite, watercolor and gouache on cream-coloured paper;
32.7 x 25.1 cm
Musée Rodin, Paris

Auguste RODIN, *Femme nue de profil, dans la posture du
port d'armes*, undated [We]
Graphite, watercolor, and gouache on cream-coloured paper;
32.7 x 25,1 cm
Musée Rodin, Paris

Auguste RODIN, *Le Génie*, undated [We]
Graphite and watercolor on beige papier; 32.5 x 24.8 cm
Musée Rodin, Paris / ADAGP

Auguste RODIN, *Trépied*, undated [We]
Graphite and watercolor on beige paper; 32.5 x 24.5 cm
Musée Rodin, Paris

Eric RONDEPIERRE, *Le Voyeur*, 1989 [You]
Black-and white photograph; 92 x 122 cm
Collection of the FRAC Lorraine, Metz

Jaroslav RÖSSLER, *Untitled*, 1933–1934 [I]
Carbro proof; 10.7 x 7.7 cm
Collections of the Centre Georges Pompidou / Musée national d'art
moderne, Paris
Photo: Photographic archive of the collections of the Centre Georges
Pompidou / Musée national d'art moderne, Paris, Adam Rzepka

Jaroslav RÖSSLER, *Untitled*, 1934–1935 [I]
Carbro proof; 8.1 x 6.2 cm
Collections of the Centre Georges Pompidou / Musée national d'art
moderne, Paris
Photo: Photographic archive of the collections of the Centre Georges
Pompidou / Musée national d'art moderne, Paris

Jaroslav RÖSSLER, *Cérès*, ca. 1935–1939 [I]
Carbro proof; 8.5 x 6.3 cm
Collections of the Centre Georges Pompidou / Musée national d'art
moderne, Paris
Photo: Photographic archive of the collections of the Centre Georges
Pompidou / Musée national d'art moderne, Paris

Jaroslav RÖSSLER, *Thymolin*, 1935–1939 [I]
Carbro proof; 6.6 x 5.8 cm
Collections of the Centre Georges Pompidou / Musée national d'art
moderne, Paris
Photo: Photographic archive of the collections of the Centre Georges
Pompidou / Musée national d'art moderne, Paris

Mark ROTHKO, *Untitled*, 1951 [You]
Oil on canvas; 112.5 x 95.1 cm
Gift of the Mark Rothko Foundation
© 2000 Board of Trustees, National Gallery of Art, Washington

Robert RYMAN, *Untitled # 1004*, 1960–1961 [You]
Oil painting, gesso on unstretched linen canvas; 39.4 x 36.8 cm
Collection of the Artist, Courtesy Galerie Xavier Hufkens, Brussels
Photo: Bill Jacobson

Robert RYMAN, *Untitled*, 1961 [You]
Oil painting, gesso on unstretched linen canvas; 27.3 x 27.9 cm
Courtesy Galerie Xavier Hufkens, Brussels
Photo: Bill Jacobson

Robert RYMAN, *Untitled*, 1965 [You]
Oil on canvas; 23 x 23,5 cm
Collection Lambert, Musée d'art contemporain d'Avignon
Photo: Philip Bernard

Rudolf SCHÄFER, *Totengesicht*, 1986 [You]
Platinotype; 50 x 40 x 23.5 cm
Collection of the FRAC Rhône-Alpes, Villeurbanne

Kurt SCHWITTERS, *Collage # 47–22*, 1920 [I]
Paper, carboard, photo on carboard; 14.2 x 10.8 cm
Private collection

Kurt SCHWITTERS, *Weisser Kreis*, 1922 [I]
Glued pieces of paper with paint; 15.2 x 11.9 cm
Private collection

Kurt SCHWITTERS, *Untitled*, ca. 1939–1944 [I]
Collage, wood, stone, metal, glass, ceramic, carboard, plywood, and
paint; 35 x 27 x 14 cm
Musée d'art moderne, Saint-Etienne, Photo: Yves Bresson

David SMITH, *Tanktotem IX*, 1960 [I]
Painted steel; 231.1 x 85.1 x 35.6 cm
©2000 Estate of David Smith
Photo: Jerry L. Thompson, Courtesy: Gagosian Gallery

Kiki SMITH, *Virgin Mary*, 1992 [I]
Wax, muslin, and wood with steel base; 171.5 x 66 x 36.8 cm
Collection of the Artist, Courtesy Pace Wildenstein

* Robert SMITHSON, *Enantiomorphic Chambers*, 1965 [You]
Steel, mirrors; twice 61 x 76 x 79 cm
Museet for Samtidskunst, Oslo

Robert SMITHSON, *Afterthought Enantiomorphic Chambers*, 1965 [You]
Photocollage (gelatin silver prints), staples, coloured pencil, squared paper, ink; 27 x 21 cm
Fundação de Serralves Collection, Porto

Michael SNOW, *Authorisation*, 1969 [You]
Black-and-white photographs and fabric ribbon on mirror in metal frame; 54.6 x 44.4 cm
National Gallery of Canada, Ottawa
Photo: Leo Cave

Michael SNOW, *That / Cela / Dat*, 2000 [I]
DVD; 54' (3 parts of 18')
Collection of the Artist

Nancy SPERO, *Acrobat Totem*, 1988 [We]
Stamp on paper and Japanese paper; 303.5 x 49.5 cm
Collection of the FRAC Nord-Pas de Calais, Dunkirk
Photo: E. Watteau

Léon SPILLIAERT, *Autoportrait au miroir*, 1908 [You]
Gouache, watercolor, and pastel; 48 x 63 cm
Museum voor Schone Kunsten, Ostend

Léon SPILLIAERT, *Miroir*, 1913 [You]
Pastel on paper; 32 x 24 cm
Collection Johan A.H. van Rossum, Brussels

Nikolai SUETIN, *Composition avec la raie jaune*, 1930 [You]
Oil on veneer; 39.8 x 39.5 cm
© Tret'jakovskaja Galerja, Moscow

Hiroshi SUGIMOTO, *Akron Civic Theatre*, 1980 [You]
Silver-salt proof; 41.7 x 54 cm
Collection of the FRAC Lorraine, Metz

Hiroshi SUGIMOTO, *Marion Palace*, 1980 [You]
Silver-salt proof; 41.7 x 54 cm
Collection of the FRAC Lorraine, Metz

* William Henry Fox TALBOT, *Lace*, 1839–1840 [I]
Photogenic drawing glued on carboard; 17.1 x 22 cm
National Gallery of Art, Washington, Patrons' Permanent Fund

** William Henry Fox TALBOT, *Lace*, ca. 1840 [I]
Photogenic drawing glued on carboard; 22.4 x 18.5 cm
National Museum of Photography, Film and Television, UK

Pavel TCHELITCHEV, *Tête de jeune homme*, 1925 [You]
Oil on canvas; 61 x 50 cm
Musée de Grenoble

Clifford Possum TJAPALTJARRI, *Warlugulong*, 1992 [We]
Acrylic on canvas; 450 x 180 cm
Strehlow Research Centre, Alice Springs, Northern Territory, Australia

Niele TORONI, *Travail / Peinture (Empreintes de pinceau n° 50)*, 1969 [You]
Oilcloth/roll, marks of red glycerophtalic paint; 1000 x 140 cm
Collection Herman Daled, Brussels

Rosemarie TROCKEL, *Cogito, ergo sum*, 1988 [You]
Knit wool on canvas; 210 x 160 cm
De Pont Stichting, Tilburg
Photo: Henk Geraedts

Richard TUTTLE, *Pink Oval Landscape*, 1964 [You]
Painting on canvas on wooden frame; twice 29 x 8.5 x 6 and twice 43.5 x 9 x 6 cm
Collection Lambert, Musée d'art contemporain d'Avignon

Günther UECKER, *Das gelbe Bild*, 1957–1958 [You]
Wood, nails and oil on canvas; 87 x 87 cm
Collection of the Artist

Günter UMBERG, *Untitled*, 1999 [You]
Pigment and dammar on wood; 32 x 27 cm
Collection of the Artist
Photo: Alistair Overbruck, Cologne

Günter UMBERG, *Untitled*, 1999 [You]
Pigment and dammar on wood; 40 x 38 cm
Collection of the Artist
Photo: Alistair Overbruck, Cologne

Günter UMBERG, *Untitled*, 1999–2000 [You]
Pigment and dammar on wood; 59 x 33 cm
Collection of the Artist
Photo: Alistair Overbruck, Cologne

VALIE EXPORT, *Untitled, 12,1*, 1989 [You]
Digital photograph, black-and-white, silver gelatine print; 40.5 x 29.5 cm
Galerie Fotohof, Salzburg

VALIE EXPORT, *Untitled, 12,2*, 1989 [You]
Digital photograph, black-and-white, silver gelatine print; 30 x 30 cm
Galerie Fotohof, Salzburg

Marijke Van WARMERDAM, *Voetbal*, 1995 [We]
VHS video, 9'02", wooden palette
Stedelijk Van Abbemuseum, Eindhoven

Angel VERGARA, *Straatman*, 2000 [We]
Oil on plaster; 100 x 100 x 100 cm
Collection of the Artist

Didier VERMEIREN, *Le Baiser*, 1984 [I]
Plaster and metal; 50.5 x 133.5 x 132.5 cm
Private collection

Didier VERMEIREN, *Untitled (commonly called Chariot)*, 1986 [I]
Plaster, steel; 165 x 78 x 83 cm
Private collection

Jacques VILET, *Deux pommes*, 1992 [I]
Silver-bromide photograph; 10 x 13 cm
Collection of the Artist

Jacques VILET, *Cinq abricots*, 1993 [I]
Silver-bromide photograph; 10 x 13 cm
Collection of the Artist

Jacques VILET, *Deux sardines et un merlan*, 1994 [I]
Silver-bromide photograph; 10 x 13 cm
Collection of the Artist

Jacques VILET, *Bouquet emballé*, 1996 [I]
Silver-bromide photograph; 10 x 13 cm
Collection of the Artist

Jacques VILET, *Deux poires*, 1996 [I]
Silver-bromide photograph; 10 x 13 cm
Collection of the Artist

Jacques VILET, *Deux sacs galbés*, 1996 [I]
Silver-bromide photograph; 10 x 13 cm
Collection of the Artist

** Jacques VILET, *Sept navets*, 1996
Silver-bromide photograph; 10 x 13 cm
Collection of the Artist

Jeff WALL, *A Ventriloquist at a Birthday Party in October 1947*, 1990 [We]
Slide, light box with inscription; 229 x 352.4 cm
Collection Groupe Lhoist, Ottignies – Louvain-la-Neuve

** Andy WARHOL, *Barne*, 1950s
Gold leaf and ink on colored graphic paper; 46 x 32.2 cm
The Andy Warhol Museum, Pittsburgh

Andy WARHOL, *Male Couple*, 1950s [We]
Ink on paper; 39 x 32 cm
The Andy Warhol Museum, Pittsburgh. Founding Collection, Contribution The Andy Warhol Foundation for the Visual Arts, Inc.
Photo: Richard Stoner

* Andy WARHOL, *Two Heads and Clasped Hands*, 1950s [We]
Oil and ink on canvas; 39 x 32 cm
The Andy Warhol Museum, Pittsburgh. Founding Collection, Contribution The Andy Warhol Foundation for the Visual Arts, Inc.
Photo: Richard Stoner

Andy WARHOL, *False Teeth*, 1982–1983 [I]
Color polaroid; 7.2 x 9.5 cm
Collections of the Centre Georges Pompidou / Musée national d'art moderne, Paris
Photo: Photographic archive of the collections of the Centre Georges Pompidou / Musée national d'art moderne, Paris, Philippe Migeat

Andy WARHOL, *Dolly Parton*, 1985 [You]
Painted synthetic polymer and sikscreen printing on canvas; 106.7 x 106.7 cm
The Andy Warhol Foundation for the Visual Arts, Inc., New York

Andy WARHOL, *Dolly Parton*, 1985 [You]
Painted synthetic polymer and sikscreen printing on canvas; 106.7 x 106.7 cm
The Andy Warhol Foundation for the Visual Arts, Inc., New York

James WELLING, *Gilded Frame (93)–July 13 1981*, 1981 [I]
Photograph, selenium-tinted; 24 x 19 cm
Courtesy Galerie Xavier Hufkens, Brussels

James WELLING, *Untitled 61*, 1981 [I]
Photograph, selenium-tinted; 24 x 19 cm
Courtesy Galerie Xavier Hufkens, Brussels

Marthe WÉRY, *Peinture Venise 82*, 1982 [You]
Acrylic on canvas, 30 canvases of 120 x 24 cm, 39 canvases of 200 x 24 cm, 24 canvases of 320 x 24 cm
Collection of the Artist

Sue WILLIAMS, *Woman with Kitten*, 1991 [We]
Acrylic on paper on canvas; 107 x 122 cm
Lisa Liebmann & Brooks Adams, New York
Photo: Courtesy 303 Gallery, New York

WOLS, *Canaille sur la palissade*, 1951 [I]
Black-and-white photograph; 22.6 x 22.6 cm
Musée d'art moderne, Saint-Etienne
Photo: Yves Bresson

WOLS, *Loupes et centimètre*, 1951 [I]
Black-and-white photograph; 22.4 x 15.5 cm
Musée d'art moderne, Saint-Etienne
Photo: Yves Bresson

René ZUBER, *Sèvres, tasses en porcelaine*, 1937 [I]
Silver-salt proof; 25.4 x 22 cm
Collections of the Centre Georges Pompidou / Musée national d'art moderne, Paris
Photo: Photographic archive of the collections of the Centre Georges, Pompidou / Musée national d'art moderne, Paris, Adam Rzepka

Piet ZWART, *Untitled*, ca. 1934 [I]
Silver-salt proof; 33.3 x 24.2 cm
Collections of the Centre Georges Pompidou / Musée national d'art moderne, Paris
Photo: Photographic archive of the collections of the Centre Georges Pompidou / Musée national d'art moderne, Paris, Philippe Migeat

LIST OF THE WORKS AND DOCUMENTS REPRODUCED IN THE TEXT

Sylvie BLOCHER, *Living Pictures / L'Annonce amoureuse*, 1995 [We]
Video installation, 15', floating screen 300 x 250 cm, plywood painted in trompe-l'œil
Photo: André Morin

Sylvie BLOCHER, *Three of Us*, 2000 [We]
Video installation, 9', 3 floating screens with 190 cm Ø
Photo: Aurélien Conty

Marcel BROODTHAERS, *Section des figures (Der Adler vom Oligozän bis heute)*, 1972 [I]
Detail 7: anonymous, Eagle with spread wings, Roman Bronze; 5.6 x 5.3 cm
Staatlichen Museen Stiftung Preußischer Kulturbesitz, Berlin
Photo: Maria Gilissen-Broodthaers

Marcel BROODTHAERS, *Section des figures (Der Adler vom Oligozän bis heute)*, 1972 [I] (double page in the catalog)
Städtliche Kunsthalle Düsseldorf

Marcel BROODTHAERS, *Untitled (commonly called Le Général au cigare)*, 1970 [I]
Collection Nicole Daled-Verstraeten, Brussels

Marcel DUCHAMP, *Fountain*, 1917 [I]
From: The Blind Man, May 1917, Philadelphia Museum of Art, Arensberg Archives
Photo: Alfred Stieglitz

Marcel DUCHAMP's studio, 33, West 67th Street, New York, 1917–1918 [I]
Private collection
Photographer unknown

Dan FLAVIN, *Icon V (Coran's Broadway Flesh)*, 1962 [You]
Oil on masonite, lit light bulbs; 107 x 107 x 25 cm
DIA Center for the Arts, New York

Jean-Louis FORAIN, *Le Bar aux Folies-Bergère*, 1878 [We]
Gouache on paper; 31.8 x 20.3 cm
The Brooklyn Museum of Art

Édouard MANET, *Nymphe surprise*, 1859–1861 [You]
Oil on canvas; 146 x 114 cm
Museo Nacional de Bellas Artes, Buenos Aires
From: Manet 1832–1883. Catalogue d'exposition – Galeries nationales du Grand Palais, Paris, avril-août 1983, Ministère de la Culture. Editions de la Réunion des musées nationaux, 1983, p. 85

Édouard MANET, Study for *Nymphe surprise* (*Moïse sauvé des eaux*), 1860–1861 [You]
Oil on canvas; 33.5 x 46 cm
Nasjonalgalleriet, Oslo
From: Manet 1832–1883. Catalogue d'exposition – Galeries nationales du Grand Palais, Paris, avril-août 1983, Ministère de la Culture. Editions de la Réunion des musées nationaux, 1983, p. 87

Édouard MANET, *L'Enfant à l'épée*, 1861 [You]
Oil on canvas; 131.1 x 93.3 cm
Metropolitan Museum of Art, New York
From: Manet 1832–1883. Catalogue d'exposition – Galeries nationales du Grand Palais, Paris, avril-août 1983, Ministère de la Culture. Editions de la Réunion des musées nationaux, 1983, p. 77

Édouard MANET, *Portrait de Victorine Meurent*, 1862 (detail) [You]
Oil on canvas; 43 x 43 cm
Museum of Fine Arts, Boston
From: Manet 1832–1883. Catalogue d'exposition – Galeries nationales du Grand Palais, Paris, avril-août 1983, Ministère de la Culture. Editions de la Réunion des musées nationaux, 1983, p. 104

Édouard MANET, *Olympia*, 1863 [You]
Oil on canvas; 130.5 x 190 cm
Musée d'Orsay, Paris
From: Manet 1832–1883. Catalogue d'exposition – Galeries nationales du Grand Palais, Paris, avril-août 1983, Ministère de la Culture. Editions de la Réunion des musées nationaux, 1983, p. 175

Édouard MANET, *Le Christ mort et les anges (Le Christ aux anges)*, 1864 [I]
Oil on canvas; 179 x 150 cm
Metropolitan Museum of Art, H.O. Havemeyer Collection, Bequest of Mrs. H.O. Havemeyer, New York
Photo: Malcolm Varon

Édouard MANET, *Le Christ mort et les anges (Le Christ aux anges)*, ca. 1865–1867 [I]
Graphite, watercolor, gouache, pen, and Indian ink; 32.4 x 27 cm
Paris, Musée du Louvre, Cabinet des Dessins
From: Manet 1832–1883. Catalogue d'exposition – Galeries nationales du Grand Palais, Paris, avril-août 1983, Ministère de la Culture. Editions de la Réunion des musées nationaux, 1983, p. 204

Édouard MANET, *Le Chemin de fer*, 1872–1873 [You]
Oil on canvas; 93 x 114 cm
National Gallery of Art, Washington
From: Manet 1832–1883. Catalogue d'exposition – Galeries nationales du Grand Palais, Paris, avril-août 1983, Ministère de la Culture. Editions de la Réunion des musées nationaux, 1983, p. 341

Édouard MANET, Study for *Un bar aux Folies-Bergère*, 1881 [We]
Oil on canvas; 47 x 56 cm
Private collection, London

Édouard MANET, *Un bar aux Folies-Bergère*, 1881–1882 [You] [We]
Oil on canvas; 96 x 130 cm
Courtauld Institute, London

X-ray photograph of *Un bar aux Folies-Bergère* [We]
Courtesy The Courtauld Gallery, London
Drawing: Thierry de Duve

Scenographic plan of *Un bar aux Folies-Bergère* [We]
© Thierry de Duve

Piet MONDRIAN, *Nature morte au pot de gingembre II*, 1912 [You]
Oil on canvas; 91.5 x 120 cm
Solomon R. Guggenheim Museum, New York
From: Joop M. Joosten, Piet Mondrian. Catalogue Raisonné of the Work of 1911–1914, Mercatorfonds, Antwerp, 1998, p. 16

Piet MONDRIAN, *Le Grand Nu*, 1912 [You]
Oil on canvas; 92.3 x 158.2 cm
Gemeentemuseum, The Hague
From: Joop M. Joosten, Piet Mondrian. Catalogue Raisonné of the Work of 1911–1914, Mercatorfonds, Antwerp, 1998, p. 13

Piet MONDRIAN, *Tableau n° 3 (Composition en ovale)*, 1913 [You]
Oil on canvas; 94 x 78 cm
Stedelijk Museum, Amsterdam
From: Joop M. Joosten, Piet Mondrian. Catalogue Raisonné of the Work of 1911–1914, Mercatorfonds, Antwerp, 1998, p. 21

Piet MONDRIAN, *Tableau n° 1 (Composition avec lignes et couleur)*, 1913 [You]
Oil on canvas; 96 x 64 cm
Kröller-Müller Museum, Otterlo
From: Joop M. Joosten, Piet Mondrian. Catalogue Raisonné of the Work of 1911–1914, Mercatorfonds, Antwerp, 1998, p. 24

Piet MONDRIAN, *Compositie 10 in zwart wit (Pier et Océan)*, 1915 [You]
Oil on canvas; 85 x 108 cm
Kröller-Müller Museum, Otterlo
From: Joop M. Joosten, Piet Mondrian. Catalogue Raisonné of the Work of 1911–1914, Mercatorfonds, Antwerp, 1998, p. 31

Piet MONDRIAN, *Composition*, 1916 [You]
Oil on canvas; 119 x 75 cm
Solomon R. Guggenheim Museum, New York
From: Joop M. Joosten, Piet Mondrian. Catalogue Raisonné of the Work of 1911–1914, Mercatorfonds, Antwerp, 1998, p. 32

Piet MONDRIAN, *Compositie in lijn*, 1916–1917 [You]
Oil on canvas; 108 x 108 cm
Kröller-Müller Museum, Otterlo
From: Joop M. Joosten, Piet Mondrian. Catalogue Raisonné of the Work of 1911–1914, Mercatorfonds, Antwerp, 1998, p. 33

Piet MONDRIAN, *Composition n° 3 avec plans colorés*, 1917 [You]
Oil on canvas; 48 x 61.5 cm
Museum Boijmans Van Beuningen, Rotterdam
From: Joop M. Joosten, Piet Mondrian. Catalogue Raisonné of the Work of 1911–1914, Mercatorfonds, Antwerp, 1998, p. 35

Pablo PICASSO, *Femme aux poires*, 1909 [You]
Oil on canvas; 92 x 73 cm
Museum of Modern Art, New York
From: Brigitte Léal, Christine Piot, Marie-Laure Bernadac, The Ultimate Picasso, Harry N. Abrams, New York, 2000, p. 143

Pablo PICASSO, *Guitariste*, 1910 [You]
Oil on canvas; 100 x 73 cm
Collections of the Centre Georges Pompidou / Musée national d'art moderne, Paris
From: Brigitte Léal, Christine Piot, Marie-Laure Bernadac, The Ultimate Picasso, Harry N. Abrams, New York, 2000, p. 150

Pablo PICASSO, *Les Jumelles*, 1910 [You]
Oil on canvas; 22 x 27 cm
Collection Stephen Hahn, New York
From: William Rubin, Picasso, and Braque. Pioneering Cubism, The Museum of Modern Art, New York, 1989, p. 180

Pablo PICASSO, *Nu*, 1910 [You]
Ink and watercolor; 74 x 46.5 cm
Private collection
From: William Rubin, Picasso and Braque, Pioneering Cubism, The Museum of Modern Art, New York, 1989, p. 160

Pablo PICASSO, *Nu debout*, 1910 [You]
Charcoal; 48.3 x 31.4 cm
Metropolitan Museum of Art, New York, Alfred Stieglitz Collection
From: William Rubin, Picasso and Braque, Pioneering Cubism, The Museum of Modern Art, New York, 1989, p. 167

Pablo PICASSO, *L'Homme à la mandoline*, 1911–1912 [You]
Oil on canvas; 158 x 71 cm
Musée Picasso, Paris
From: Brigitte Léal, Christine Piot, Marie-Laure Bernadac, The Ultimate Picasso, Harry N. Abrams, New York, 2000, p. 153

Pablo PICASSO, Photo of Marie Laurencin at Picasso's studio, 1911 ou 1912 [You]
Musée Picasso, Paris
From: T. J. Clark, Farewell to an Idea, Episodes from a History of Modernism, Yale University Press, New Haven, 1999, p. 188

Robert RAUSCHENBERG, *Mother of God*, ca. 1950 [We]
Oil, enamel, printed plans, newspaper, copper, and metal on hardboard; 121.9 x 81.6 cm
Collection of the Artist
From: Walter Hopps and Susan Davidson, Robert Rauschenberg. A Retrospective, Guggenheim Museum, New York, 1997, p. 51

Engraving after RIBALTA, *Dead Christ Held by Two Angels*, in l'Histoire des peintres, by Charles Blanc [I]
From: Manet 1832–1883. Catalogue d'exposition – Galeries nationales du Grand Palais, Paris, avril-août 1983, Ministère de la Culture. Editions de la Réunion des musées nationaux, 1983, p. 201

Gerhard RICHTER, *Spiegel (619)*, 1987 [You]
Mirrored glass; 200 x 180 cm
From: Gerhard Richter, 100 Bilder, Carré d'Art, Musée d'art contemporain de Nîmes, 1996, p. 23

Robert RYMAN, *Untitled*, 1961 [You]
Oil painting, gesso on unstretched linen canvas; 27.3 x 27.9 cm
Courtesy Galerie Xavier Hufkens, Brussels
Photo: Bill Jacobson

Robert RYMAN, *Untitled Painting # 10*, 1963 [You]
Oil painting, graphite, and gesso on unstretched linen canvas; 45.7 x 45.7 cm
Courtesy Galerie Xavier Hufkens, Brussels
Photo: Bill Jacobson

Robert RYMAN, *Two Paintings (A)*, ca. 1964 [You]
Oil painting and gesso on unstretched linen canvas; 20.9 x 22.2 cm
Courtesy Galerie Xavier Hufkens, Brussels
Photo: Bill Jacobson

Robert RYMAN, *Untitled*, ca. 1964 [You]
Acrylic and charcoal on stretched linen canvas; 22.9 x 22.9 cm
Courtesy Galerie Xavier Hufkens, Brussels

Robert RYMAN, *12'' Square*, 1965 [You]
Oil on cardboard; 30.5 x 30.5 cm
Courtesy Galerie Xavier Hufkens, Brussels
Photo: Bill Jacobson

Michael SNOW, *Presents*, 1980 [I]
16-mm film, colour, sound, 90'

Michael SNOW, *So Is This*, 1982 [I]
16-mm film, colour, silent, 43'

STOP, "Une marchande de consolation aux Folies-Bergère", caricature in Le Journal amusant, 1882 [We]
From: Manet 1832–1883. Catalogue d'exposition – Galeries nationales du Grand Palais, Paris, avril-août 1983, Ministère de la Culture. Editions de la Réunion des musées nationaux, 1983, p. 481

Diego VELÁZQUEZ, *Rokeby Venus*, 1650 [You]
Oil on canvas; 122.5 x 177 cm
National Gallery, London
From: Antonio Domínguez Ortiz, Alfonso E. Pérez Sánchez, Julián Gállego, Velázquez, The Metropolitan Museum of Art, New York, 1989, p.48

Diego VELÁZQUEZ, *Las Meninas*, 1656 [You]
Oil on canvas; 318 x 276 cm
Museo del Prado, Madrid
From: Alessandro Bettagno, Christopher Brown, Francisco Calvo Serraller, Francis Haskell, Alfonso E. Pérez Sánchez, Le Musée du Prado, Mercatorfonds, Antwerp, 1996, p. 115

Vorsterman, after Rubens, *Suzanne et les vieillards* (reproduced mirror-reversed) [You]
Photo courtesy of Metropolitan Museum of Art, New York
Centrum voor kunsthistorische documentatie, Nijmegen

Jeff WALL, *The Destroyed Room*, 1978 [We]
Cibachrome slide in light box; 159 x 234 cm
National Gallery of Canada, Ottawa
From: Art in America, April 1996, p. 88

Jeff WALL, *Picture for Women*, 1979 [We]
Cibachrome slide in light box; 161.5 x 223.5 cm
Musée national d'art moderne, Paris
From: Fémininmasculin. Le sexe de l'art, Gallimard/Electa, Centre Georges Pompidou, Paris, 1996, p. 177

Scenographic plan of *Picture for Women* [We]
From: Arielle Pelenc, Thierry de Duve, Boris Groys, Jeff Wall, Phaidon, London, 1996, p. 31

This book is the revised and enlarged edition of the book published in French and Dutch
on the occasion of the exhibition *Voici, 100 ans d'art contemporain*,
Palais des Beaux-Arts, Brussels, 23 November 2000 – 28 January 2001.

EXHIBITION
Production: *Bruxelles/Brussel 2000—Ville européenne de la culture de l'an 2000*
Curator: *Thierry de Duve*
Management, Press and Communication: *Françoise Wolff*
Administration: *Ninon Poncelet*
Public Relations: *Jacqueline Tulkens*
Assistant: *Erika Wautelet*
Scientific Commitee: *Lynne Cooke*, director of the DIA Center for the Arts, New York;
Eliane De Wilde, Chief Conservator of the Royal Museums of Fine Arts of Belgium;
Chris Dercon, director of the Museum Boijmans Van Beuningen, Rotterdam;
Jürgen Harten, director of the Stiftung Ehrenhof, Dusseldorf; and
Thomas Messer, director emeritus of the Solomon R. Guggenheim Museum, New York.

Thierry de Duve conveys his most affectionate thanks to the small team of his close
collaborators, to the artists who created a new work for the show, as well as to *Roger
Vandermeulen* and the team of devoted workers who set up the exhibition at the Palais des
Beaux-Arts. He also wishes to express his profound gratitude to all the lenders—artists,
private collectors, museums and institutions. He is deeply indebted to Bruxelles/Brussel
2000, its director, Robert Palmer, the Coordinator for Visual Arts, Annick de Ville, and
her assistant, Brigitte De Clercq. His gratitude also goes to the Scientific Commitee for
their advise and moral support, to AXA Royale Belge for its generous sponsoring, to the
Banque Bruxelles Lambert for having purchased Dan Graham's new work, and, last but
not least, to *Piet Coessens*, director of the Société des Expositions, *Bruno van Lierde*, its
president, and *Marie-Thérèse Champesme*, in charge of exhibitions. He has received the
kind help of *Judith Gintz-Aminoff* in revising the translation of the book and wishes to
thank her too, as well as *Simon Pleasance* and *Fronza Woods*, who did the bulk of the work.
Sylvie Blocher wholeheartedly thanks the men and women from Brussels who kindly
agreed to present themselves before her camera.

PUBLICATION
Design and typesetting: *Filiep Tacq*, Ghent
Color separations and printing: *Die Keure*, Bruges

Copyright © 2001 Ludion, Ghent-Amsterdam; Thierry de Duve
Copyright © 2001 SABAM Bruxelles, 2001 SOFAM Bruxelles, Charly Herscovici Bruxelles,
VG Bildkunst Bonn, ADAGP Paris, VAGA New York, SIAE Roma, Lichtenstein New York,
Succession Matisse Paris, Beeldrecht Amsterdam, ARS New York, Succession Picasso Paris,
Pro Litteris Zürich, CKD/KU Nijmegen.
All the installation photos are by Philippe De Gobert, with the exception of the photo on
page 298, which is by Alain Géronnez.

Every effort has been made to contact copyright-holders of photographs. Any
copyright-holders we have been unable to reach or to whom inaccurate
acknowledgement has been made are invited to contact the publisher: Ludion,
Muinkkaai 42, B-9000 Ghent; Herengracht 376, NL-1016 CH Amsterdam

ISBN 90-5544-316-6
D/2001/6328/40